Celebra

Review

Multistate Performance Test Book 1

Certain publicly disclosed questions from past MPT examinations have been included herein with the permission of NCBE, the copyright owner. These questions are the only actual MPT questions included in Celebration Bar Review's Multistate Performance Test Book. Permission to use the NCBE's questions does not constitute an endorsement by NCBE or otherwise signify that NCBE has reviewed or approved any aspect of these materials or the company or individuals who distribute these materials.

This book is provided for the exclusive use of:

This Registered Celebration Bar Review Student

And may not be used by any other person without written permission of Celebration Bar Review

TABLE OF CONTENTS

FILE

LIBRARY

ANSWER

INSTRUCTIONS

1 You will have 90 minutes to complete this session of the examination. This performance test is designed to evaluate your ability to handle a select number of legal authorities in the context of a factual problem involving a client.

2. The problem is set in the fictional state of Columbia, one of the United States. Columbia is located within the fictional United States Court of Appeals for the Fifteenth Circuit.

3. You will have two sets of materials with which to work: a File and a Library. The File contains factual information about your case. The first document is a memorandum containing the instructions for the task you are to complete.

4. The Library contains the legal authorities needed to complete the task. Any cases may be real, modified, or written solely for the purpose of this examination. If the cases appear familiar to you, do not assume that they are precisely the same as you have read before. Read them thoroughly, as if all were new to you. You should assume that cases were decided in the jurisdictions and on the dates shown. In citing cases from the Library, you may use abbreviations and omit citations.

5. Your response must be written in the answer book provided. In answering this performance test, you should concentrate on the materials provided, but you should also bring to bear on the problem your general knowledge of the law. What you have learned in law school and elsewhere provides the general background for analyzing the problem; the File and Library provide the specific materials with which you must work.

6. Although there are no restrictions on how you apportion your time, you should probably allocate at least 45 minutes to organizing and writing.

7. This performance test will be graded on your responsiveness to instructions and on the content, thoroughness, and organization of your response.

COLUMBIA PRISON ASSISTANCE PROGRAM
An Equal Justice Project of the Columbia Bar Association

MEMORANDUM July 29, 1993

To: Applicant

From: Melissa Woodward, General Counsel

Re: Xenophanes v. James Thompson, Warden, et al.

Our severe budget crisis requires me to attend an emergency meeting of the Board of Directors. As a result, I need your help representing Xenophanes, an inmate at the Columbia Correctional Center (CCC), in a federal court proceeding now in recess. Xenophanes (who refers to himself as "Xeno") was convicted of forgery (as a 3rd offender) under his "birth name," Bryson Hamilton, and is serving a ten to 20-year sentence.

While in prison, Xeno converted to an ancient polytheistic religion based on the teachings of the Oracle of Delos. One of the tenets of the religion is that a member of the faith must adopt a single Greek name, discarding forever any other non-religious names. Upon his conversion, Xeno took the name of an ancient Greek philosopher who taught that "all things are arisen from earth and water." Last year, we were assigned to represent him and succeeded, in an action entitled Xenophanes v. CCC, in getting the CCC to recognize Xenophanes as his "religious name," adding it to his "birth name" on all prison records and making it his "official" name. The facts that Xeno's religious beliefs are genuine and that the cult to which he belongs is legitimately established were adjudicated in his favor in last year's action and are, therefore, res judicata.

In Xeno's present lawsuit, testimony concluded earlier today and I must make my closing argument tomorrow. In this matter, Xeno's § 1983 suit charges the warden and others with violating the "cruel and unusual punishment" provision of the Eighth Amendment by denying him access to out-of-cell physical exercise for several months, and he seeks an order requiring them to grant him such access at a minimum of three days per week, one hour per day. CCC officials respond that administrative and other reasons justified keeping Xeno in his cell during this period. The transcript of this very short trial proceeding is in the File.

Please do the following:

Draft my closing argument to the jury. Judge Gebippe, before whom this action is pending, empaneled an advisory jury pursuant to Federal Rule 39(c) and has said he will adopt the jury's finding on whether Xeno's constitutional rights have been violated. He also told us at the conclusion of the testimony that he intends to base his instructions to the jury on two opinions of the Court of Appeals. I have included those opinions, Hall v. Williams and Mitchell v. Rice, in the Library.

This task must be completed when I return later in the day from my meeting with the Board. I have attached an office policy memorandum that describes the appropriate format for this task. Many thanks for your assistance.

COLUMBIA PRISON ASSISTANCE PROGRAM
An Equal Justice Project of the Columbia Bar Association

MEMORANDUM April 10, 1991

To: To All Lawyers

From: Director of Litigation

Re: Closing Arguments/Jury Trials

You should begin with an understanding of the legal principles that will be applied to the facts in the case. In some cases, you will be provided with jury instructions. In other cases, the instructions will not yet be drafted and you will have to rely upon an analysis of legal authority. The instructions or legal authority will give you the framework for your closing argument. However, the closing argument should not discuss or make reference to these authorities; a closing argument is not a legal brief or an essay. The argument must show how the evidence presented meets the legal standards which are or will be set forth in the jury instructions. The argument is based on the evidence presented, not histrionics or personal opinion. Write out your argument exactly as you plan to give it.

It's important that the argument be in your own words, but remember that you're communicating with a group of lay people. Your job is to help them understand how the law relates to the facts presented, and to persuade them that they have no choice but to find for your client. In doing that, you should consider the following:

- State explicitly the ultimate facts that the jurors must find in order for your client to prevail.
- Organize the evidence in support of the ultimate facts.
- Incorporate relevant legal principles or jury instructions into your argument.
- Discuss the sufficiency of the evidence and the credibility of witnesses.
- Draw reasonable inferences from the evidence to support positions you have taken.
- Anticipate opposing counsel's arguments and point out weaknesses in his case.
- Refer to equities or policy considerations that merit a finding for our client.

The most important factors are organization and persuasiveness; if you immerse the jury in a sea of unconnected details, they won't have a coherent point of view to discuss in the jury room. Never hold back any argument assuming that you will have a second opportunity to make it on rebuttal.

UNITED STATES DISTRICT COURT
NORTHERN DISTRICT OF COLUMBIA

Xenophanes,

Plaintiff

Case No. 1119-93

v.

UNDER CIVIL RIGHTS ACT
42 U.S.C. § 1983

James Thompson, Warden, et al.,

Defendants

PARTIAL TRANSCRIPT OF TRIAL PROCEEDINGS, JULY 29, 1993

COURT: Members of the jury, we are about to begin what I expect will be a very short trial. You've heard the opening remarks of counsel. What plaintiff Xenophanes seeks in this case is an order requiring the defendants to grant him certain exercise privileges. Ordinarily in equity cases like this, we don't have a jury. However, I've empaneled you as an advisory jury, and I will rely on you to make the basic factual finding on whether or not there has been a violation of plaintiff's constitutional rights, and I will make my final order accordingly. Now I want to read to you a statement stipulated to by the parties, one that you are to accept as given.

> The plaintiff, Xenophanes, an inmate at the Columbia Correctional Center, is confined to Cellhouse-C, a section in which certain prisoners are administratively segregated from the general population. Many inmates are in administrative segregation because they have violated prison regulations. Plaintiff, however, was assigned to this section at his request and in an attempt to protect him from possible physical attack by other inmates.

Now we'll begin the testimony with the plaintiff.

THE PLAINTIFF, Xenophanes, WAS SWORN AND IDENTIFIED.

MS. WOODWARD: How long have you been incarcerated at Columbia Correctional Center?

XENOPHANES: A little more than four years.

Q: And how long have you been in administrative segregation?

A: Counting today it's 234 days, almost eight months.

Q: While you were living with the general population, did you have the opportunity to engage in physical exercise?

A: You bet, every day.

Q: Describe your exercise program.

A: Well, I had rehabilitation exercises. You know, after my back operation in 1991. But that was only about six months. Before and after that I exercised just about every day, not because I had to but because I wanted to. We played ball indoors and out, depending on the season. And then there was jogging on the indoor and outdoor track. And weight lifting too.

Q: How much time did you devote to exercise when you were in the general population?

A: At least an hour a day, sometimes more if the guards would let us.

Q: What impact did the exercises have on you?

A: It made me feel great. You know, alive and in good shape, my back getting better and all. That's important when you're locked up. Feeling like a human being gives you the strength to make it. And exercising and being fit made me feel like a human being.

Q: How about other men in the general prison population? Did they exercise on a regular basis?

A: Sure, there were lots of guys who worked as much as me, some a whole lot more. About ten of us followed the same basic program and so we did it together most of the time.

Q: Now, tell us the exercise opportunities available to you in administrative segregation.

A: Nothing, almost none at all. We hardly ever even get out of our cells, except to eat and twice a week showers. I've been outdoors not more than once a week in the last six months, I bet. And there's no indoor recreation allowed. So you can say that there's really no exercise opportunities in admin seg.

Q: Since you've been in administrative segregation, how many times have you played football, basketball or baseball?

A: Not more than ten times, for sure.

Q: How about jogging or running?

A: Another ten times or so, maybe.

Q: Weight lifting, how often since you've been in C-Block?

A: Zero. Haven't had any chance to lift weights.

Q: What effect has the reduction in exercise had on you?

A: Terrible. I get headaches all the time, my muscles are stiff and they're getting flabby, I seem to have a cold or the sniffles constantly. I was in great shape, now I'm in terrible shape. And most of all, I'm having trouble with my back again and I can't do the proper exercises they told me to do after the operation.

Q: Has it had any impact on you mentally, your morale?

A: Sure. I'm always depressed and upset, you know, feeling defeated. And I think it's caused me to get written up more often for disciplinary infractions.

Q: Have you asked for more exercise opportunities?

A: All the time, all the time.

Q: Have you filed a formal grievance with prison officials?

A: Three or four.

Q: What results?

A: Turned down cold. No resources, no staff. They don't care.

MS. WOODWARD: Nothing further.

COURT: You may inquire, Mr. Metzger.

MR. METZGER: Thank you, Your Honor. Mr. Xenophanes, you ...

XENOPHANES: It's just Xenophanes.

Q: Pardon me?

A: It's just Xenophanes. No mister.

Q: Oh. Sorry. You've been in administrative segregation for about eight months?

A: Correct.

Q: For almost six of those eight months you've complained of severe back pain, haven't you?

A: Probably not that long.

Q: Didn't you write up an infirmary slip on ... let's see, on January 26, in which you said, quote, "I am having bad lower back pain" unquote?

A: Yeh, I suppose that was the date.

Q: And that was the first of 23 such complaints of back pain that you filed in the CCC infirmary, isn't that so?

A: If you say so.

Q: No, sir. What do you say?

A: Yeh, I guess that's right.

Q: And on two occasions you were issued crutches, the first time for three days and the second time for five days. Is that correct?

A: (INAUDIBLE)

Q: What was that?

A: I said, yes.

Q: Thank you. And on three other occasions, infirmary staff ordered complete bed rest for two days at a time. Right?

A: Right.

Q: And you're on medically ordered bedrest right now, aren't you?

A: Yeh, but I can get around.

Q. Now you've testified that there is a significant difference between the exercise opportunities in administrative seg and that available to the general population.

A: You bet there is. It's like night and day.

Q: And you think the exercise options in admin seg are inadequate, right?

A: Totally and absolutely inadequate. No doubt.

Q: And the exercise opportunities given to the general prison population, that's okay. Is that correct?

A: Well, I wouldn't go quite that far. They could still give us the chance to do more things and to use the athletic facilities even more time. But other than that, I don't have any real complaints.

Q: Sir, on April 6, you were offered the opportunity by CCC officials to return the general population, weren't you?

A: Well, you see . . .

Q: Sir, that question can be answered yes or no.

MS. WOODWARD: Objection, Your Honor. The witness is entitled an opportunity to explain the answer.

MR. METZGER: Any explanation to such a simple question can be obtained during redirect.

COURT: Well, he's entitled to an explanation. But it's a simple issue, if he wants to explain he can do it on your examination, Ms. Woodward. Overruled.

MR. METZGER: You were provided the chance to return to the general population. Correct? Just yes or no, please.

XENOPHANES: Yes.

Q: I have no further questions of this witness.

MS. WOODWARD: Just a few questions, Xenophanes. Except those days when you were on crutches or confined to bed, could you have exercised if you had been given the opportunity?

XENOPHANES: Sure. And on some of those bed and crutch days I could've done something, like at least walk around in the fresh air, if they'd given me a chance.

Q: Okay. Now tell us what you tried to say about the supposed offer to return to the general population.

A: That wasn't a real offer, they just wanted me to shut up about exercising. The warden knew that if I left C-Block I was as good as dead. There were numerous threats on me before I was transferred to admin seg. And then, because I tried to assert my rights based on guidance from the Gods on Olympus, prison staff has recruited inmates to carry out my execution. So if I leave Cellhouse-C, I'm history. Period. I'm not signing my own death warrant, no way.

MS. WOODWARD: That's it. Nothing further and the plaintiff rests, Your Honor.

COURT: See, members of the jury. I told you it would be a short trial. Mr. Metzger, what's your pleasure?

MR. METZGER: The State calls Warden James Thompson.

THE DEFENDANT, James Thompson, WAS SWORN AND IDENTIFIED.

MR. METZGER: Warden Thompson, how long have you been at CCC?

MR. THOMPSON: Almost 13 years. Seven as a Correctional Officer, including Supervising Captain, and the last six years as Warden of CCC.

Q: Your educational background, Warden?

A: My undergraduate degree in Criminal Justice was earned at Columbia State University and I have a masters in Penology from Johns Hopkins.

Q: Are you acquainted with the plaintiff, Xenophanes?

A: I certainly am. Of course, I knew him originally as Bryson Hamilton, the name under which he was admitted to CCC. That was before his conversion and adoption of his religious name.

Q.: Please give us some idea of the nature of the administrative segregation unit at CCC.

A: Administrative segregation is a section of the institution where we house inmates who have violated prison regulations, ones with special needs or those that require special protection. It's not for the dangerous individuals like those who've tried to kill an inmate or guard; they're placed in solitary confinement in the isolation unit. Admin seg is for inmates who committed minor violations of the rules or for those accused of more serious violations who are awaiting disciplinary hearings.

Q: How about the ones with special needs and protection?

A: Well, there are some medical cases, recuperation and the like, where admin seg provides reduced activity levels and more constant observation. Special protection cases, like Xenophanes', are those where the inmate or our supervision personnel believe that other inmates may harm him if he remains in the general population.

Q: Okay. Do you have standards for inmate exercise for those in administrative segregation?

A: Well, they're not written down but there are standards known to all personnel and most inmates.

Q: What are those standards?

A: Inmates in administrative segregation are to have outside exercise opportunities three days per week for at least one hour unless there are circumstances that prevent such activity.

Q: What are the circumstances that would prevent exercise?

A: Inclement weather, absence of sufficient personnel because of sickness, etc., prison disturbance or lockdown situation, those kind of things.

Q: Have those exercise standards been in operation during the past year?

A: Yes, sir.

Q: Have those exercise standards been followed by supervisory personnel during the past year?

A: Yes sir, to the best of my knowledge.

Q: Thank you. Nothing further.

COURT: Ms. Woodward?

MS. WOODWARD: Warden Thompson, the exercise standards for the general population are quite different, aren't they?

JAMES THOMPSON: Well, I wouldn't call them major differences. For the general population we have out-of-cell exercise one hour per day with the same special exceptions.

Q: So inmates in the general population have more than twice the exercise time of those in administrative seg, right?

A: That's true. But the differences are due primarily to staffing needs and resources.

Q: Oh, that means you don't have enough guards assigned to administrative segregation to allow those persons the same amount of exercise?

A: Well, that's not exactly it. Administrative segregation requires a much higher ratio of guards because of discipline and security needs and because those with medical problems require more observation and attention. So you see, we have more guards per inmate in administrative seg than in the general population.

Q: But not enough to allow those inmates exercise every day?

A: No, not enough for that. You've got to remember that the State's fiscal crisis resulted in a 28% cut in the Corrections Department budget over the last couple of years. That's made it even harder to arrange adequate supervision.

Q: That hasn't stopped the general population from exercising every day, has it?

A: Well, I know they haven't exercised quite every day.

Q: When you say discipline needs, you mean that because most inmates in administrative seg are there because they've violated some rule that they require more guards per inmate than the general population, right?

A: That's correct.

Q: And when you say medical needs, you mean that because some of them are sick and might have an emergency or need attention that they too require more guards than the general population?

A: Yes.

Q: You stated on direct that the exercise regulations for admin seg have been followed "to the best of your knowledge." That means you don't have personal knowledge of whether that's true.

A: Well, I'm not actually there in administrative segregation.

Q: So you're relying on staff reports, right?

A: Of course. That's all I have.

Q: Are you aware that Xenophanes has filed several grievances claiming that his exercise opportunities average only one day per week?

A: Ms. Woodward, there are 1,375 inmates at CCC and we average 131 grievances a week. That means almost one prisoner in ten grieves us each week.

Q: That's interesting, Warden, but not responsive. Are you aware of Xenophanes' grievances about exercise?

A: Yes. They were reviewed and dismissed.

Q: Were his allegations about the number of exercise times accurate?

A: No, my staff reported they were understated.

Q: But inmates in administrative segregation did not have three exercise opportunities per week the last six months, did they?

A: They did, except on those occasions because of staff needs or otherwise, like inclement weather, when they couldn't go out.

Q: How many times was that?

A: I don't know exactly.

Q: So it could be that prisoners in admin seg only got out of their cells for exercise one day a week?

A: I don't think so, no.

Q: Let's talk about cells, Warden. Xenophanes' cell is nine feet by seven and one-half feet, right?

A: Yes, just like all single person cells in C-Block.

Q: But that's smaller than the general population cells?

A: Yes, the basic cell at CCC is 9' by 11 ', slightly larger.

Q: And in Xenophanes' cell there is a bunk, a washstand and a toilet, correct?

A: That is so.

Q: CCC has a gymnasium, doesn't it Warden?

A: Yes, it does.

Q: And that gym has exercise equipment, tumbling mats, half-court basketball and a small elevated track, right?

A: True.

Q: But you don't permit administrative segregation inmates to use the gym, do you?

A: We can't usually. With 1,300 men in the general population, the gym is booked solid from 7 a.m. to 9 p.m. We can't mix the 50 or so from admin seg with the general prisoners for security reasons. Sound penological theory precludes such mingling. That's why we have administrative segregation. Occasionally, a slot opens up and we get some of the men from admin seg into the gym.

Q: I have nothing more. Thank you.

COURT: Mr. Metzger.

MR. METZGER: Call Officer Biaggi.

THE WITNESS, Michael Biaggi, WAS SWORN AND IDENTIFIED.

MR. METZGER: How long have you been a Correctional Officer at CCC?

MR.BIAGGI: Fifteen years, next month.

Q: Your specific assignment is?

A: Senior officer in charge of Cellhouse-C, administrative segregation.

Q: Summarize your duties, please.

A: Overall supervision of Corrections staff in the Cellhouse. I apply and adjust general institution rules in the block, post all shift assignments, monitor leaves, review performance, pass on inmate grievances. I run the block essentially.

Q: Are you acquainted with the plaintiff?

A: Xenophanes? Yes, sir. He's been assigned to C-Block for the better part of the last year.

Q: Directing your attention to the exercise policy, what are the rules for administrative segregation?

A: Three times per week, one hour, except for circumstances that interfere and would cause disruption to the integrity and operation of the block.

Q: What kind of circumstances?

A: Inclement weather, staff shortages, unit or institution disturbance, lockdown and other ...

Q: What's a lockdown?

A: That's where the population is confined to their cells during a search for weapons or contraband or in the aftermath of a disturbance where we're trying to bring calm and order back.

Q: Now, during the time that the plaintiff has been in C-Block has an exercise period been canceled for any reason other than those circumstances you've just mentioned?

A: No, sir, not according to my personal knowledge and reports I've received from my staff.

Q: Please characterize the exercise policy followed in C-Block in the period of plaintiff's assignment there.

A: We've followed the standard established by the Warden for administrative segregation, that is, three exercise periods per week unless stated circumstances exist.

Q: Nothing further.

COURT: Cross examination.

MS. WOODWARD: Thank you, Your Honor. Officer Biaggi, let's see if I have the exercise exceptions down correctly. One, staff shortages; two, inclement weather; three, disturbances, including lockdowns. Is that it?

MR. BIAGGI: That's basically it, yes.

Q: How about punishment?

A: Pardon me?

Q: Isn't it true, Officer Biaggi, that withdrawal of exercise is a form of punishment for the men in C-Block if one or more of them does something to irritate or annoy the guards?

A: Absolutely not. The Department and the Warden have forbidden retaliation like that. If there's a problem with an inmate, he has to be written up for a violation on an individual basis. Maybe that stuff went on in the old, old days, but not now.

Q: Let's focus on staff shortages. That means if a guard calls in sick then exercise for that day is canceled, right?

A: Well, not always. One guard off during the 8 to 4 shift won't usually cause a cancel except at those times of the month, around the first and fifteenth, when reports are due. Most times we're a go with only one off.

Q: Okay, but if two call in sick, it's a cancel, isn't it?

A: Yeh, we have to cancel then. With the budget reductions, we're pretty shorthanded as it is.

Q: And staff earn one day of sick leave each month and they can accumulate up to a total of 36 days, right?

A: Right.

Q: And Correctional Department personnel take off an average of seven sick days a year, isn't that so?

A: I think that's right, about there.

Q: And C-Block operates with four guards per shift, right?

A: Three on midnight to eight, four on the other two. That's down from five before the budget cuts, sometimes six.

Q: How many days have you canceled exercise because of staff shortages, let's say in the past six months?

A: I'm not sure. We don't keep any kind of exercise log or nothing. We've got so many other records we have to maintain. I'd estimate six to ten maybe, somewhere in there.

Q: Thank you. And you cancel exercise for inclement weather?

A: Right. Rain, snow, hail, cold. Like that.

Q: And you make that decision, right? You don't check with anyone, do you?

A: The senior officer on duty makes a weather decision, me or someone else who's on. But we don't check with anyone.

Q: And any precipitation causes a cancellation, right?

A: Sure, I can't have guards standing around in the rain or snow and most inmates don't want to be outside then.

Q: And the rule you follow is that there's no exercise if the temperature falls below 33 degrees, correct.

A: Right, we cancel at freezing.

Q: How many days have you canceled exercise because of weather in the last six months?

A: I'm not sure. I'd say half a dozen or so at the most. Some of those could've been when staff was short, too.

Q: And how many exercise days have been lost in the last six months because of disturbances or lockdown?

A: Well, we had an institutional lockdown for five days in February after a general disturbance. And I can recall three or four days when we had a weapon or contraband lockdown in C-Block in the past few months. Not very much, really.

Q: Isn't it true, Officer Biaggi, that in the last six to eight months the inmates in Cellhouse-C, administrative segregation, have had only about one day per week of exercise?

A: It's more than that, I'm sure.

Q: Officer Biaggi, you have no records to substantiate that estimate, do you?

A: No, but based on my experience I'm confident we're closer to the three a week standard.

Q: But it's not three a week in the last six months or so given the cancellations you've identified, right?

A: That's probably so. We've had to cancel some.

Q: So actual exercise in C-Block has been, according to your estimate, above once but less than three times per week, right?

A: Close to three a week.

Q: I have no more questions.

MR. METZGER: Defendants rest, Your Honor.

COURT: Excellent. Ladies and gentlemen, I've arranged with counsel in this case to recess at this stage and have us all come back tomorrow for their closing arguments, my instructions to you and your deliberations. That will allow me to deal with another emergency issue. Let me remind you that you are not to discuss this matter among yourselves or with anyone else, including your family. Save any discussion until tomorrow when you'll decide this case. Any questions? We're adjourned until 9:30 a.m. Counsel, remain a moment, please.

JURY REMOVED FROM COURTROOM

COURT: Counsel, I intend to give the standard instructions on the basics, preponderance of the evidence, burden of proof, role of judge and jury, and the like. On the critical question of the alleged Eighth Amendment violation, I'm going to fashion my instructions based on the two 15th Circuit cases you both have cited, Hall v. Williams and Mitchell v. Rice. Of course, I'll be covering the totality-of-the-circumstances test, reasonable alternatives, if any, available to prison officials, and whether there was deliberate indifference. That should be of some guidance to you in developing your closing arguments. Nothing further? Okay, we're adjourned till tomorrow.

FEDERAL RULES OF CIVIL PROCEDURE

Rule 39. Trial by Jury or by the Court

(c) Advisory Jury and Trial by Consent. In all actions not triable of right by a jury the court upon motion or of its own initiative may try any issue with an advisory jury or, except in actions against the United States when a statute of the United States provides for trial without a jury, the court, with the consent of both parties, may order a trial with a jury whose verdict has the same effect as if trial by jury had been a matter of right.

Hall v. Williams

United States Court of Appeals for the Fifteenth Circuit
(1992)

Plaintiff Carl Edward Hall appeals the grant of summary judgment in favor of defendants, who are officers and employees of the Columbia Department of Corrections. Hall was confined at Powhatan Correctional Center, a maximum security facility, when there was a prison riot. The entire facility was put on "lockdown" status, which confines inmates to their cells.

Hall and other inmates in Cellblock C-2 were on lockdown from the date of the riot, November 26, 1989, until they were allowed to return to the mess hall and out-of-cell exercise on April 16, 1990. Hall brought this action under 42 U.S.C. § 1983[1] alleging violation of the Eighth Amendment because of the confinement to his cell for a period of four and one-half months with no out-of -cell exercise. The district court found that the selection of appropriate security measures is left to the discretion of prison officials and that the decision to lock down C-2 was within the discretion of the defendants and did not violate any of plaintiff's constitutional rights.

We hold that there are disputes as to material facts on the Eighth Amendment claim and that the granting of summary judgment at this stage was error. We reverse and remand for further proceedings on the Eighth Amendment claim.

The lockdown of Powhatan Correctional Center followed a riot or disturbance in its mess hall on November 26, 1989. The entire facility was locked down immediately after the mess hall riot. Six weeks later, all cell blocks were reopened except C-2, which remained locked down until the middle of April 1990.

Hall contends that he was in his cell when the mess hall disturbance occurred. The Institutional Classification Committee (ICC) received "confidential information from an informant that Hall had participated" in the disturbance. The ICC conducted a hearing on January 11 ,1990, at which time Hall was cleared of the charge that he was involved in the riot. The ICC recommended that he be returned to the prison's general population, but the defendants contended that there was no bed space available, and Hall remained confined to C-2 and subject to the lockdown until mid-April 1990.

The defendants contend that the lockdown was monitored and evaluated daily and that limited activities and privileges were restored in each cell block as security concerns permitted. Under the facts surrounding this disturbance, the prison administrators determined that recreation was precluded because of security concerns.

Hall alleges that the defendants acted in bad faith in locking down all of C-2 when the warden knew that most of the pris-

1 "Every person who, under color of any statute, ordinance, regulation, custom, or usage, of any State or Territory or the District of Columbia, subjects, or causes to be subjected, any citizen of the United States, or other person within the jurisdiction thereof to the deprivation of any rights, privileges, or immunities secured by the Constitution and laws, shall be liable to the party injured in an action at law, suit in equity, or other proper proceeding for redress."

oners in that block had nothing to do with the riot. He further claims that the lockdown was maintained as a retaliatory measure against the inmates of C-2 because of acts that occurred prior to and unconnected with the riot.

The warden denied that leaving Hall in C-2 was a retaliatory measure, but instead claimed that it was based upon security needs and the orderly operation of the institution. He asserted that Hall remained in C-2, after the ICC recommendation, because there was no other bed available.

In Wilson v. Seiter (1991), the Supreme Court adopted a two-part test for claims of Eighth Amendment challenges to conditions of confinement. The test consists of an objective component (was the deprivation sufficiently serious?), and a subjective component (were the prison officials deliberately indifferent to the conditions?).

In evaluating the objective component, we-note that it is not disputed that Hall was denied any out-of-cell exercise for almost five months, and he alleges that his cell was too small for exercise. Our analysis begins with Wilson's observation that physical exercise is an "identifiable human need." But even prior to Wilson, the law was clear that prisoners had a constitutional right to out-of-cell exercise. In Clay v. Miller (15th Cir. 1980), we held that restricting an inmate's opportunity for physical exercise could rise to the level of cruel and unusual punishment, and that courts must look to the totality of the circumstances in deciding this issue.

The duration of the exercise deprivation is an essential element in determining if there is a constitutional violation. It is clear that complete deprivation of exercise for an extended period of time can violate the Eighth Amendment. Courts have considered duration in terms of days or weeks when setting a constitutional limit, but we have found no case holding that complete exercise denial for as long as four and one-half months is constitutionally insignificant. Hall's allegations make out a prima facie case (complete deprivation of exercise for four and one-half months) as to the objective component, subject of course to the defendants' rebuttal.

The subjective component defined in Wilson v. Seiter is the intent of the responsible prison officials. An inquiry into a prison official's state of mind is required when it is claimed that the official has inflicted cruel and unusual punishment. The subjective element mandates proof of deliberate indifference by prison officials to the plaintiff's basic need for regular exercise.

In Eighth Amendment cases involving conditions of confinement, deliberate indifference may be shown when prison authorities were aware of the objectively cruel conditions and failed to remedy them. The long duration of a cruel prison condition may make it easier to establish knowledge and hence some form of intent.

The affidavits of Hall and Warden Williams create factual issues on the question of intent. There is a dispute as to the reason the warden kept all C-2 inmates on lockdown for almost five months, Hall contending that it was the warden's intent to punish all of the inmates in C-2 for reasons unrelated to the mess hall disturbance. There were 140 inmates in C-2 and even the warden admits that only 41 were charged with offenses arising out of the riot. Keeping all 140 inmates locked down with no effort to segregate those not involved could be viewed as evidence of retaliation. There is a factual dispute as to whether arrangements could reasonably have been made to allow Hall, and the other 98 non-offenders, to exercise out of their cells on a regular basis.

Since there are disputes as to genuine issues of material fact, summary judgment was inappropriate and this case must be remanded for further proceedings.

United States Court of Appeals for the Fifteenth Circuit

(1989)

In December 1 973, James Calvin Mitchell began serving a thirty-year sentence for second degree murder and armed robbery. He was incarcerated at Central Prison in Mission, Columbia. While confined from 1973 to 1983, Mitchell was convicted of three separate incidents of assault with deadly weapons with intent to kill. His prison term was extended for another twenty years as a result of these convictions. Additionally, from 1973 to 1986 Mitchell incurred over seventy prison rule infractions, many of which were violent in nature.

As a result of his July 1983 assaults, prison officials ordered Mitchell shackled in full restraints (hand and leg cuffs) any time he was outside his cell. Despite these physical restraints, Mitchell's menacing behavior persisted. In September 1983, while outside his cell in full restraints, Mitchell attacked the window of a Control Station with a broom handle. This episode led to Mitchell being confined to his cell except for showers twice weekly, and, even then, in full restraints. In accordance with regulations, prison officials provided Mitchell with an exercise manual demonstrating in-cell exercises. In February 1984, seven months after the imposition of full out-of-cell restrictions, Mitchell was allowed to leave his cell for regular exercise, however, still in full restraints.

One year after full restrictions were relaxed, Mitchell's assaultive behavior resumed. In February 1985, Mitchell, in arm and leg restraints, again attacked the Control Station with a mop wringer after refusing to return to his cell. As a result, full out-of-cell restrictions were again imposed.

In March 1986, after eleven months of full restrictions, Mitchell filed a pro se complaint charging various prison officials under 42 U.S.C. § 1983 with numerous Eighth Amendment violations. In total, Mitchell had been subjected to out-of-cell arm and leg restraints for a period of two years and eight months. For eighteen of those months, he was confined to a seventy-two square foot cell without any regular opportunity to exercise outside his cell or any regular exposure to different surroundings, fresh air or sunshine. The district court granted defendant's motion for summary judgment.

It may generally be considered that complete deprivation of exercise for an extended period of time violates Eighth Amendment prohibitions against cruel and unusual punishment. However, there can be exceptional circumstances where the general rule does not apply. This Court has repeatedly stated that when reviewing Eighth Amendment claims, courts must consider the totality of the circumstances. In considering the totality of conditions, elements including the overall duration of incarceration, the length of time for which prisoners are locked in their cells each day, and the practical opportunities for the institution to provide prisoners with increased exercise opportunities must be considered. Thus, confinement conditions imposed under one set of circumstances may constitute an Eighth Amendment violation; yet the same conditions, imposed under different circumstances, would not.

By adopting a totality of the circumstances test, we have never held that denial of out-of -cell exercise opportunities is per se unconstitutional cruel and unusual punishment. However, our decisions at the time of the incidents in this case indicated that generally a prisoner should be permitted some regular out-of-cell exercise.

Although the cases in this area have generally established the necessity for some out-of-cell exercise, courts concede that penological considerations may, in certain circumstances, justify restrictions. The one court to specifically address justifications for exercise restrictions limited them to "unusual circumstances," or circumstances where "disciplinary needs made [outdoor exercise] impossible." Spain v. Procunier (9th Cir. 1979). In that case, the court did not accept the state's justification that outdoor exercise was withheld to prevent attacks on prison staff and other inmates. It agreed on the necessity of segregating violent inmates from the population in general, but questioned why "other exercise arrangements were not made." Further, it would not allow cost to excuse constitutional violations. It seems to us proper to require a similar showing of infeasibility of alternatives.

Having set forth the applicable law, we now consider the actions of the prison officials in this case. We find that a reasonable official should have known that in most circumstances withholding all exercise opportunities from a prisoner over an extended period of time, such as seven or eleven months, violates the Eighth Amendment. Without additional evidence, these conditions could be said to violate our evolving constitutional standards of decency for penal confinement.

Prison officials contend, however, that even if regular exercise opportunities are constitutionally required for prisoners as a general matter, their actions in this case were not unconstitutional. They claim that Mitchell's incorrigibly assaultive nature demanded the imposed restrictions. The officials further claim that the in-cell exercise manual provided Mitchell a meaningful substitute to out-of-cell exercise.

Mitchell's unmanageable, violent nature may present exceptional circumstances, justifying the deprivation. The facts on the record, however, are inadequate for such a determination. We are not penologists and, without more than the record before us, cannot properly judge the necessity or adequacy of officials' actions. But a mere assertion of necessity cannot relieve prison officials of Eighth Amendment requirements. A detailed review of the feasibility of alternatives in this case, such as solitary out-of-cell exercise periods or the adequacy of in-cell exercise, would need to precede a final judgment.

Because the record does not adequately address all the issues necessary to determine whether prison officials violated clearly established law, we cannot affirm a grant of summary judgment. We remand this case for further findings of fact in order to determine whether prison officials' conduct in this case constituted cruel and unusual punishment under the principles stated.

NATIONAL CONFERENCE OF BAR EXAMINERS
Xenophanes Performance Test

Outline for a Minimum Acceptable Answer

Xenophanes v. James Thompson, Warden, et al.

1. Introductory remarks

   - Short statement that sets the framework

11. Argument in plain English (as opposed to legalese)

    A. Demonstrate that the legal framework will be drawn from the two cases in the library

       1. **A** long term deprivation is legally an 8th Amendment violation (Mitchell v. Rice)

          - Determined based on "totality of circumstances"

       2. There's a two-part test (Hall v. Williams)

          - Objective - i.e., duration and extent of deprivation

          - Subjective - i.e., "deliberate indifference"

    B. Make a reasonable attempt at applying the facts in the record to the principles extracted from the cases

       1. Xeno's exercise was severely curtailed

       2. The prison officials knew of the deprivation

       3. The prison's evidence lacks substance

FILE

GVP Non-Disclosure Agreement

Blevin, Edmonds & Victor, P.A.

BEV, pa

Attorneys & Counselors at Law
1000 Commercial Boulevard
Webville, Franklin 33883

www.bevlaw.org
bev@paris.com
(555) 349-0890

TO: Applicant
FROM: Tom Edmonds
RE: *GVP Non-Disclosure Agreement*
DATE: August 1, 2002

We represent General Vision Processing, Inc. (GVP), a closely held research and development company. Dr. Nabeel Adsani, GVP's President and Chief Executive Officer, is a former Professor of Computer Science at the University of Franklin. He developed a breakthrough discovery known as the *iChip*™, and GVP has a patent pending.

Dr. Adsani is exploring a strategic alliance with MicroSystems (Micro), a high tech incubator company that acquires leading edge technologies, evaluates whether there is a market for them, and spins off new companies to produce them. Micro and GVP are evaluating whether the *iChip*™ is something on which the two companies should collaborate to create applications for use in computerized transportation safety systems.

In undertaking this strategic alliance, GVP realizes that it needs to disclose confidential information about the *iChip*™ to Micro. Therefore, GVP faces both substantial risks and benefits in this collaboration. A non-disclosure agreement (NDA) is one mechanism GVP can use to reduce the risks associated with disclosures made during this alliance.

Dr. Adsani is concerned that the "boilerplate" NDA proposed by Micro fails to adequately protect GVP from unauthorized use and disclosure of its trade secrets. You can glean from the transcript of my interview with Dr. Adsani the points that he is worried about. I have reviewed Micro's proposed NDA and excerpted several provisions. I would like your help in preparing an opinion letter to Dr. Adsani. Other members of the team are working on other aspects of the proposed NDA. I want you to analyze the NDA and focus on the following three concerns expressed by Dr. Adsani:

1. Restrictions as to the persons or entities (receiving parties) to whom disclosure can be made;
2. The conditions or limitations that should be placed on the disclosures to those receiving parties; and

3. GVP's ability to enforce its rights as a third-party beneficiary against persons or entities who obtain confidential information but who are not signatories to the GVP/Micro NDA.

Write the portion of the opinion letter that analyzes whether and how effectively the excerpts from Micro's proposed NDA address from GVP's perspective each of those concerns and whether the existing language adequately protects GVP.

In addressing each of the three concerns I've set forth above

- Examine each paragraph of the NDA provision by provision;
- Explain why particular language protects or fails to protect GVP's interests, including how the language of each provision relates to the concerns and suggestions Dr. Adsani expressed during the interview;
- If particular language fails to protect GVP's interests, suggest a solution using the materials in the File and the authorities in the Library.

You need not rewrite the entire NDA, but you do need to explain in narrative form the points you believe we should be concerned about and the changes you would suggest. For example, I noted the following about the preamble: "The preamble as written suggests that Micro is seeking protection for its own confidential information as well as GVP's. As Dr. Adsani said in the interview, he is not interested in protecting Micro's trade secrets. If the language is left as is, it might unwittingly impose some obligations on GVP. The language should be changed to make clear that Micro is the party that wishes to evaluate the technology and that it is GVP's confidential information that needs the protection."

I want you to analyze the rest of the NDA excerpts in the same manner. You should identify and recommend any and all changes you believe are necessary. I will decide which ones to communicate to Dr. Adsani. Please avoid conclusive, non-explanatory statements of the ultimate facts, such as: "The NDA does not adequately define to whom Micro may disclose information and it should be clarified."

computer vision research. It emphasizes the perception aspect of sight instead of concentrating on the understanding process.

Q: I hope I don't need to understand the nuances of Perception Tracing theory to advise you!

A: You don't, Tom. Suffice it to say that every computer vision engineer who graduates from a leading technology university today is exposed to the theory. The GVP *iChip* is premised on Perception Tracing. That's one of the reasons Shaw is investigating a partnership with us.

Q: Tell me more about Micro's interest in the *iChip*.

A: Micro's Transportation Safety Division has two breakthrough products. *InterSect* is a system that controls traffic lights by estimating vehicle traffic and maximizing green light time. *LaneTrac* is a device mounted on the dashboard that signals a driver who is veering out of the traffic lane.

Q: So, that's the link with the *iChip*?

A: Right. Shaw wants to find out if the *iChip* is a more efficient system than Micro's. If it is, then Micro will propose a strategic alliance between the two companies to enhance Micro's existing products and to develop new products, like the driver drowsiness detector.

Q: What does GVP gain from a strategic alliance with Micro?

A: A ton! Micro will front most, if not all, of the product development costs. Micro also has existing relationships with the tier one auto parts manufacturers. That means that GVP/Micro's products will have a clear path directly into the market. Moreover, Micro is a well-known and well-respected company. Partnering with Micro gives GVP instant credibility.

Q: Are there risks associated with a strategic alliance?

A: Many, and they're high. Our *iChip* patent is pending, and we copyrighted our software source code. But as we get into technical demonstrations of the *iChip*, showing what it can do and how it's done, we're bound to reveal some of our trade secrets and our know-how. My greatest fear is that Shaw is on a fishing expedition, trying to learn as much as possible about the *iChip*, then dumping GVP. If that happens, the next thing we know, we'll see subtle but important improvements in Micro's products based on GVP technology. But it'll be almost impossible to trace them back to the confidential information we provided to Micro.

Q: There's that and there's also the possibility that GVP and Micro will create an alliance but somewhere down the road, following successful or unsuccessful technology development, the relationship sours. If Micro and GVP split, won't Micro's employees have some understanding of GVP's trade secrets and know-how?

A: Well, you can't purge their minds of what they've learned from us, although I'd sure like to if I could! How about making Micro return the information, the documents, we've given them? And, of course, I'd want to get back the evaluation of the *iChip* itself. Can you do these things?

Q: We certainly can put together a non-disclosure agreement that will afford you as much protection as possible.

A: Oh—I nearly forgot to mention that Shaw sent us Micro's non-disclosure form. She said it's their standard agreement whenever they're evaluating technology.

Q: Let me take a quick peek at it.

A: Here's what I'm most concerned about. Can we limit how Micro can use the confidential information we give them and to whom they can disclose it?

Q: Let me get some more details. Exactly what will you reveal to Micro?

A: The *iChip* is a board about the size of a business card consisting of a .25 micron chip with a built-in microprocessor. We'll demonstrate to Micro how the *iChip* can measure and analyze eye blinking as well as track the left and right lane markers.

Q: Will the demos reveal any trade secrets or know-how?

A: Some. I hope not too much. But the Micro engineers will have dozens of follow-up questions about everything, from the architecture of the chip to programming protocols.

Q: Is there a way to limit the people associated with Micro who have access to GVP's information?

A: I'm not sure. I want Micro to give the *iChip* a full examination. So I want GVP information to go to those at Micro who have the knowledge and expertise to do a full and fair evaluation of the technology's potential. That may go beyond Micro's employees. All high tech companies draw on outside consultants as independent contractors. I'm sure Micro will use consultants on the review of *iChip*. I'd sure like to be able to find out ahead of time what consultants they're using and when they're using them.

Q: OK, we'll think about that issue. Anything else?

A: There's a huge employee turnover in the technology field. Competitors are always trying to pick off engineers from other companies. What do we do if a Micro employee who has received GVP confidential information leaves and ends up with a competitor of both Micro and GVP?

Q: Well, Micro has an interest in protecting itself against the loss of trade secrets. They're sure to have Micro employees under a non-disclosure agreement, just as you do at GVP.

A: Maybe, but I'm not interested in protecting Micro's trade secrets. I'm nervous about relying on Micro to protect GVP's rights. Can we be more proactive if a Micro employee leaves after having access to GVP data?

Q: I'm sure there's a way to empower GVP to act on its own to preserve its trade secrets. Is that it?

A: Micro has a pattern of spinning off successful divisions as independent companies. In its annual SEC report, Micro said it plans to transform its Transportation Safety Division into a public company in which it holds a significant interest. Micro's plans, however, are dependent on its ability to acquire or develop more sophisticated technology to support its products. Could that be a problem?

Q: It could be. We'll evaluate GVP's alternatives and make a recommendation on how best to protect your interests if Micro makes such a move.

A: Great. I want to protect our confidential information but I don't want to scare Micro off. I've always wanted to work with J.P. Shaw, and this may be my only chance. I've heard she plans to retire soon.

Q: I'm sure we can come up with language that will balance your desire to create an alliance with Micro and your need to guard GVP's confidential information. When I have had a chance to review the entire NDA, we'll get together and go over it line by line.

A: Thanks, Tom. I appreciate your assistance.

Excerpts from the Non-Disclosure Agreement (NDA)
Drafted and Proposed by MicroSystems

* * * *

This agreement is intended to allow General Vision Processing (GVP) and MicroSystems (Micro) to evaluate the feasibility of possible cooperation in the development of GVP's *iChip*™ technology (hereinafter referred to as the "Project") while protecting their confidential information against unauthorized use or disclosure.

IT IS AGREED AS FOLLOWS:

1. CONFIDENTIAL INFORMATION means any item or information, including electrical/electronic schematic and circuit diagrams, documentation, specifications, formulas, manufacturing processes, know-how, computer programs, technology, technical descriptions and other technical and economic data, records and information pertaining to the Project that is disclosed by GVP (hereinafter the DISCLOSING PARTY) to Micro (hereinafter the RECEIVING PARTY) under this Agreement, whether disclosed orally, in writing, or in any other form, provided it is clearly and conspicuously marked or designated in writing by the DISCLOSING PARTY as being CONFIDENTIAL INFORMATION or if originally disclosed orally, it is confirmed in writing as CONFIDENTIAL INFORMATION by the DISCLOSING PARTY within ten (10) calendar days after oral disclosure.

2. During the term of this Agreement, the RECEIVING PARTY undertakes to apply to all CONFIDENTIAL INFORMATION the same degree of care with which it treats and protects its own proprietary information against public disclosure. The RECEIVING PARTY further undertakes to restrict its use of CONFIDENTIAL INFORMATION to the Project. However, the RECEIVING PARTY reserves the right to disclose the CONFIDENTIAL INFORMATION to persons working as employees of an Affiliated Company, provided the RECEIVING PARTY shall ensure that such persons comply with the provisions of this Agreement. For the purpose of this Agreement, an Affiliated Company shall mean any company, owned or controlled, directly or indirectly, now or hereafter, by the RECEIVING PARTY.

3. Information is not considered CONFIDENTIAL INFORMATION if the RECEIVING PARTY can prove that such information is

a) in or passes into the public domain other than by breach of this Agreement; or,
b) known to the RECEIVING PARTY prior to disclosure by the DISCLOSING PARTY; or,
c) disclosed to the RECEIVING PARTY by one having the full right to disclose it; or,
d) independently developed by an employee of the RECEIVING PARTY; or,
e) approved for release by written authorization of the DISCLOSING PARTY; or
f) required to be disclosed as a result of a Court order or pursuant to government action.

* * * *

Library

AL Limited v. Glass Glo Corporation

United States Court of Appeals for the Fifteenth Circuit (1995)

Per Curiam: This interlocutory appeal was certified by the district court after it dismissed, for failure to state a claim, one of the claims in a suit by AL Limited against Glass Glo Corporation.

AL Limited, a United Kingdom corporation, owns the worldwide rights to the "Aluglas Process," a coating system by which a thin layer of metalized aluminum is applied to products such as greeting cards, gift wrapping, and labels. Part of the Aluglas Process is patented, but major portions of the process are trade secrets. AL has consistently taken great care to protect its trade secrets, principally by the use of non-disclosure agreements between it and its licensees.

AL licensed the Aluglas Process to Prodicom, a Mexican company that used the process to manufacture its products and was familiar with all aspects of the process, including AL's patent and trade secret information. The licensing agreement between AL and Prodicom contained a non-disclosure provision that prohibited Prodicom from disclosing any "confidential information," which was defined in the agreement, to any person or entity without the express, prior written consent of AL. Moreover, any such disclosures were to be made under terms at least as restrictive as the non-disclosure terms of the AL/Prodicom agreement.

Robert Faris, chief executive officer of Glass Glo Corporation, a Franklin corporation, was interested in evaluating whether the Aluglas Process could be applied beneficially to the products manufactured by Glass Glo. He met with officials of Prodicom and requested that he be permitted to examine Prodicom's manufacturing methods using the Aluglas Process. Prodicom communicated with AL and received approval to allow Faris to receive formulas, documentation, and other information vital to the use of the process. All the information Faris sought fell within the definition of "confidential information" as defined in the AL/Prodicom agreement. The condition upon which AL agreed to let Prodicom disclose to Faris, however, was that Faris and Glass Glo first enter into a non-disclosure agreement with Prodicom restricting Faris' and Glass Glo's right to disclose information relating to the Aluglas Process to the same extent that Prodicom was prevented from disclosing such information.

Consequently, Prodicom and Faris, on behalf of Glass Glo, entered into a written agreement defining "confidential information and trade secrets" consistent with the definitions in the AL/Prodicom agreement and containing a non-disclosure clause that stated: "Prodicom reveals the confidential information and trade secrets ('information') relating to the Aluglas Process upon the express undertaking of Glass Glo Corporation that it receives the information from Prodicom in confidence and that it will not disclose any of the information to any person or entity [other than certain specified scientific and engineering personnel of Glass Glo] for any purpose whatsoever without first obtaining the written consent of Prodicom." The Prodicom/Glass Glo agreement did not mention or otherwise refer to AL Limited.

Faris later concluded that the Aluglas Process was not suited to Glass Glo's purposes and decided not to use it. However, one of the members of Glass Glo's board of directors was the chief executive officer of Shining Light, Inc., a manufacturer of ornamental papers. Believing that Shining Light might be able to use the Aluglas Process and without getting Prodicom's approval, Faris turned over to Shining Light the files and materials he had obtained from Prodicom.

When AL discovered Faris' disclosure to Shining Light, AL sued Glass Glo on a number of claims, including one for breach of the Prodicom/Glass Glo nondisclosure agreement. AL asserted that it was an intended beneficiary of the Prodicom/Glass Glo agreement.

It is ancient law in Franklin that, to succeed on a third-party beneficiary theory, a non-party to an agreement "must be the intended beneficiary of the contract, not merely an incidental beneficiary to whom no duty is owed." *Lawrence v. Fox* (Franklin Supreme Court, 1895). More recently, the Franklin Supreme Court, applying principles declared in the Restatement (Second) of Contracts, stated, "essential to the status as an intended beneficiary are circumstances indicating that the promisee intends to give the beneficiary the benefit of the promised performance." *Goldman v. Belden* (Franklin Supreme Court, 1995).

The non-disclosure agreement that Faris signed makes no reference to a licensing agreement between AL and Prodicom, nor does it purport by its terms to run to the benefit of AL. Mere mention of the Aluglas Process in the Prodicom/Glass Glo agreement does not satisfy the requirement that the contract must expressly identify the intended third-party beneficiary and provide that the promises of the promisee run to that intended beneficiary.

The contract upon which AL sued Glass Glo does not satisfy these requirements. Accordingly, the court below did not err in dismissing this cause of action for failure to state a claim.

We affirm.

Celeritas Technologies v. Rockwell International Corporation

United States Court of Appeals for the Fifteenth Circuit (1998)

In July 1993, Michael Dolan filed a patent application for a "de-emphasizer" apparatus to increase the rate of data transmission over analog cellular telephone networks. The resulting patent, assigned to Celeritas, was issued in January 1995.

In September 1993, Dolan and other officials of Celeritas met with representatives from Rockwell to demonstrate their proprietary de-emphasis technology. Rockwell entered into a non-disclosure agreement (NDA) with Celeritas which provided that Rockwell "shall not disclose or use any Proprietary Information except for the purpose of evaluating possible business arrangements between Celeritas and Rockwell."

The agreement also provided that proprietary information "shall not include material which . . . was in the public domain on the date hereof or comes into the public domain other than through the fault or negligence of Rockwell . . . or information independently developed by Rockwell or Rockwell's employees who had no access to the Information disclosed hereunder."[1]

In March 1994, AT&T began to sell a modem that incorporated de-emphasis technology. In that same month, Rockwell informed Celeritas it would not license the use of Celeritas' proprietary technology and concurrently began a development project to incorporate de-emphasis technology into its modem chip sets. In January 1995, Rockwell began shipping its first prototype chip sets that contained de-emphasis technology.

Celeritas' subsequent suit against Rockwell on breach of contract resulted in a jury verdict in its favor and a judgment in excess of $57 million.[2] Rockwell's motion for judgment as a matter of law was denied by the district court. Rockwell appeals.

Rockwell argues the de-emphasis technology disclosed to Rockwell was already in the public domain before Rockwell used it, specifically when AT&T began selling its modems. Rockwell asserts that the technology was "readily ascertainable" because "any competent engineer could have reverse-engineered the AT&T modem." Rockwell further argues that any confidentiality obligation under the NDA regarding

[1] The full text of the clause setting forth the exclusions from proprietary information reads as follows:

"Such Information shall not include material which Rockwell can by reasonable proof: (1) Show was in the public domain on the date hereof or comes into the public domain other than through the fault or negligence of Rockwell; (2) Show was contained in a written record in Rockwell's files prior to the date of receipt from Celeritas; (3) Show was lawfully obtained under circumstances permitting its disclosure and use; (4) Show was disclosed by Celeritas to others on an unrestricted basis; and (5) Demonstrate was independently developed by Rockwell or Rockwell's employees who had no access to the Information disclosed hereunder."

[2] The term of the confidentiality agreement was designated "perpetual" as opposed to a set number of years in duration. Permanent confidentiality signifies that the parties assigned high value to the information that was to be disclosed to Rockwell and supports the amount awarded to Celeritas by the jury. *See Stamats v. Concord Tech* (Franklin Supreme Court, 1991).

de-emphasis technology was extinguished once the Celeritas patent was issued in January 1995. Substantial evidence supports the jury's conclusion that Rockwell breached the NDA. The jury implicitly found the information given to Rockwell by Celeritas was covered by the NDA. Unrebutted testimony established that Celeritas disclosed to Rockwell implementation details and techniques that went beyond the information disclosed in the patent. Accordingly, Rockwell's reliance on the issuance of the Celeritas patent is misplaced.

There was substantial evidence on which the jury could find that Rockwell used Celeritas' proprietary data to develop its modem chip sets. Significantly, when Rockwell initiated its de-emphasis development program it did not erect an organizational barrier to protect the confidential information of Celeritas. In place of a "clean room,"[3] Rockwell assigned the same engineers who had learned of Celeritas' technology under the NDA to its own de-emphasis development project.

The jury also found that the technology had not been placed in the public domain by the sale of the AT&T modem. Franklin law appears somewhat unsettled regarding whether a trade secret enters the public domain when it is "readily ascertainable" or whether it must also be "actually ascertained" by the public. Because the judgment is supportable under either standard, we need not attempt to resolve this issue of state law. Suffice it to say that substantial evidence supports a finding that the technology implementing the de-emphasis function in the modem was not "readily ascertainable."

Accordingly, the court did not err in denying Rockwell's motion for judgment as a matter of law regarding its breach of the NDA.

Affirmed.

[3] A "clean room" involves a development team working under a set of strict written procedures to control the transfer of data from other research efforts to the team, thereby protecting the development team from exposure to confidential information or trade secrets of third parties. *See* K. Copenhaver, *Structuring, Negotiating & Implementing Strategic Alliances* (PLI 1997).

Nilsen v. Motorola, Inc.

United States District Court (D. Franklin 1997)

In mid-1987, Joseph Nilsen, the president of Innovation Center, Inc., approached Motorola about an alliance to produce electronic ballasts, devices used to power fluorescent lamps. Nilsen offered Motorola an "exclusive licensing of proprietary technology that permits the development of electronic ballasts at substantially reduced cost as compared with the least costly of presently available electronic ballasts."

In September 1987, Nilsen and Motorola executed a non-disclosure agreement (NDA) to establish the terms under which Nilsen would provide confidential information to Motorola. Essential provisions of the NDA included these:

• "Confidential Information" was defined as "any device, graphics, written information, or information in other tangible forms that is disclosed, for evaluation purposes, to Motorola by [Nilsen] relating to [electronic ballasts] and that is marked at the time of disclosure as being 'Confidential' or 'Proprietary.'"

• Information disclosed orally or visually and identified at the time of such disclosure as "Confidential" was to be considered as "Confidential Information" only if reduced to tangible form, marked "Confidential," and transmitted to Motorola within 30 days of such oral or visual disclosure.

• "Confidential Information" was explicitly defined to exclude "any information which: (a) is or becomes publicly known through no wrongful act on Motorola's part; or (b) is, at the time of disclosure under this Agreement, already known to Motorola without restriction on disclosure; or (c) is, or subsequently becomes, rightfully and without breach of this Agreement, in Motorola's possession without an obligation restricting disclosure; or (d) is independently developed by Motorola without breach of this Agreement; or (e) is furnished to a third party by [Nilsen] without a similar restriction on the third party's rights; or (f) is explicitly approved for release by written authorization of [Nilsen]."

• Motorola undertook "to apply to all 'Confidential Information' the same degree of care with which it treats and protects its own proprietary information against public disclosure but no less than reasonable care."

• Motorola also agreed that "Disclosure of confidential information is limited to Motorola employees and Motorola is not to disclose the 'Confidential Information' to any third party" nor was it to "use the 'Confidential Information' for any purpose" other than "evaluation purposes, which evaluation is to be completed within two months from [September 1, 1987]."

• In the event of termination, Motorola undertook to deliver to Nilsen all of the 'Confidential Information' it had received from Nilsen, or to certify its destruction, at

Nilsen's option.

Within a short time after executing the NDA, Motorola wrote to Nilsen "to confirm the various 'to-dos' that you agreed to address during our meeting last Monday. . .

> 2. Review your documents and determine whether any of them should have been stamped 'confidential.' Our mutual intent is to specifically identify confidential information."

Motorola reminded Nilsen of this "to do" item a number of times.

From September 1987 to May 1988, Motorola personnel evaluated its possible entry into the electronic ballast business. Nilsen provided Motorola personnel with a prototype ballast in a "black box"[1] that Motorola used as a test device. He later built another prototype based on a set of Motorola performance specifications.

During that same period, Motorola engaged two non-Motorola employees as consultants. David Bergman, a marketing specialist, and William Alling, an electronics specialist, were asked to prepare a report detailing financial and technical objectives for Motorola's potential entry into the electronic ballast industry. Motorola shared with Bergman and Alling all the material Nilsen had provided to Motorola from the onset of their relationship. Based on the Bergman-Alling report, Motorola decided to "put on hold" the decision whether to enter the electronic ballast business and wrote to Nilsen informing him of that decision.

In 1990, Motorola reconsidered the Bergman-Alling report and concluded that Motorola should go forward with the business, using Nilsen's technology.

Over the next several months, Nilsen and Motorola engaged in what can only be described as "arm's-length bargaining." Motorola offered Nilsen several compensation packages and business models. Nilsen rejected all of them as inadequate. In light of the "significant gap" between them, Motorola sent Nilsen a letter in November 1990 terminating their discussions. Motorola later returned to Nilsen all documents that Motorola had received, but retained an "archive copy" for Motorola's files that included documents that Nilsen had failed to mark "confidential."

Once discussions with Nilsen were terminated, Motorola communicated with Carl Stevens, an engineer who had developed his own "Super Ballast," a design that he had earlier licensed to Calmont Technologies. Motorola hired Stevens as its chief engineer and executed a Licensing Agreement for the exclusive use of his electronic ballast technology. Stevens and other Motorola engineers participated in the improvement of electronic ballast design until December 1993, at which time Motorola completed its

---

[1] A "black box" is a unit whose internal structure is unknown but whose function can be documented. The internal mechanics of a device do not matter to the engineer who uses the unit to evaluate the device's function. A memory chip, for example, can be viewed as a black box so that its function can be ascertained without disclosing its structure. Many people use memory chips and even design them into computers, but generally only the memory chip designer needs to understand the chip's internal operation.

final design and proceeded to production.[2] Nilsen thereafter filed suit, claiming Motorola breached the non-disclosure agreement it had with him.

Before this case proceeds to a jury trial, one matter that must be decided is whether, as a matter of law, Motorola breached its contractual obligations of limited disclosure under the NDA when it revealed confidential information provided by Nilsen to third parties. Construction of the parties' written agreements is, of course, a question of law for this Court and not one of fact for the jury.

As a preliminary matter, however, this Court concludes that there was no implied duty imposed on Motorola to maintain the confidentiality of any of Nilsen's documents that he himself had failed to designate as "confidential." The "to-do" list (*supra*) afforded Nilsen the full opportunity to stamp his documents as "confidential." Since he failed to stamp a number of documents, he cannot now contend that the trade secret concept extends to any implied duty stemming from his delivery to Motorola of any information that had not been marked as "confidential."

Franklin courts have repeatedly held that any disclosure believed to be proprietary—including previous disclosures that had not been so marked—must be in written form and stamped "confidential" (*e.g., In re Andrea Dumon* (Franklin Supreme Court, 1994)). Motorola, therefore, was under no duty to maintain the confidentiality of any of Nilsen's disclosures (whenever made) that were not so marked.

[2] Discovery during the course of this litigation has uncovered several of Nilsen's disclosures, designated as "confidential" per the NDA, in Stevens's files.

Nilsen also contends that, as a matter of law, Motorola violated the NDA when it provided information marked as "confidential" to Alling and Bergman, who were not employees of Motorola. Motorola presses the view that the section of the NDA that reads "Disclosure of Confidential Information is limited to Motorola employees" and "Motorola is not to disclose the 'Confidential Information' to any third party" should be interpreted expansively. It contends that customary business practice in situations where companies are evaluating technologies and commercial opportunities includes passing the information on to non-employee consultants and experts for review and analysis. Therefore, argues Motorola, the clause in the NDA must be read to allow it to share the confidential information it received from Nilsen with non-employees who had a "need to know" in order to provide Motorola with essential advice.

Courts have traditionally held that non-disclosure agreements restricting dissemination of confidential information to employees of the receiving party permitted disclosure to legal counsel (*Matters v. Siddown Corporation* (Franklin Court of Appeal, 1980)), and other professionals normally engaged by the receiving company (e.g., technical consultants, *Otone, Inc. v. Chambers* (Franklin Supreme Court, 1984)). More recently, however, the Franklin courts have concluded that an NDA clause restricting disclosure of information to employees "is a very clear expression that the intent of the parties was employees only and not employees and others to whom the Disclosing Party might have foreseen that the Receiving Party would make disclosures." *Den-Tal-Ez, Inc. v. Siemens Capital*

49

Corp. (Franklin Supreme Court, 1993). That interpretation is all the more appropriate here, where the clause not only restricts disclosure to employees but goes on to explicitly prohibit disclosure "to any third party."

The parties had the opportunity to craft conditions under which confidential information could have been revealed by Motorola to third parties who were providing assistance in the evaluation of the data it received from Nilsen. They could have, for example, allowed disclosure to those with "a need to know"; or to those individuals specifically identified; or to third parties who were under a confidentiality agreement the terms of which were at least as restrictive as the terms of the Nilsen-Motorola agreement; or, on an *ad hoc* basis, to those third parties approved in advance by Nilsen. These options and more were available to the contracting parties and would have permitted at least some disclosure to third parties.

Motorola and Nilsen, however, did not avail themselves of such options. Instead they agreed to a flat ban on the disclosure of "'Confidential Information' to any third party." Therefore, the Court concludes, as a matter of law, that Motorola breached its duty under the NDA when it disclosed confidential information to the third parties identified above.

GVP Non-Disclosure Agreement
DRAFTERS' POINT SHEET

In this test item, the applicants' firm represents General Vision Processing, Inc. (GVP), the developer of an electronic device known as the *iChip*. GVP is about to enter into an arrangement with Microsystems (Micro), by which GVP will give Micro access to the *iChip* so Micro can evaluate whether the *iChip* can be used to enhance its computerized transportation safety systems. GVP's immediate concern is the protection of the trade secrets and know-how (confidential information) that it will necessarily have to disclose to Micro in the course of Micro's evaluation of the *iChip*.

Micro has supplied its standard form non-disclosure agreement (NDA), and Dr. Nabeel Adsani, GVP's President and Chief Executive Officer, is concerned that this "boilerplate" agreement may not adequately protect GVP from the unauthorized use and disclosure of GVP's trade secrets and confidential information. Dr. Adsani has expressed his concerns in an interview with the supervising partner.

The File contains the instructing memorandum from the supervising partner, a transcript of the interview with Dr. Adsani, and selected excerpts from Micro's NDA. The Library contains three federal court opinions that bear upon different aspects of the problem. Using these materials, the applicants are instructed to write part of an opinion letter to Dr. Adsani.

The following discussion covers all of the points the drafters intended to raise in the problem. Applicants need not cover them all to receive passing or even excellent grades. Grading decisions are within the discretion of the graders in the user jurisdictions.

Overview: No particular format is prescribed for the applicants' work product. It should be a narrative exposition that can be incorporated into an opinion letter being prepared by the supervising partner, written in language suitable to communication with a non-lawyer. The applicants are told specifically to focus their analysis of Micro's NDA on three concerns:

- The NDA's restrictions as to the persons or entities (receiving parties) to whom disclosure can be made;
- The conditions or limitations that should be placed on disclosures to those receiving parties; and
- GVP's ability to enforce its rights as a third-party beneficiary against persons or

entities who obtain confidential information but who are not signatories to the GVP/Micro NDA.

Applicants are to explain whether the excerpted parts of Micro's NDA provide GVP with adequate protection on the foregoing issues. If applicants answer "yes," they should explain how the NDA provides adequate protection. If they answer "no," they should explain why and indicate the changes they would recommend to address GVP's concerns.

In the interview, Dr. Adsani says, "I don't want to scare Micro off." In other words, he doesn't want to require changes to the NDA that will make the confidentiality burden on Micro so onerous that Micro will refuse to go forward with the deal. Nevertheless, applicants should push the envelope and let the partner decide, after consultation with Dr. Adsani, which suggestions to adopt and which ones to reject.

There are a number of ways in which applicants can organize their answers. The best way is probably to analyze each of the paragraphs in the NDA, in serial order.

The Preamble: The preamble is adequate as an introductory statement of the purpose of the agreement.

- It identifies the parties and the technology (i.e., the *iChip*);
- It states that the purpose is to protect the use and disclosure of confidential information.

An applicant might suggest that the "project" be defined a bit more carefully, e.g., "exploring the feasibility of possible cooperation in the development of GVP's *iChip* technology for use in transportation safety products being developed by Micro."

As currently written, the preamble suggests that Micro is also seeking to protect its own confidential information. It would not be out of order for an applicant to suggest that the thrust of the language should be changed to make it clear that Micro is the party that wishes to evaluate the technology and that it is *GVP's* confidential information that is sought to be protected. It might also help in ascribing the proper relationship of the parties to identify Micro as the "Receiving Party" and GVP as the "Disclosing Party" in the preamble rather than later on.

Paragraph 1: The language of this paragraph adequately defines "confidential information."

- It clearly states that it pertains to the litany of subjects potentially to be disclosed by the Disclosing Party, GVP, to the Receiving Party, Micro.

- Applicants can analogize to the definition found in the *Nilsen* case and conclude that the definition in Micro's form NDA is sufficiently broad to cover any conceivable type of tangible and intangible information given by GVP regarding the *iChip*.
- In *Celeritas*, the court rejected the claim that the confidentiality obligation was extinguished once a patent was issued, finding that the information furnished by the disclosing party went far beyond that which could have been gleaned from the patent documents.
    - To guard against a similar claim by Micro, a perceptive applicant might suggest an expansion of the definition of "confidential information" by including a recitation to the effect that the information that will be disclosed by GVP on this "project" includes information that cannot be obtained from GVP's patent application. This might be helpful later on if Micro asserts that it obtained the information from GVP's patent documents.

Other parts of this paragraph of Micro's form NDA are problematic in two respects:

- The proviso that information must be "clearly and conspicuously marked or designated in writing" by GVP as being confidential information places a burden on GVP; and
- The obligation that GVP "confirm[ ] in writing . . . within ten (10) calendar days" information that was communicated orally is too restrictive.

- The clue for the applicants that these points are issues to deal with is found in *Nilsen*, where the court refused to find a breach of the agreement because the disclosing party had failed to mark certain documents.
    - Applicants should suggest changes that will ease the burden on GVP and make it less likely that mere oversight by GVP will let something fall between the cracks. For example:
        - The agreement could recite that *all* information communicated by GVP in connection with the "project" shall be deemed confidential unless otherwise designated; or
        - It could require Micro to maintain a log of all information communicated by GVP, to identify that which has not been "marked or

designated" confidential, and give periodic notice to GVP so that GVP might have the option of so marking or designating it.

  - The clue for this approach is also found in *Nilsen*.

- In any event, the 10-day limitation is too short.
  - The time for marking and designating should be lengthened to, perhaps, 30 days or to a period more consistent with when it can reasonably be expected that GVP could react to the notice.

Paragraph 2: This is the paragraph that needs the most work. In their comments, applicants should address each of the following concerns expressed by the client in the interview:

- How to ensure that Micro's employees observe and are bound by the NDA;
- How to protect information disclosed to people (e.g., outside consultants) "associated with" Micro;
- How to take into account the risks associated with turnover in Micro's workforce;
- How to protect the information in the likely event that Micro spins off its Transportation Safety Division into a separate entity; and
- How to protect the information if GVP and Micro are not able to make a deal and they end up going their separate ways.

- The first sentence in this paragraph requires Micro to apply to GVP's confidential information "the same degree of care with which it treats its own proprietary information against public disclosure."
  - The language should go beyond that and set a base standard, e.g., "but not less than reasonable care."
    - The clue for this change is found in the court's recitation of the provisions of the NDA in *Nilsen*.
- The next sentence, the one that restricts Micro's use of the confidential information to the "project" (i.e., the evaluation of the *iChip* for use in Micro's traffic safety products), appears adequate to protect GVP from having Micro use the information for other purposes, especially if the definition of the "project" is augmented as suggested above.
- There is no language specifically stating that Micro will limit access to GVP's confidential information to Micro employees and others assigned or retained to work on the "project." This deficiency goes directly to several of the concerns expressed by Dr. Adsani, i.e.:
  - How to ensure that Micro's employees observe and are bound by the NDA.

- To address this concern, language should be inserted into the NDA that either requires all Micro employees who work on the "project" to subscribe to the Micro/GVP NDA as signatories or, if that is impractical because of the numbers of such employees, that requires them to execute separate NDAs specifically acknowledging that the NDAs are for the benefit of GVP.
  - The latter approach would satisfy the third-party beneficiary requirement set forth in *AL Limited v. Glass Glo Corporation.*

How to protect information disclosed to people "associated with" Micro (e.g., outside consultants).

- Dr. Adsani recognizes that Micro is likely to want to use outside consultants to assist in the evaluation of the *iChip* but says he would like to know ahead of time who they are and when they would be used. To address this concern and avoid the problem encountered in *Nilsen*, the NDA should specifically provide that Micro may disclose confidential information to such consultants but under strict controls, e.g.:
  - The information should be disclosed only to outside consultants who have a need to know (see *Nilsen*);
  - The outside consultants should be identified to GVP before any confidential information is communicated to them, with GVP having the right to object;
  - GVP should be told what information will be disclosed to the consultants and for what purposes;
  - All documents and other tangible forms of information disclosed should be marked confidential and a log maintained by Micro, with a copy to GVP;
  - At the conclusion of the consultancy, all information communicated to the consultants in written or other tangible form, including archival copies, should be returned to Micro; and
  - All outsiders should be required to execute NDAs at least as restrictive as that between GVP and Micro, specifically recognizing that GVP is the third-party beneficiary of those agreements.

How to take into account the risks associated with turnover in Micro's workforce.

- Anticipating the reality that employees who have worked on the "project" will leave Micro's workforce and others will enter,
    - Micro should be obligated to require all new employees to subscribe to or sign NDAs;
    - The NDAs signed by all employees assigned to the "project" should provide that they will preserve the confidentiality of the information in perpetuity (*cf. Celeritas*) and that when they leave they will not take with them any of the written or otherwise tangible confidential information.
        - These agreements, too, should recognize that GVP is the third-party beneficiary.

How to protect the information in the likely event that Micro spins off its Transportation Safety Division into a separate entity.

- An eventual spinoff appears to be a certainty, and Micro's form NDA deals somewhat with this eventuality. However, the form language does not go far enough.
- Under Micro's form NDA, Micro reserves the right to disclose the confidential information to employees of the "Affiliated Company" and undertakes to require those employees to comply with the GVP/Micro NDA.
    - To address Dr. Adsani's concerns, the GVP/Micro NDA should provide that, in the event of a spinoff;
        - Micro will require the new entity (not just the employees of the new entity) to execute an NDA incorporating all the protections that exist in the GVP/Micro NDA;
        - The employees of the new entity who are assigned to work on the evaluation of the ***iChip*** will be required to either execute NDAs or subscribe to the one entered into by the new entity; and
        - In all events, the new NDAs must specifically make GVP the intended beneficiary. *See AL Limited v. Glass Glo Corporation.*

- How to protect the information if GVP and Micro are not able to make a deal and they end up going their separate ways.
  - In expressing this concern during the interview, Dr. Adsani himself suggests the solution, i.e., require Micro to return to GVP all the documents and other tangible forms of information, including the *iChip* itself.
  - Accordingly, the NDA should include such a requirement.
  - It should also include a requirement for Micro's "certification of destruction" of documents and other things that have not been returned. *Nilsen.*
- In addition, in the event GVP and Micro are unable to work out a deal, the NDA should contain a provision stating for how long the information should remain confidential once the "project" has concluded.
  - As suggested in *Celeritas*, it may depend on the value of the information, but it would not be out of order for an applicant to suggest that the NDA should provide for perpetual confidentiality. Presumably, if GVP were unable to make a deal with Micro, GVP would want to offer the opportunity to others. In that event, Micro's continued confidentiality would be necessary.
- Along these same lines, an applicant might want to suggest that there be an agreed-upon time frame within which the evaluation of the *iChip* must take place, i.e., when the "project" must end. (See the NDA in *Nilsen*, which included such a provision.)
  - This would prescribe the period during which GVP would be required to make disclosures and make it easier to manage the flow of information.

Paragraph 3: This part of the NDA attempts to articulate categories of information that are not considered "confidential," and, while an applicant might suggest removing them completely from the NDA, the likelihood is that Micro would insist on this language or similar language for its own protection.

Subparts a, b, and d of this paragraph require the applicants' scrutiny. Subparts c, e, and f need not be altered.

- Subpart a excludes information that is "in or passes into the public domain other than by breach of this agreement."

- This might be a good place for applicants to suggest inserting language to the effect that the information disclosed by GVP is above and beyond that which is contained in the patent application. This would prevent Micro from asserting that it obtained it information from the public domain, i.e., the patent application. (*Cf. Celeritas.*)

The exclusions in subparts b (information that was known to Micro before GVP disclosed it) and d (information that was independently developed by a Micro employee) are related.

- Recall that in the interview, Dr. Adsani pointed out that Micro is in the process of developing two "perception tracing" products—*Intersect* and *LaneTrac*—which might make efficient use of the *iChip*.
- This suggests that certain research and development work has been underway at Micro and that there is a potential for claims by Micro that it already knew certain things disclosed by GVP and that those things were independently developed by Micro. (These problems are suggested in *Celeritas* and *Nilsen.*)
- To prevent disputes arising from such claims, applicants might suggest that:
    - Micro should be required to disclose to GVP the status of its "perception tracing" research and development efforts on the *Intersect* and *LaneTrac* products so it can be ascertained whether and what *iChip*-type information may already be known to Micro.
        - GVP would agree to receive the information under a non-disclosure obligation.
    - Micro should be required to identify to GVP all Micro employees who have worked on the "perception tracing" aspects of *Intersect* and *LaneTrac* and to describe the status of their research and development so it can be ascertained whether any of them have "independently developed" any of the *iChip* information.
        - Again, GVP would agree to receive this information under a non-disclosure obligation.

- Applicants should recognize that this proposal will present two risks: (1) that GVP will be polluted by Micro's confidential information, and (2) that Micro might be so turned off by the requests that it will balk at the deal.

Micro should be required to establish a "clean room" (*see Celeritas*) so that Micro employees who have been working on Micro's products will not be exposed to GVP's information.

Likewise, Micro should be required to agree that employees and outside consultants it assigns to work on the *iChip* evaluation project (*cf. Nilsen*) shall not be allowed to work on Micro's *Intersect* and *LaneTrac* projects for the duration of the evaluation period and perhaps even for a number of years into the future.

FILE

In re Al Merton

Locher, Lawson & Klein, P.A.
Attorneys and Counselors at Law
6714 Tulsa Cove
Munster, Franklin 33448

To: Applicant
From: Catherine Locher
Date: July 30, 2002
Subject: Al Merton's Will

Al Merton came in earlier today to talk about updating his will. I've attached a transcript of my interview with him. I've also charted his family tree insofar as it is relevant to our task.

Mr. Merton is going to have heart surgery tomorrow. He is apprehensive and wants us to draft a new will in accordance with the wishes he expressed when I interviewed him. He will come in and sign the will later today.

Eventually, we may need to draft additional documents necessary to carry out Mr. Merton's testamentary scheme, but the main thing now is to get the will done in time for Mr. Merton to execute it before his surgery. I would like you to complete the following tasks:

1. Draft the introductory clauses and all dispositive clauses for Mr. Merton's new will. Follow our firm's Will Drafting Guidelines and set forth the clauses in separately labeled paragraphs, using the headings set forth in the guidelines. Do not concern yourself with the definitional and boilerplate clauses.

2. I'm particularly concerned about how you deal with Stuart Merton and the gifts of the corporate stock. Once you draft the provisions regarding those issues, please explain why you drafted them the way you did.

Another associate is researching the tax implications, so you need not concern yourself with them.

Locher, Lawson & Klein, P.A.

MEMORANDUM

September 8, 1995

To: All Attorneys
From: Robert Lawson
Re: Will Drafting Guidelines

Over the years, this firm has used a variety of formats in drafting wills. Effective immediately, all wills drafted by this firm should follow this format:

PART ONE: Introduction.

1. Set forth the first of the introductory clauses with a statement declaring it to be the testator's will and the name and domicile of the testator.
2. Include an appropriate clause regarding the revocation of prior testamentary instruments.
3. Include a clause naming the testator's immediate family members and identifying their relationship to the testator (parents, siblings, spouse, children, grandchildren, nephews, and nieces).

PART TWO: Dispositive Clauses (to be set forth in separate subdivisions or subparagraphs by class of bequest.) See the attached excerpt from *Walker's Treatise on Wills* for the definitions of the different classes of bequests. Bequests should be set forth in the following order, using the appropriate heading:

1. Specific bequests
   a. Real property
   b. Tangible personal property
   c. Other specific bequests
   d. Any other clauses stating conditions that might affect the disposition of specific bequests
2. General bequests
3. Demonstrative bequests
4. Residuary bequests

PART THREE: Definitional Clauses. Clauses relating to how words and phrases used in the will should be interpreted.

PART FOUR: Boilerplate Clauses. Clauses relating to the naming of fiduciaries and their administrative and management authority, payment of debts and expenses, tax clauses, attestation clauses, and self-proving will affidavits.

Walker's Treatise on Wills

CLASSIFICATION OF BEQUESTS:

Section 500. All bequests under wills are classified as either (1) specific, (2) general, (3) demonstrative, or (4) residuary.

Section 501. A *specific* bequest is a bequest of a specific asset.

Section 502. A *general* bequest (typically a gift of money) is a bequest payable out of general estate assets or to be acquired for a beneficiary out of general estate assets.

Section 503. A *demonstrative* bequest is a bequest of a specific sum of money payable from a designated account. To the extent that the designated account is insufficient to satisfy the bequest, the balance is paid from the general funds of the estate.

Section 504. A *residuary* bequest is a bequest that is neither general, specific, nor demonstrative and includes bequests that purport to dispose of the whole of the remaining estate.

Merton Family Tree

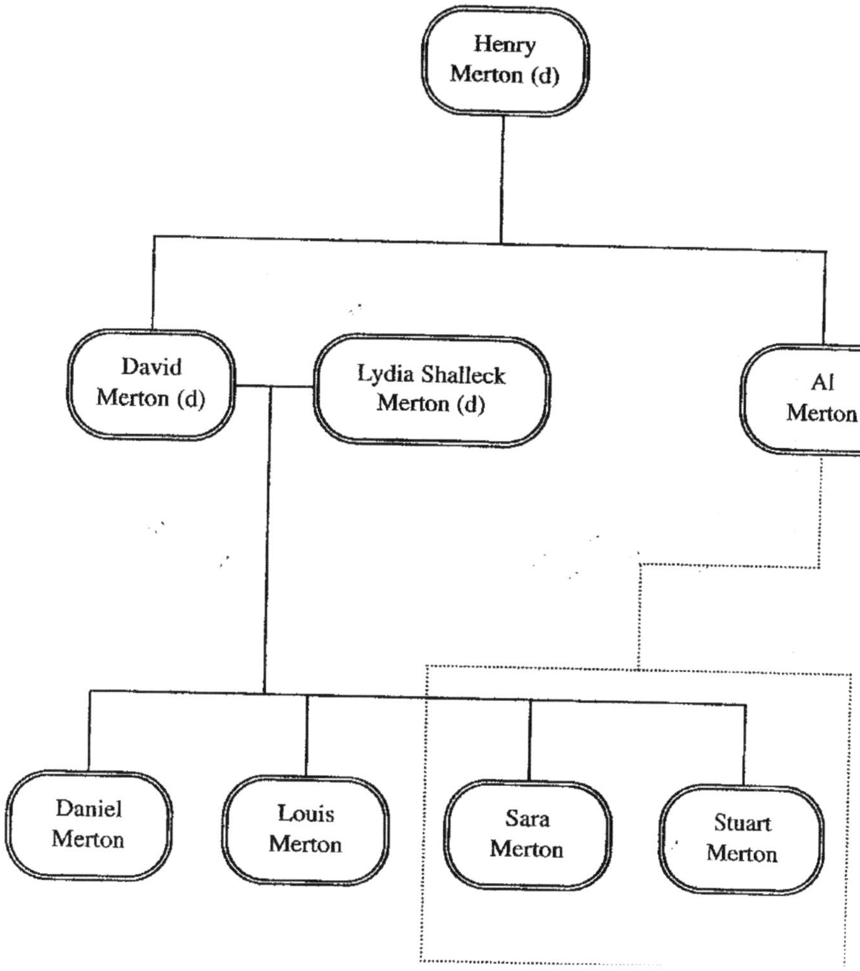

Transcript of Interview with Al Merton

July 30, 2002

* * * *

Q: What brings you here today?

A: Tomorrow I will have open heart surgery and I'm thinking some about death. The surgery is very risky, plus I lost my father last year.

Q: Sounds like a scary time for you.

A: I can't think about anything else. My will is more than 20 years old and so much has happened since it was drafted, I'm sure that it needs to be revised. When my father passed away, I inherited his office supply business, and I need to figure out how to deal with it in case I die. I know I've left everything to the last minute. I just couldn't force myself to deal with this task.

Q: Did you bring your old will with you?

A: Yes. I also brought my father's.

Q: Tell me more.

A: When my brother David and his wife died three years ago in an auto accident, I became responsible for their two youngest children, the twins, Sara and Stuart. At the time their parents died, the twins were 17 years old.

Q: What do you mean you were responsible for them?

A: Well, there was no one else to take care of them so I adopted the twins. I was reluctant to adopt Stuart because he has always been trouble. About a year ago, he left home and I only hear from him when he wants money. David also had two older children, Daniel, who is 27 and has become very wealthy in the software business, and Louis, who is 25 and somewhat irresponsible. There was no point in adopting them.

Q: Tell me about the business you inherited from your father.

A: At least 40 years ago, my father, Henry Merton, inherited from his own father Merton Office Supply and the Lincoln Street land and building where the business is located. Dad incorporated the business, but he retained ownership of the Lincoln Street Property in his individual capacity. The rental income he received from the corporation for the Lincoln Street Property supported him when he retired.

Dad had two children, David and me. I earned a Ph.D. in business strategy and joined the faculty of Franklin College 30 years ago. My brother began working at Merton Office Supply 26 years ago, shortly after earning his B.B.A. in marketing.

Q: And David is the brother who died?

A: Yes. David and his wife Lydia died three years ago without a will. Although their debts effectively wiped out most of their assets, they left a trust holding $75,000 in life insurance proceeds for each child. Each child began receiving the income at age 18 and will receive the principal at age 25. Daniel and Louis have already received their $75,000.

Q: Do you have children of your own?

A: Nope, I never married or had kids. My students at the college keep me young.

Q: Can you tell me about your resources?

A: Well, there is Dad's business, Merton Office Supply Corporation. I brought an appraisal that was done in the year after Dad died. I think it is very accurate. There is a net profit of around $100,000 on sales of $3 million.

Q: I want to learn a lot more about the business, but tell me what else you own.

A: I inherited the Lincoln Street land and building that are leased to the office supply corporation. I also have a savings account of about $50,000 and a stock portfolio worth a little more than $2.5 million. I also own my house in Highland, worth around $450,000.

Q: Now can you tell me about the business?

A: Dad would have left the business to my brother David because he worked there for his whole life and ran it after Dad retired, but that was not to be. I inherited it from Dad and have been running it, but I really want to go back to teaching and the important pro bono work I was doing in Franklin College's small business program. Since David died, Sara has become more interested in the business and has worked there after school and in the summers. Neither of David's two older kids ever had any interest in the business. Sara really seems to have a head for it and is majoring in business in college. She will graduate at the end of this semester. I am reluctant to sell the business as long as she has an interest in running it, and it really may be that her interest in it is a way of dealing with the death of her father when she was so young. The older boys just want me to sell it. Indeed, I have an unsolicited offer of $900,000 for the Lincoln Street Property already.

Q: So let me see if I understand. There are twins, age 20, one of whom is interested in the business and the other of whom is not. There are two older boys—one is wealthy and the other?

A: Ahh, Louis. Louis has yet to graduate from college after six years and can't seem to focus. He just switched to his fourth major and his grades are terrible. He took part of the insurance money and bought a fancy car. I don't think he will ever amount to very much, and I am sure he will want a lot of money if he can get it without hard work.

Q: What about Sara's twin, Stuart?

A: It is heartbreaking, but I have given up. He hung around with a bad crowd, and I know they were into drugs and motorcycles. I tried but couldn't reach him, and now he is out of contact. I think that if I left him anything it would only exacerbate his worst behaviors, and so I can't in good conscience give him anything in my will.

Q: So you want to permanently disinherit him?

A: Yes, but if he turns around, then I may change my mind. Besides, he'll get his share of the proceeds from his parents' life insurance.

Q: And have you thought about what you want to do with your assets?

A: I am torn. My father wanted the business to continue in the family. I want to go back to teaching. Only one of the kids, Sara, could conceivably carry on the business. Louis and Stuart would sell it and waste the money, and Daniel doesn't need another penny. Also, the college has been my home for the last 30 years and I want to support it. I also need to protect Sara until she can support herself and, if she really wants to run the business, I need to give her a chance. To do that, the assets of the business plus the Lincoln Street Property must be kept intact, but it would be unfair to leave the whole thing to Sara and cut out the others completely.

Q: So . . . ?

A: I need some advice about how to do it. I want to give the three kids other than Stuart an equal share of the business but be sure that Sara has the power to make the decisions she will need to make in order to be successful. I would like her to be able to have all of the votes and for the three of them to share in the profits, but if either Louis or Daniel won't agree to give her the power, then that person's shares should go to Sara.

Q: There is such a thing as a voting trust, and I think it might be useful here. We can't create a voting trust in a will, but we can attach enough conditions to the gifts of the corporate stock to Sara, Daniel, and Louis to lay the groundwork for the trust. We can formalize the voting trust later.

A: That's fine. That's exactly what I want you to do. Sara's going to need at least 15 years to make a success of the business.

Q: Do you know if the articles of incorporation of Merton Office Supply say anything about voting trusts?

A: I just looked at them yesterday, and they say nothing at all about voting trusts.

Q: Okay. What would you like to do with the rest of the property?

A: I want to leave Franklin College $1 million in assets to endow the small business program and name it for my dad—The Henry Merton Small Business Assistance Program.

Q: There is still a sizable amount left. What would you like to do with it?

A: Well, I want to pay whatever taxes I owe. Then, I want to leave Sara some money so she can finish college—say $25,000, which should be paid first out of whatever is left in my savings account. Then, I want to leave Sara, Louis, and Daniel $100,000 each. If there is anything left, I want to leave it to the Franklin College Faculty Development Fund.

Q: Is there anything else?

A: Well, both the land and the building that comprise the Lincoln Street Property are absolutely essential to the successful operation of Merton Office Supply. Is there some way to make sure they remain linked?

Q: Well, the simplest thing would be to give the Lincoln Street Property to the corporation.

A: That sounds okay.

Q: All right. Anything else?

A: No, I think that covers it.

Q: In light of how you are feeling about your surgery, we will put a priority on revising your will so that you can sign it before you go to the hospital. In the long run, you will need to have a more sophisticated estate plan that includes tax planning, but for now let us get to work and get this done. Can you come back late this afternoon, and we will have it ready?

A: Okay. I'll be back later.

Last Will and Testament

Henry Merton

I, Henry Merton, a resident of Griffin County, Franklin, do make, publish and declare this my last will and testament. I revoke all wills and codicils previously made by me. I am widowed and have two adult sons, Al and David, and two grandchildren, Daniel and Louis.

Article One. I bequeath my real property to my son David. If my son David predeceases me, I bequeath my real property to my son Al. If both sons predecease me, I bequeath my real property to Franklin College.

Article Two. I bequeath my stock in Merton Office Supply Corporation to my son David. If my son David predeceases me, I bequeath said stock to my son Al. If both sons predecease me, I bequeath said stock to Franklin College.

Article Three. I bequeath the sum of $10,000 to my secretary Mary Jones if she survives me.

Article Four. I leave all the rest, residue, and remainder of my estate in equal shares to my sons David and Al or to the survivor of them.

Article Five. I appoint my son David to serve as my personal representative. If he is unable or unwilling to serve as personal representative, I appoint Franklin State Bank to serve. I direct my personal representative to pay as soon as practicable all of the following sums: all debts owed by me at my death; the expenses of my last illness; the expenses of my funeral; any unpaid charitable pledges, whether or not these are enforceable; and the costs of administering my estate.

Date: July 21, 1978

Signed: Henry Merton

Witnesses: Liza Marchant
Anna Miller
Charles Adams

Last Will and Testament

Al Merton

Introduction

A. I am Al Merton, a resident of Griffin County, Franklin. This is my last will and testament.

B. I revoke all wills and codicils previously made by me.

C. My father is Henry Merton. I have one brother, David, and two nephews, Daniel and Louis.

Article One. I bequeath all my real property to Franklin College.

Article Two. I bequeath all other property owned by me at my death to those individuals who would inherit my property under the laws of Franklin if I died intestate.

Article Three. I appoint my brother David to serve as my personal representative. If my brother David is unable or unwilling to serve as my personal representative, I appoint Franklin State Bank as my personal representative. I direct my personal representative to pay, as soon as practicable, all of the following sums: all debts owed by me at my death; the expenses of my last illness; the expenses of my funeral; any unpaid charitable pledges, whether or not these are enforceable; and the costs of administering my estate. My personal representative shall have the power to sell property as needed for the payment of debts and expenses and to distribute property to those individuals who take under Article Two.

Date: September 19, 1980

Al Merton

Witnesses:

Appraisal of Merton Office Supply Corporation
by Expert Appraisals LLC
October 24, 2001

Executive Summary

Merton Office Supply Corporation (MOSC) has operated at the same Lincoln Street location since its founding as an unincorporated business in 1917. Henry Merton, the second owner, incorporated the company in 1946 and, until his death, owned all 150 of the issued and outstanding shares of stock. He retained individual ownership of the Lincoln Street land and the building on that land. Henry's executor valued the MOSC stock at $800,000 and the land and the building (i.e., the Lincoln Street Property) at $1,000,000. On Henry's death, his son, Al Merton, inherited Henry's corporate stock and the Lincoln Street Property. Al now owns all 150 shares.

MOSC has not responded well to the challenges posed by large chains and the Internet. Because Henry did not expand into larger quarters, open additional stores, or even join a buying cooperative, MOSC foregoes economies of scale with respect to inventory buying, insurance rates, and other costs. The existence of competitors limits its ability to increase prices.

Last year's $100,000 profit on sales of $3 million would have been wiped out if Al Merton had received a salary as his father and brother had before him. Neither his brother David nor his father Henry received a salary reflecting anywhere near the amount of effort required to run this business.

MOSC's assets consist only of the inventory, the lease on the Lincoln Street Property, and the corporate name. Potential purchasers of the stock would discount the price offered unless they could be guaranteed a long-term lease option on the Lincoln Street Property. Without that guarantee, Al Merton would be fortunate to receive even $800,000 for his stock. With the guarantee of a long-term lease, the value of the stock would be $1.1 million. If he sold the business and the land and invested in no-risk certificates of deposit, Al Merton could easily earn 5% per year on the sale proceeds. Unless he is willing to undertake significant expansion activities, MOSC's value will not grow at even that conservative rate.

LIBRARY

In re Al Merton

Franklin Probate Code

Article One. Succession

§ 101. Definitions.

* * * *

(e) Lineal Descendant. An adopted person is a lineal descendant of the adopting parent and is not a lineal descendant of his or her biological parents.

* * * *

Article Two. Wills

* * * *

§ 206. Pretermitted Heirs.

(a) Surviving Spouse. If the decedent's will fails to provide for a surviving spouse who marries the decedent after the will is made, the surviving spouse shall receive an amount equal to what he or she would have received if the decedent had died intestate. This provision shall not apply if the surviving spouse waived that share in a valid prenuptial or postnuptial agreement.

(b) Surviving Children. If the decedent's will fails to provide for children born or adopted after the will is made, each omitted child shall receive the share that he or she would have received had the decedent died intestate. This provision shall not apply if language in the will indicates that the omission was intentional.

* * * *

Franklin Probate Code

Article One. Succession

§ 101. Definitions.

* * * *

(e) Lineal Descendant. An adopted person is a lineal descendant of the adopting parent and is not a lineal descendant of his or her biological parents.

* * * *

Article Two. Wills

* * * *

§ 206. Pretermitted Heirs.

(a) Surviving Spouse. If the decedent's will fails to provide for a surviving spouse who marries the decedent after the will is made, the surviving spouse shall receive an amount equal to what he or she would have received if the decedent had died intestate. This provision shall not apply if the surviving spouse waived that share in a valid prenuptial or postnuptial agreement.

(b) Surviving Children. If the decedent's will fails to provide for children born or adopted after the will is made, each omitted child shall receive the share that he or she would have received had the decedent died intestate. This provision shall not apply if language in the will indicates that the omission was intentional.

* * * *

Barry v. Allen

Franklin Supreme Court (1992)

This case arises out of Paul Barry's attempts to protect his daughters' disparate interests. Lisa Barry appeals the lower court's determination that a voting trust was void *ab initio.*

Paul Barry founded Eon Corporation 30 years ago. Eon issued only voting common stock.

Paul had three children, Lisa, Dorothy, and Judy. Only Lisa ever worked for Eon. As Paul contemplated retirement, he considered methods of ensuring that Lisa would retain operating control.

Paul could have bequeathed all of his shares to Lisa. Because the shares represented virtually all of his intangible personal property and because he had no tangible personal or real property, he would have effectively disinherited Dorothy and Judy. His attorney suggested using a voting trust for the shares.

When Paul retired, he transferred 150 shares to each daughter and retained 150 shares for himself. Lisa, Dorothy, and Judy transferred their shares into a voting trust. Each signed a trust agreement that provided for voting all of their shares according to Lisa's wishes for the next 15 years and that bound subsequent takers of these shares.

As president, Lisa operated the company successfully. Eon continued to pay the $300 annual per-share dividend that it paid before Paul's retirement. Paul and his daughters each received $45,000 in each of the next five years.

When Paul died, he bequeathed his remaining shares equally to each daughter conditioned upon their agreement to transfer those shares to the voting trust. The shares of any daughter who did not agree would be divided equally between the ones who did. All three daughters agreed. Two years later, Lisa decided that Eon should cease paying such large dividends and instead should use corporate profits to expand the company. The board cut the dividend to $3 per share.

Dorothy and Judy concluded that Lisa was acting in her own interests, rather than those of the entire family. Only the trust prevented them from electing a board that might be more amenable to their wishes.

In the eighth year of the trust, Dorothy and Judy sued to have the voting trust dissolved because it was not limited to a 10-year term, as provided in Franklin Corporations Code § 102(b). The corporation's articles do not specifically mention voting trusts.

Lisa argues that her father's primary goal was preserving her control, which he could have achieved in a number of ways. She claims the trust is valid for at least 10 years because the language in § 102(b) that mandates invalidity does not appear in the sentence limiting the term of such trusts.

This court must decide whether § 102 voids the voting trust *ab initio* or operates only to limit it to a 10-year term.

Paul could have carried out his plan in several ways. For example, he could have re-capitalized the corporation and transferred voting stock only to Lisa. That action would have avoided the requirements applicable to voting trusts.

Alternatively, he could have bequeathed the remaining stock on the condition that the daughters agree to vote for an amendment of the articles of incorporation to validate the 15-year voting trust. That conditional bequest could also have provided that any daughter who failed to vote for the amendment would be divested of her shares, with a gift over to Lisa. There are few limits on the conditions a testator can place on bequests in a will.

We cannot determine which of Paul's goals *vis-à-vis* his children governed his actions. Even if we could, we will not validate the voting trust merely because he could have accomplished the same goal using a different means. Paul chose a voting trust, and we must determine its validity under § 102.

At common law, courts invalidated voting trusts because they separated the voting power from the ownership of the stock. Because statutory authorization changes the common law rule, many courts will not enforce a voting trust unless it strictly complies with the statutory language. We interpret the last sentence of § 102(b) as validating voting trusts exceeding 10 years only if the corporate articles authorize a longer term.

We agree with the trial court that the voting trust was void *ab initio*.

We affirm.

In re Estate of Henry K. Tourneau

Franklin Court of Appeal (1920)

This case presents the problem of whether the bequest to the testator's wife of one-fifth of the residuary estate is burdened by the conditions set out in Paragraph Five of the will. This paragraph reads:

> Five: With respect to my interests in the corporation known as Tourneau, Inc., and as a condition precedent to turning over my stock interests in such business to my brother and sisters as hereinabove set forth, I direct that such beneficiaries enter into a voting trust agreement in favor of my brother, Pierre S. Tourneau. The voting trust agreement shall give to my brother the full voting rights for a minimum of ten (10) years with respect to the stock interests of all of the beneficiaries. The voting trust agreement shall further provide that, if my brother dies prior to the expiration of the voting trust agreement, the voting trust shall cease, and the stock certificates shall be delivered to the beneficiaries thereof.

Paragraph Five clearly shows the intention of the testator to give his brother the voting rights to the stock in question for the specified period.

The cases cited by the siblings challenging the will under the proposition that the condition precedent is illegal under the Franklin Corporations Code do not involve the right of a testator who owns stock in a corporation to impose conditions precedent upon a bequest of such stock. That the testator has the right to impose conditions is unquestioned. The donee must take the gift with the condition imposed or not at all, so long as the condition does not offend public policy or statutory enactment.[1] We hold, therefore, that the bequest is valid.

[1] The same result would be reached with a condition subsequent, as long as there was an express gift over to another person if the condition were breached.

In re Al Merton

DRAFTERS' POINT SHEET

On the day before he is scheduled to undergo open heart surgery, the client, Al Merton, meets with the supervising partner in the firm about getting his will updated. He is concerned that he might not survive the surgery and wants to set his affairs in order.

The task for the applicants is to draft the introductory and dispositive clauses of a will in accordance with the wishes expressed by Mr. Merton in his interview with the partner. In addition, applicants must deal with Stuart Merton (the adopted son whom Mr. Merton wants to disinherit) and the disposition of the corporate stock and explain why they have dealt with these issues as they have. The applicants are also told to follow the instructions in the firm's Will Drafting Guidelines, which are included in the File.

The File contains the will of Henry Merton, from whom Al Merton inherited the Merton Office Supply Corporation ("MOSC") and associated property, and the latest will of Al Merton himself. These documents are in the File to give the applicants some idea of what a will looks like and the sort of language that might be used to express a disposition of property. The two wills are sufficiently different from the one the applicants are assigned to write so that the exercise does not become one of simply copying from the wills of Henry and Al Merton.

The File also contains an excerpt from a treatise, *Walker's Treatise on Wills*, explaining the classifications of bequests, to aid the applicants in placing Mr. Merton's bequests in the proper order in the new will. It also contains an appraisal of MOSC. The appraisal furnishes some background information regarding the corporation's assets, the number of shares owned by Mr. Merton, and the history and future prospects for carrying on the business, but is otherwise irrelevant to the task. Finally, the File contains a family tree to assist the applicants in keeping the parties straight.

The Library contains some relevant, definitional statutes on descent of property and basic corporations law, including a provision regarding voting trusts, which is relevant to Mr. Merton's desire to vest control of MOSC in Sara, one of his adopted children.

The Library also contains two cases, including *Barry v. Allen*, a Franklin case that stands for the proposition that a voting trust cannot last longer than 10 years unless certain conditions exist. The applicants should use that case in molding the will language regarding the establishment of a voting trust.

The following discussion covers all of the points the drafters intended to raise in the problem. Applicants need not cover them all to receive passing or even excellent grades. Grading decisions are within the discretion of the graders in the user jurisdictions.

Overview: There are two things the applicants are required to do:

(1) Draft the introductory and dispositive provisions of a new will for Mr. Merton. In doing so, applicants must follow the instructions in the firm's guidelines and adhere to Mr. Merton's wishes as expressed in the transcript of the interview.

The will should include numbered paragraphs setting forth the provisions in the order prescribed in the guidelines. That organization will require the applicants to determine the character of each bequest as defined in the excerpt from *Walker's Treatise on Wills* and to order them according to the guidelines.

The provisions should be stated concisely and written in the structure and format of a will.

(2) Follow the dispositive provisions regarding the disposition of the MOSC stock with a short explanation of why the dispositive language says what it does. This part of the exercise offers the applicants the opportunity to state in narrative, expository form what the language they have drafted means and why. They must also explain how they have dealt with Stuart Merton, and why, irrespective of whether they included language about Stuart in the will *(see infra)*.

Graders can decide for themselves how much weight, if any, to ascribe to artful exposition and facial format.

PART ONE - The Introductory Clauses: This should be a fairly easy task. The Will Drafting Guidelines are clear. These clauses should recite that:

- The document is Mr. Merton's will;
- He is a resident of Griffin County, Franklin; this comes from his prior will and information contained in the interview.
- His immediate family consists of the two adopted children, Sara and Stuart, and his two nephews, Daniel and Louis.
- He revokes all prior wills and codicils.

PART TWO - The Dispositive Clauses: The order of bequests should follow the directions set forth in the guidelines. First the specific bequests: real property (of which the only one is the land and the building comprising the Lincoln Street Property); tangible personal property (none); and other specific bequests (the stock in MOSC).

The guidelines also tell applicants that they are to set forth "any other clauses stating conditions that might affect the disposition of specific bequests." It is unclear whether such clauses should be part of the dispositive clauses themselves or whether they should be separate clauses referring back to the dispositive clauses. Either way will work, but it will be more efficient if the applicants state the conditions in the dispositive clauses themselves.

Then, in sequence, applicants should set forth the general bequests (gifts of money to Sara, Daniel, and Louis, and to Franklin College for the Henry Merton Small Business Assistance Program); next, the demonstrative bequest to Sara to be paid from the savings account; and, finally, the residuary bequest.

At some point in the exercise, they must also deal with Mr. Merton's desire to disinherit Stuart.

SPECIFIC BEQUESTS

- **Real Property—Disposition of the Lincoln Street Property:** The interview and the business appraisal make it clear that the Lincoln Street Property consists of the land and the building and that it is not among the assets of MOSC. In order to "link" the Lincoln Street Property with the business, Mr. Merton has decided simply to will the Lincoln Street Property to MOSC. Thus, the applicants should simply draft a clause giving the land and buildings to MOSC.
    - NOTE: It would be erroneous to mention Mr. Merton's residence in this section because it falls into the residuary bequest.
- **Other Specific Bequests—Disposition of the Corporate Stock:** Under the facts, Mr. Merton wants to leave "an equal share of the business" to Sara, Daniel, and Louis and have them all share in the profits but wants to ensure that Sara retains the power to "make the decisions" for at least 15 years. This will require, as the supervising attorney put it, laying the groundwork in the will for the later creation of a voting trust. Drawing upon the wishes Mr. Merton expressed in the interview, § 102 of the Franklin Corporations Code, and the holdings in *Barry v. Allen* and *In re Estate of Tourneau*, the applicants should draft language reflecting that:
    - Sara, Daniel, and Louis are each to receive one-third (or 50 shares) of the MOSC stock;
    - Sara is to have the right to vote all shares, a goal that is to be accomplished by the later creation of a voting trust;
        - Accordingly, Sara, Daniel, and Louis must agree that their respective shares will be placed in a voting trust for up to 15 years and that Sara is to have the sole right to vote the shares.

- They will also have to agree that, if MOSC's articles of incorporation do not provide that a voting trust can last for more than 10 years (which they appear not to), the articles will be amended so to provide. (*See Barry v. Allen, In re Estate of Tourneau*, and Franklin Corporations Code § 102(b).)
- If either Daniel or Louis should refuse to agree to these conditions, the shares of the corporate stock that each would receive under the will would go to Sara.
- This would be the "gift over" that appears as a requirement in *Tourneau*.

- The applicants might also draft language specifying that Mr. Merton wants all three to share in the profits. However, omission of such language is not fatal because the statute (§102(c)) provides that dividends paid on account of stock in a voting trust shall be paid to the beneficial owners (Sara, Daniel, and Louis). If applicants omit such language they should cover it in their explanations.

- **Explanation:** Applicants should explain that the language used in the dispositive provisions is intended to make sure that Sara retains the right to run the business for up to 15 years even though all three of them will share in the profits (and, unless applicants have explicitly included "share-the-profits" language, they must explain that sharing results automatically by operation of § 102(c)); that, although each beneficiary is getting one-third of the stock, it is on the condition that they all agree to put it into a 15-year voting trust giving Sara the sole power to vote the stock; that the beneficiaries must agree that the articles of incorporation may be amended to carry out that intent; and that if either Daniel or Louis refuses to agree to these conditions, that beneficiary will lose his shares to Sara.
  - It should be implicit in applicants' treatment of this subject that they understand that a bequest of the corporate stock conveys ownership of the assets of the corporation, i.e., the inventory, the lease, and the corporate name (see the appraisal of the corporation). Applicants who attempt to bequeath these assets separately have missed the point and should receive reduced credit.

- It should also be implicit that applicants recognize that this bequest falls into the category of "other specific bequests" as opposed to a bequest of "tangible personal property," i.e., stock in a corporation is not tangible personal property in the ordinary sense of the word. *See Barry v. Allen.*

GENERAL BEQUESTS

- **The general gifts of money or estate assets:** There are two categories of such gifts: the bequest of $100,000 each to Sara, Daniel, and Louis; and the gift of $1,000,000 to Franklin College to endow a specific entity.
  - The gifts of $100,000 each to Sara, Daniel, and Louis can be stated in a single dispositive paragraph (e.g., "I give Sara, Daniel, and Louis $100,000 each.") or in separate paragraphs reciting the gift for each of them.
  - The gift of $1,000,000 out of general estate assets to Franklin College should recite that it is to endow the small business program and is conditioned on the program's being named after Mr. Merton's father: The Henry Merton Small Business Assistance Program.

DEMONSTRATIVE BEQUEST

- **The gift to Sara to be paid from the savings account:** This is a demonstrative bequest because its payment is to be made from a designated fund—the savings account.
  - The language of the bequest should state that the gift is to be paid first out of the savings account and that it is a separate bequest to furnish money to enable Sara to finish college.

RESIDUARY BEQUEST

- **The gift of the remainder of the estate:** The language of this clause should recite clearly that the remainder of the estate goes to the Franklin College Faculty Development Fund (e.g., "the rest, residue, and remainder" or "all my property not otherwise disposed of by this will.")
  - Note that the residue also contains Al Merton's home, which is realty. It is not disposed of as a specific bequest because Mr. Merton did not direct that it be given to the Faculty Development Fund separately and distinctly from the residue.

DISINHERITING STUART

- **The intent to disinherit Stuart:** At some point in the exercise, applicants will have to deal with Mr. Merton's desire to disinherit Stuart. It can be done either at the beginning or at the end of the document.
    - It can be accomplished by an express statement in the will that Mr. Merton wants to disinherit Stuart. (e.g., "It is my intention that my adopted child, Stuart Merton, take nothing under my will.") It can also be accomplished by saying nothing in the will, inasmuch as Stuart had been adopted several years before Mr. Merton's visit with the partner and therefore he is the legal equivalent of a child in being before the will was written. Better applicants will definitely opt to make the express statement rather than leave it open to interpretation.
    - **Explanation:** This is the only point in the exercise, other than a reference in the introductory clause, where the fact that Mr. Merton adopted Sara and Stuart is called into play. As to Sara, it makes no difference because she is a named beneficiary and takes under the terms of the will, irrespective of the adoption.
        - With regard to Stuart, applicants should discuss whether he would be a pretermitted heir if he is not provided for in the will. Under Franklin Probate Code § 101(e), Stuart is deemed for all purposes to be Mr. Merton's lineal descendant. Section 206 raises the issue of pretermission, and it is abundantly clear that Stuart would not be pretermitted because he was not adopted after the will was made. Applicants should make it clear that they understand this. An applicant who includes language expressly disinheriting Stuart so to prevent Stuart from claiming as a pretermitted heir shows a lack of understanding. If, on the other hand, an applicant chooses to leave the will silent as to Stuart, it is essential that he or she explain why, i.e., that there is no need to mention him because the will was made after Stuart became a child of Mr. Merton and, therefore, Stuart is not pretermitted.

FILE

State v. Tweedy

Office of the District Attorney

DeSoto County
83645 Washington Street
DeSoto, Franklin 33123
(901) 555-1294

TO: Applicant

FROM: Shirley Clay Scott, Assistant District Attorney

RE: Tweedy, James A.

DATE: July 30, 2002

I have been asked to recommend whether we should prosecute James A. Tweedy. The District Attorney has stated his belief that the case will be difficult to try and that it is unlikely that a conviction can be obtained. I, however, believe that this case is worth pursuing and want to seek a felony indictment against Mr. Tweedy for two counts of endangering the welfare of a child under Penal Code § 4304.

Please prepare for my signature a two-part memorandum to the District Attorney. The first part should persuade the District Attorney that we have sufficient admissible evidence to prove all the elements necessary to obtain a conviction. You may assume that we can avoid any hearsay problems that might arise. I know that additional facts may facilitate prosecution, but in this first part you should address only the question of whether we have enough evidence to proceed based on what we *already* know.

In the second part of the memorandum, which should be brief, identify any conflicting or incomplete facts in the File that we will need to further investigate or clarify to facilitate prosecution. Recommend the investigative steps this office should take to develop these additional facts.

INCIDENT NO. 02-3105	DeSoto Police Department Incident Report			Date of Statement 7/17/02
NAME (LAST, FIRST, MIDDLE) OF PERSON GIVING STATEMENT Tweedy, James A.		DOB/AGE 8/3/76	RESIDENCE PHONE None	BUSINESS PHONE None
STREET ADDRESS 1376 Archer Ave, Apt. 27		CITY DeSoto	STATE Franklin	ZIP CODE 33123
STATEMENT TAKEN BY (NAME/BADGE) Mary Lou Higgerson #1361		IN PRESENCE OF		

On the evening of July 16, 2002, and the early morning hours of July 17, officer called to the scene of a fire to investigate possible criminal neglect. Two minor children (the older child three (3) years of age and the younger twenty (20) months) were left in their apartment unattended while father, James A. Tweedy, participated in a social evening with friends.

Before leaving, Tweedy put the children in the bedroom. According to his statement, he secured the bedroom door by inserting two table knives between the door and the jamb. In addition, he locked the main door to the apartment. Tweedy claims he spoke to neighbor, Mrs. England, who had consented to watch out for the children in his absence.

According to another neighbor, Glen Poshard, at approximately 12:05 a.m. a fire started in the building, possibly originating as a result of a defective television set in Tweedy's apartment. Tweedy returned to premises at 3:00 a.m. at which point investigating officer briefly interviewed Tweedy before Tweedy left for the hospital to see if he could find the children.

Firefighter Albert Malone informed officer that unknown visitor to the building, learning from a neighbor that the youngsters were trapped in the bedroom, attempted to remove them but was prevented from doing so by the manner in which the bedroom door had been fastened. Firefighters, upon entry, found the children apparently dead in the bedroom of the apartment.

Signature Mary Lou Higgerson

2

INCIDENT NO. 02-3105	DeSoto Police Department Incident Report Addendum			Date of Statement 7/18/02
NAME (LAST, FIRST, MIDDLE) OF PERSON GIVING STATEMENT Wirthin, Harry P.		DOB/AGE 9/2/46	RESIDENCE PHONE 555-5678	BUSINESS PHONE same
STREET ADDRESS 1376 Archer Ave, Apt. 22		CITY DeSoto	STATE Franklin	ZIP CODE 33123
STATEMENT TAKEN BY (NAME/BADGE) Mary Lou Higgerson #1361		IN PRESENCE OF		

Addendum to Incident Report dated July 17, 2002.

I spoke with Harry P. Wirthin, owner and superintendent of the building occupied by James Tweedy and family. He stated that Tweedy was a typical tenant. Only problem was that 4 years ago a small electrical fire occurred in Tweedy's apartment. Apparently, Tweedy's wife, who is now deceased, left a curling iron on in the bathroom and it overheated causing a short that started a fire. No one was in the apartment at the time.

Mr. Wirthin did indicate that on at least two prior occasions he knew the children were left alone in the apartment. He also indicated that the neighbor two floors up, a Mrs. England, occasionally watched the children. I spoke with Mrs. England who indicated that on one or two occasions she had watched the children. She indicated that she had been asked to watch them on the night in question, but that she declined.

A check of DeSoto Licensing & Inspection records indicates that Mr. Wirthin has been cited on 5 occasions within the last 5 years for code violations related to wiring problems in the building. All citations resulted from complaints from tenants about faulty wiring.

Signature Mary Lou Higgerson

INCIDENT NO.	DeSoto Fire Marshal Report	DATE OF INVESTIGATION
02-3105	DeSoto, Franklin	7/17/02

An investigation was conducted on the above-referenced date into the fire at 1376 Archer Ave, Apt. 27.

Cause of fire was electrical problem located in defective television set. This conclusion was easily reached with examination of set and surrounding area. There existed little actual fire damage. Damage was limited to television set and curtains located near the set. Internal part of television set received extensive damage.

Smoke and water damage in contrast was extensive. Level of smoke commensurate with high use of synthetic materials in apartment.

NAME (LAST, FIRST, MIDDLE) OF PERSON MAKING REPORT	TITLE		BUSINESS PHONE
Gatton, Phil	Deputy Fire Marshal		555-8463
STREET ADDRESS OF INVESTIGATION	CITY	STATE	ZIP CODE
1376 Archer Ave, Apt. 27	DeSoto	Franklin	33123
Signature [signature]			

OFFICE OF THE DESOTO COUNTY MEDICAL EXAMINER

Marsha Ryan, J.D., M.D.
Chief Medical Examiner
9765 Garwin Street
DeSoto, Franklin 33123

July 22, 2002

TO: Shirley Clay Scott, Assistant District Attorney

FROM: Marsha Ryan, Chief Medical Examiner

RE: Alma & Fred Tweedy

I got your voice mail concerning the autopsies on the Tweedy children. The autopsies are complete, and I'll send you a copy of the report. The important details, however, are pretty straightforward.

Fred: White male, approximately three years old. General health was good. No evidence of any disease process. Cause of death was smoke inhalation resulting from fire.

Alma: White female, approximately twenty months old. General health was poor. Evidence of congenital heart malformation, which if remained undetected would be life threatening. Cause of death was smoke inhalation resulting from fire.

Let me know if you need anything else.

Transcript of Interview of James Tweedy
by Officer Higgerson
July 22, 2002

Officer: Thank you for coming down, Mr. Tweedy. The night of the fire was horrible and I understand your difficulty in answering all my questions then.

Tweedy: Well, of course, I wanted to get to the hospital as soon as possible, but it was too late.

Officer: Yes, I know. I'm sorry. Now, Mr. Tweedy, I want to state on the record that you do not have to talk with me. Anything you say can and will be used against you. You have the right to be represented by a lawyer. If you cannot afford to hire a lawyer, one will be appointed to represent you.

Tweedy: I know my rights.

Officer: And you are willing to talk to me?

Tweedy: Yes.

Officer: Why did you leave the children alone?

Tweedy: I didn't.

Officer: What do you mean?

Tweedy: I asked Mrs. England to watch them. She said she would be happy to.

Officer: But she didn't come down to the apartment, did she?

Tweedy: Not right when I asked, but she said she'd be down there in a few minutes, after she finished her dishes.

Officer: Then why did you jam the bedroom door the way you did?

Tweedy: This is not a safe neighborhood. The landlord doesn't keep the place in the best shape and I could not trust the locks on the door to the apartment. Look, I did what I could. I even left the TV on to make people think I was home.

Officer: But, it was the bedroom door jamb that you stuck the knives into.

Tweedy: Well, I couldn't very well do that on the outside door.

Officer: Was it your habit to leave the children unattended?

Tweedy: No.

Officer: Had you ever done it before?

Tweedy: Like I said, I didn't do it this time. I'd asked Mrs. England to watch them.

Officer: Mrs. England denies being asked.

Tweedy: Well, she's lying. Obviously she's afraid that she's going to be blamed. In fact, rather than sitting here and accusing me, you should be asking her why she didn't do what she said she would.

Officer: Mr. Tweedy, were you drinking the night of the fire?

Tweedy: I went to a club that night. Yes, I had a couple beers. I was not drunk. I'm sorry, I think I should talk to an attorney.

LIBRARY

State v. Tweedy

Franklin Penal Code

§ 4304. Endangering Welfare of a Child

(a) Offense defined. A parent, guardian, or other person supervising the welfare of a child under 18 years of age commits an offense if he knowingly endangers the welfare of the child by violating a duty of care, protection or support.

(b) Grading. An offense under this section constitutes a felony of the third degree.

Franklin Rules of Evidence

Rule 401. Definition of "Relevant Evidence"

"Relevant evidence" means evidence having any tendency to make the existence of any fact that is of consequence to the determination of the action more probable or less probable than it would be without the evidence.

Rule 402. Relevant Evidence Generally Admissible; Irrelevant Evidence Inadmissible

All relevant evidence is admissible, except as otherwise provided by the Constitution of the State of Franklin, by Act of the Franklin Legislature, by these rules, or by other rules prescribed by the Franklin Supreme Court pursuant to statutory authority. Evidence which is not relevant is not admissible.

Rule 403. Exclusion of Relevant Evidence on Grounds of Prejudice, Confusion, or Waste of Time

Although relevant, evidence may be excluded if its probative value is substantially outweighed by the danger of unfair prejudice, confusion of the issues, or misleading the jury, or by considerations of undue delay, waste of time, or needless presentation of cumulative evidence.

Rule 404. Character Evidence Not Admissible To Prove Conduct; Exceptions; Other Crimes

(a) Character evidence generally. Evidence of a person's character or a trait of character is not admissible for the purpose of proving action in conformity therewith on a particular occasion, except:

(1) Character of accused. Evidence of a pertinent trait of character offered by an accused, or by the prosecution to rebut the same;

(2) Character of victim. Evidence of a pertinent trait of character of the victim of the crime offered by an accused, or by the prosecution to rebut the same, or evidence of a character trait of peacefulness of the victim offered by the prosecution in a homicide case to rebut evidence that the victim was the first aggressor;

* * * *

(b) Other crimes, wrongs, or acts. Evidence of other crimes, wrongs, or acts is not admissible to prove the character of a person in order to show action in conformity therewith. It may, however, be admissible for other purposes, such as proof of motive, opportunity, intent, preparation, plan, knowledge, identity, or absence of mistake or accident, provided that upon request by the accused, the prosecution in a criminal case shall provide reasonable notice in advance of trial, or during trial if the court excuses pretrial notice on good cause shown, of the general nature of any such evidence it intends to introduce at trial.

State v. Miller

Franklin Supreme Court (1992)

Appellant, Rachel Miller, was convicted under Franklin Penal Code § 4304, endangering the welfare of a child, following a non-jury trial. Miller was thereafter sentenced to two years' probation. This appeal ensued.

The relevant facts are straightforward and thoroughly tragic. On the evening of November 18, 1989, Miller, with her 22-month-old son, Clarence, visited Antonio Green, the father of the child. Green and Miller are not husband and wife. Green resided in a three-story rooming house. A restaurant was located on the first floor of the premises. Eugenia Orr lived on the second level and Green occupied the top floor.

Father, mother, and child met at a neighbor hood tavern and then returned to the rooming house. Earlier in the day, Green had accompanied Orr on a shopping trip; father, mother, and child went directly to Orr's apartment to examine that day's purchases. Miller was not well acquainted with Orr. After some time, Miller went upstairs to Green's room, leaving the child in Orr's apartment in the care of Green because the child was playing with his father's new shoes. When the child tired of this activity, Green took him upstairs to Miller and then returned to the Orr apartment.

Miller washed and changed the child and prepared him for bed. Green's room contained a double bed. Nearby was an electric space heater, which turned out to be in a damaged condition but was then operating. Miller put the child in the bed and then lay down with the child until he fell asleep. Once her son was asleep, Miller decided to go down to the first-floor restaurant to buy some juice for the child. She left Green's apartment with the child asleep in the bed, the space heater operating, and the door to the hallway stairs open. She also left her sweater in the apartment.

When Miller stopped on the second floor en route to the restaurant, Green asked Miller if she would "go clubbing" (visiting bars or nightclubs) with him. She declined, explaining that she had to watch the child and that she was tired and not dressed for the occasion anyway. While she was on the first floor, Green yelled down to her through the common hallway, repeating his request and saying that Orr had agreed to watch the child. Miller agreed to accompany him. She asked Green to bring down her sweater and did not return upstairs. Green brought her the sweater. He had, in fact, not spoken to Orr about watching the child and Orr did not do so.

Green and Miller left the rooming house at approximately 1:00 a.m. and visited two clubs. During this time, they were joined by friends. One of these friends was called as a witness and testified that Miller continually fretted about the child. Returning to the rooming house after 3:00 a.m., Green and

Miller discovered police and fire trucks in the street outside and the building ablaze. The only death resulting from the conflagration was Miller's infant son, who died of smoke inhalation and burns. The space heater was determined to be the cause of the fire. Green was convicted of various criminal charges in connection with the child's death. Miller was convicted of endangering the welfare of her child.

We must consider whether the evidence was sufficient to uphold the verdict of the trial court. We must accept all the evidence and all reasonable inferences that may be drawn from that evidence upon which the factfinder could have based its verdict. If the evidence, viewed in the light most favorable to the state, is not sufficient to establish guilt beyond a reasonable doubt of the crime charged, then the conviction should be overturned.

Miller claims that the evidence presented at trial was insufficient to prove the intent element of the crime with which she was charged. Under Penal Code § 4304, a parent or other person supervising the welfare of a child commits a felony if he or she *knowingly* endangers the child. Section 302(b) of the Penal Code defines knowingly:

> (2) A person acts knowingly with respect to a material element of an offense when:
>
> > (i) if the element involves the nature of his conduct or the attendant circumstances, he is aware that his conduct is of that nature or that such circumstances exist; and
> >
> > (ii) if the element involves the result of his conduct, he is aware that it is practically certain that his conduct will cause such a result.

It is clear that § 4304 contemplates endangerment either by act or by omission to act. In *State v. Cardwell* (1986), this court established a three-pronged standard for testing the sufficiency of evidence of the intent element under § 4304:

> We hold that evidence is sufficient to prove the intent element of the offense of endangering the welfare of a child when the accused is aware of his or her duty to protect the child; is aware that the child is in circumstances that are reasonably likely to result in harm to the child; and has either failed to act or has taken actions so lame or meager that such actions cannot reasonably be expected to be effective to protect the child from physical or psychological harm.

If proof fails on any one of these prongs, the evidence must be found insufficient.

Employing this test, the *Cardwell* court found sufficient evidence of intent where a mother was aware that her child was being subjected to sexual abuse by the stepfather and took wholly ineffectual remedial actions. Specifically, she wrote letters to the stepfather expressing outrage and warning that she would not tolerate such conduct and she made an aborted attempt to move the child to a relative's house.

On the other hand, in *State v. Louie* (1990), this court found insufficient evidence to convict a husband and wife where they knew that their 13-year-old daughter was engaging in sexual activity with an adult and became pregnant against the express warnings of a physician. *Louie* differed from *Cardwell* in that the parents did not allow the child to remain in a potentially dangerous situation; they simply failed to stop the child from surreptitiously seeking out sexual activity. The court was unwilling to extend culpability, noting that parents could not know everything about their child's activities nor was § 4304 intended to punish parents merely because their child becomes pregnant.

Here, the trial court, sitting as factfinder, determined that when Miller left with Green to go clubbing, she was aware that her infant son was in the third-floor room with the space heater on. The court found that by failing to question Green's statement that Orr would watch the child, Miller has evidenced the requisite intent for purposes of § 4304. We have difficulty in finding that the evidence is sufficient to satisfy the *Cardwell* tripartite test. It is undisputed that appellant was aware of her duty to protect her child. However, merely leaving the child alone is insufficient to establish the requisite intent. We cannot find as a matter of law that she was aware that she had placed her child in circumstances that were likely to result in harm to the child or that her failure to check on the alleged babysitting arrangements was unreasonable under *Cardwell*.

The trial court specifically credited Miller's testimony that she believed Green when he told her that Orr was watching her child. The logical inference based on this finding is that Miller was not aware that she had left her child unattended. There was no evidence presented at trial that Green was an inherently dishonest person or that Miller had cause to disbelieve him. The trial court has based Miller's culpability under § 4304 not on the fact that Miller knowingly left her child alone, but rather that she should not have been so gullible as to believe Green. Undeniably, Miller may have exercised poor judgment on the night in question, and perhaps she is guilty of reckless or negligent conduct in connection with her son's death. However, this is not sufficient for a finding of guilt under § 4304. If Miller in fact believed that her son was in the care of another, she did not knowingly place him in circumstances that were reasonably likely to result in harm, and her conduct cannot be adjudged criminal.

Judgment reversed. Appellant discharged.

State v. Shoup

Franklin Supreme Court (1993)

Joseph C. Shoup was tried by jury and was found guilty of homicide by vehicle while driving under the influence of alcohol. Shoup asserts that the trial court committed reversible error by refusing to give the instruction requested by the defense on the issue of causation.

On January 3, 1990, at about 8:00 p.m., appellant was operating an automobile on Oak Street, a narrow alleyway located in the town of Vienna. The passengers in appellant's vehicle were Michelle Shoup, his wife, who was seated in the front passenger seat, and Jean Moll and John Rush, who were in the back seat. Appellant was observed failing to stop for three consecutive stop signs, and the speed of his vehicle was estimated to be approximately 50 to 55 miles per hour.

Appellant drove through the intersection of Oak and Williams Streets without stopping at the stop sign. His vehicle collided with a large dump truck parked in the alleyway near a loading dock at a garment factory. The site of the accident was about 30 to 35 feet from the intersection.

Upon being summoned to the scene of the accident, Charles Harris, the Police Chief for the town of Vienna, observed that appellant smelled strongly of alcohol and that there were several beer cans on the floor of the vehicle. All of the vehicle's occupants were transported for medical treatment. Appellant's wife suffered massive internal injuries and died shortly after being taken by helicopter to Cardinal Medical Center. Appellant was taken to Ashland State Hospital, where, at 9:30 p.m., blood samples were drawn at the request of Chief Harris for the purpose of determining appellant's blood alcohol level. Two blood tests measured appellant's blood alcohol content at 0.176% and 0.175%.

At trial, the defense contended that the legal cause of Michelle Shoup's death had been the illegal parking of the dump truck with which appellant's vehicle collided. Police Chief Harris testified that there had been a no parking sign posted at the loading dock where the dump truck was parked. However, according to Chief Harris, this sign had been placed there by the garment factory and not by the town. Therefore, he was without legal authority to issue tickets for illegal parking at that location. Other testimony established that, despite poor lighting conditions, the dump truck could be seen from the intersection at Oak and Williams Streets. Additionally, both Jean Moll and John Rush described appellant's driving prior to the accident as erratic.

Causation is an essential element of a criminal charge, which the State must prove beyond a reasonable doubt. The tort concept of proximate cause plays no role in a prosecution for criminal homicide. Rather, the

State must prove a more direct causal relationship between the defendant's conduct and the victim's death. However, it has never been the law of this State that criminal responsibility must be confined to a sole or immediate cause of death. Criminal responsibility is properly assessed against one whose conduct was a direct and substantial factor in producing the result even though other factors combined with that conduct to achieve the result. Thus, a defendant cannot escape the natural consequences of his act merely because of foreseeable complications.

In this case, a jury could find that appellant's conduct was a direct and substantial factor in bringing about the death of Michelle Shoup. The evidence disclosed that, while intoxicated, appellant drove his vehicle down a narrow, dimly lit alleyway, erratically and at a high rate of speed, failing to stop at three consecutive intersections where stop signs had been posted. Moreover, the evidence suggested that had appellant obeyed the stop sign at the intersection of Oak and Williams Streets, he would have been able to observe the dump truck parked in the alleyway. The fact that the dump truck was parked in the alleyway undoubtedly contributed to the accident. Appellant's conduct started an unbroken chain of causation that directly and substantially led to his wife's death. Because the fact that another vehicle may have been parked in a hazardous manner was a foreseeable circumstance, appellant is not relieved from the natural consequences of his conduct.

Affirmed.

State v. Tweedy
DRAFTERS' POINT SHEET

In this performance test item, applicants are employed in the Office of the District Attorney. Their task is to write a persuasive memorandum to convince the District Attorney that there is enough evidence to prosecute James Tweedy on two felony counts of endangering the welfare of a child and to identify additional facts that would be helpful.

On the night of the incident, James Tweedy, a single parent of two minor children, put the children to bed, secured the bedroom door by jamming two table knives in the door jamb, locked the main door to his apartment, and went out to a night club, leaving the children alone. He claims that he asked Mrs. England, a neighbor, if she would watch the children, and he claims that she said she would. Mrs. England is reported at one place in the record to have said she declined and in another place to have said that she was not asked to watch the children on this occasion.

While Tweedy was away, a fire started in a defective television set he had left on in his apartment. An unidentified visitor to the building went into Tweedy's apartment in an attempt to rescue the two children but was unable to get into the bedroom because of the way the door had been secured. The children died of smoke inhalation.

The File contains the police incident reports, the fire marshal's report, a letter from the county medical examiner assigning the cause of death, and a transcript of a police interview with Tweedy. The Library contains the "endangering" statute, excerpts from the Franklin Rules of Evidence, and two cases.

The following discussion covers all of the points the drafters intended to raise in the problem. Applicants need not cover them all to receive passing or even excellent grades. Grading decisions are within the discretion of the graders in the user jurisdictions.

1. **Overview:** The applicants' work product should be persuasive in tone and the format should be similar to that of an office memorandum.

The problem breaks down into four logical components:

- A recognition that a conviction under the "endangering" statute requires that the accused have "knowingly" violated a duty to care for the children;
- A recognition that the accused's acts or omissions must be the direct and substantial cause of the deaths of the children;

3. **Application of the Available Facts:** Here, applicants should apply the available facts to each of the elements of the crime and argue how the facts suffice to prove each of the elements.

- The statutory definition of "knowingly" is given in *State v. Miller*.
  - Applicants should recognize that the element of the crime to which the "knowingly" standard is applied is Tweedy's violation of his duty of care or protection.
- The known facts are to be applied to the three-pronged test set forth in *State v. Miller*:
  - Tweedy was aware of his duty to protect the children.
    - He is presumed as parent to know that he has a such a duty toward his children.
    - His actual knowledge of his duty is shown by the following provable facts:
      - The police incident report and the police interview both record admissions by Tweedy that he asked Mrs. England to watch the children. This admissible evidence demonstrates that he knew he had a duty not to leave them home alone.
      - He admits having jammed the bedroom door with the table knives because it was not a safe neighborhood and the locks on the door to his apartment could not be trusted. This admission is also admissible evidence that he knew he had to protect the children.
      - He left the television set on to make it appear as if he were at home—another piece of admissible evidence that he knew the children should be supervised.
      - He admits in the police interview that in the past, when he had gone out without the children, he had asked Mrs. England to watch them. This admission is corroborated by Mrs. England's statement to the investigating officer and is also admissible evidence of his awareness of his duty.
  - Tweedy was aware that the children were in circumstances that

were reasonably likely to result in harm.

- All of the foregoing facts go equally to prove this element; i.e., his jamming the door, having asked Mrs. England in the past to babysit when he left without the children, and leaving the television set turned on also tend to prove that Tweedy was aware that leaving the children home alone was a threat to their welfare. The facts are therefore generally relevant and admissible under the Franklin Rules of Evidence, Rules 401 and 402.
- The problem, however, is that these facts are not directly relevant to the issue of whether Tweedy knew that the danger to which the children were exposed was the danger of fire.
    - It is implicit in the two cases cited internally in *State v. Miller (Cardwell* and *Louie)* that the requisite awareness must be somehow related to the danger that resulted in the harm.
- Accordingly, there is a need for evidence of Tweedy's specific awareness of the fire danger. This part of the case is problematic.
- The only *currently available* evidence that Tweedy was aware of the danger of fire (and more particularly, an electrical fire) was that four years earlier Tweedy's now deceased wife had left a curling iron plugged in and it had shorted, causing a fire in the same apartment.
- Applicants must find a way to make this fact admissible as to Tweedy's knowledge that there was a danger of fire. (See *infra* for *additional* facts to be investigated that may help prove this knowledge.)
- Evidence Rule 404(b) should furnish a clue to the applicants that evidence of the prior fire should come in to show Tweedy's knowledge of the danger of fire.

    - Starting the earlier fire is not an "other act" within the meaning of 404(b) because it was not his act. It was his wife's act.
    - Admission of the evidence of the earlier fire would be sought not to show that Tweedy was responsible for the fire but, rather, merely that he knew about it as a "similar happening."
- Applicants should recognize that admissibility of the fact of the earlier fire will be contested at trial. Nevertheless, they should argue that it will be admitted to show Tweedy's knowledge of the specific danger of fire. This evidence, together with the evidence of his knowledge about ensuring the physical welfare of his children, will suffice to convict.

<u>The actions Tweedy took to carry out his duty were so "lame or meager" as to be ineffectual</u>.

- It is disputed whether Tweedy asked Mrs. England to babysit that evening and whether, if he did ask, she agreed or declined to do so.
- Nevertheless, even if Tweedy is to be believed, he admitted to police that he left the children in the apartment knowing that it would be some time before Mrs. England would join them.
    - This is distinguishable from the situation in *State v. Miller*, where the defendant did reasonably believe that a neighbor was watching the baby when she left to go "clubbing."
- Given his knowledge of the earlier fire, his actions were antithetical to the protection of the children: leaving before Mrs. England arrived to be with them; jamming the bedroom door shut in such a way that no one could get in to rescue them in the event of an emergency; and leaving the television set on, thus risking another electrical fire.

- <u>Tweedy's actions were a direct and substantial factor in the deaths of the children</u>.
  - According to the fire marshal's report, the fire was caused by an electrical problem in the defective television set.
    - But for Tweedy's having left the TV set on, the fire would not have occurred.
    - Even though the fire itself was not extensive, smoke resulted from "high use of synthetic materials in the apartment." Under the reasoning of *State v. Shoup*, the smoke from the fire was a "foreseeable circumstance" that did not relieve Tweedy of liability.
  - Moreover, the way Tweedy secured the bedroom door prevented entry or escape.
- All of the foregoing facts, taken together with the fact that Tweedy left the children just so he could go out drinking, should suffice to obtain a conviction.

4. **Additional Facts and Investigative Steps:** The materials in the File suggest that many more facts that will help in the prosecution can be obtained and/or clarified:

- The investigating officer should be contacted to ascertain which is correct: the statement in the incident report that Mrs. England was asked but declined to babysit, or the statement in the interview transcript that Mrs. England denies she was even asked.
- Mrs. England should be contacted and asked about whether she was asked and agreed to babysit on the night of the fire as well as about past occasions when she babysat or when she was asked but declined to babysit. She should also be asked whether she knows of occasions when she had declined, but Tweedy had nevertheless gone out and left the children alone.
- In view of the fact that the outside door to the apartment was locked, Mrs. England should be asked whether she has a key.
- An investigator should interview the neighbor to whom Firefighter Albert Malone had spoken and also try to find the "unknown visitor" (see Police Incident Report), to ascertain why the jammed bedroom door prevented rescue.

- The building owner should be contacted to ascertain what he knows about the prior fire in Tweedy's apartment and the "two prior occasions [when] he knew the children were left alone in the apartment."
- An investigator should follow up on the five citations for code violations relating to wiring problems to determine whether any of them related to Tweedy's apartment and whether Tweedy was one of the tenants who complained about faulty wiring. In this connection, all the complaining tenants should be interviewed.
    - Was notice of the code violations sent to the tenants so that Tweedy can be deemed to have known about them?

INSTRUCTIONS

1. You will have 90 minutes to complete this session of the examination. This performance test is designed to evaluate your ability to handle a select number of legal authorities in the context of a factual problem involving a client.

2. The problem is set in the fictitious state of Franklin, in the fictitious Fifteenth Circuit of the United States. Columbia and Olympia are also fictitious states in the Fifteenth Circuit. In Franklin, the trial court of general jurisdiction is the District Court, the intermediate appellate court is the Court of Appeal, and the highest court is the Supreme Court.

3. You will have two kinds of materials with which to work: a File and a Library. The first document in the File is a memorandum containing the instructions for the task you are to complete. The other documents in the File contain factual information about your case and may also include some facts that are not relevant.

4. The Library contains the legal authorities needed to complete the task and may also include some authorities that are not relevant. Any cases may be real, modified, or written solely for the purpose of this examination. If the cases appear familiar to you, do not assume that they are precisely the same as you have read before. Read them thoroughly, as if they all were new to you. You should assume that the cases were decided in the jurisdictions and on the dates shown. In citing cases from the Library, you may use abbreviations and omit page references.

5. Your response must be written in the answer book provided. In answering this performance test, you should concentrate on the materials provided. What you have learned in law school and elsewhere provides the general background for analyzing the problem; the File and Library provide the specific materials with which you must work.

6. Although there are no restrictions on how you apportion your time, you should be sure to allocate ample time (about 45 minutes) to reading and digesting the materials and to organizing your answer before you begin writing it. You may make notes anywhere in the test materials; blank pages are provided at the end of the booklet. You may not tear pages from the question booklet.

7. This performance test will be graded on your responsiveness to the instructions regarding the task you are to complete, which are given to you in the first memorandum in the File, and on the content, thoroughness, and organization of your response.

INSTRUCTIONS

8. You will have 90 minutes to complete this session of the examination. This performance test is designed to evaluate your ability to handle a select number of legal authorities in the context of a factual problem involving a client.

9. The problem is set in the fictitious state of Franklin, in the fictitious Fifteenth Circuit of the United States. Columbia and Olympia are also fictitious states in the Fifteenth Circuit. In Franklin, the trial court of general jurisdiction is the District Court, the intermediate appellate court is the Court of Appeal, and the highest court is the Supreme Court.

10. You will have two kinds of materials with which to work: a File and a Library. The first document in the File is a memorandum containing the instructions for the task you are to complete. The other documents in the File contain factual information about your case and may also include some facts that are not relevant.

11. The Library contains the legal authorities needed to complete the task and may also include some authorities that are not relevant. Any cases may be real, modified, or written solely for the purpose of this examination. If the cases appear familiar to you, do not assume that they are precisely the same as you have read before. Read them thoroughly, as if they all were new to you. You should assume that the cases were decided in the jurisdictions and on the dates shown. In citing cases from the Library, you may use abbreviations and omit page references.

12. Your response must be written in the answer book provided. In answering this performance test, you should concentrate on the materials provided. What you have learned in law school and elsewhere provides the general background for analyzing the problem; the File and Library provide the specific materials with which you must work.

13. Although there are no restrictions on how you apportion your time, you should be sure to allocate ample time (about 45 minutes) to reading and digesting the materials and to organizing your answer before you begin writing it. You may make notes anywhere in the test materials; blank pages are provided at the end of the booklet. You may not tear pages from the question booklet.

14. This performance test will be graded on your responsiveness to the instructions regarding the task you are to complete, which are given to you in the first memorandum in the File, and on the content, thoroughness, and organization of your response.

Larson Real Estate File

FILE

LIBRARY

FILE

Glazer, Berten & Dreyer, LLC

1200 Kilborn Avenue
www.GBDLaw.com

Lawton, Franklin 33202
(555) 901-3899

MEMORANDUM

To: Applicant
From: Elaine Dreyer
Date: July 25, 2006
Re: Larson Real Estate File

One of our longtime business clients, Karen Larson, has contracted to sell her home located in Banford, Franklin. The closing, when transfer of title will occur, is scheduled for August 15, 2006. She has just received a letter from the attorney for the buyers, Pierre and Lisa Meridien, demanding substantial damages for claimed conditions in the house and neighborhood.

Franklin has traditionally been a "buyer beware" jurisdiction regarding the sale of residential real estate, but in 2005 the law changed substantially to impose disclosure obligations on the seller.

I've attached the interview transcript from my meeting with Ms. Larson and the letter from the buyers' attorney. Please draft a memorandum to assist me in advising Ms. Larson as to the following:

- What disclosure obligations does a seller of residential real estate have under Franklin statutory and common law?
- As to each of the problems and defects cited by the Meridiens' attorney, what, if anything, was Ms. Larson required to disclose under Franklin law, and did she comply?
- What type of relief, if any, can the Meridiens obtain against Ms. Larson under Franklin law?

A separate fact section is not necessary. However, you should incorporate the relevant facts and analyze applicable legal authority.

TRANSCRIPT OF CLIENT INTERVIEW: Karen Larson

July 24, 2006

LAWYER: Hello, Karen, it's great to see you. What can I help you with?

CLIENT: I've contracted to sell my house to Pierre and Lisa Meridien. I've just received a letter from their attorney claiming that there are some problems and I don't know what to do. Here's a copy.

LAWYER: Why don't you begin with some general information about your house.

CLIENT: The house is in the Terrapin Heights neighborhood of Banford. It's a beautiful old house, built in 1880, with amazing views of the marina and the ocean. I bought it in 2002. The previous owner spent a lot of money restoring it. I've done some work on the house myself, but not a lot. Mainly painting and carpeting the bedrooms.

LAWYER: Tell me something about the neighborhood.

CLIENT: Terrapin Heights is the oldest neighborhood in Banford. Most of the houses are as old as mine. Housing prices in the neighborhood have soared. In fact, just last year, the Banford City Council designated Terrapin Heights as a historic district, after years of pressure from the Neighborhood Association. We even have signs posted throughout the neighborhood reading "Terrapin Heights Historic District." I wish the City Council had gotten its act together before my neighbor, Ned, remodeled his house. I wasn't thrilled when he tore the back off his house and replaced it with a modern atrium with lots of glass and a steel frame. The house doesn't fit the neighborhood anymore, although he now has a great ocean view with all that glass.

LAWYER: What did you tell the Meridiens about the designation?

CLIENT: Here's a copy of my disclosure statement indicating that the house is zoned residential-historic.

LAWYER: Didn't I see something in the news about Terrapin Heights?

CLIENT: Yes. You may have read that a group home for recovering drug addicts will be opening shortly. I have to say that if I were staying in the neighborhood, I'd be concerned about the group home being just a few blocks away from my house.

LAWYER: I noticed in the letter that the Meridiens' attorney raised the group home issue. Let's now talk about the condition of the house. The Meridiens' attorney references some water stains. Have you ever had any problems with the roof?

CLIENT: The stains the attorney is talking about are in a bedroom I rarely use. I had the roof looked at. The roofers said it needed repair, but the estimate they gave me was really high. I've been meaning to get another estimate. In the meantime, I just had the ceiling repainted so it's less noticeable.

LAWYER: What about the fire damage?

CLIENT: That claim about fire damage completely confused me—there's never been a fire while I've lived there. After I got this letter, I called up the prior owner and he said that, about fifteen years ago, while doing some remodeling upstairs he discovered charred wood beams behind the plaster walls. He thought it was just a cosmetic issue, so he covered over the walls with new plaster and didn't worry about it.

LAWYER: The last item listed in the letter is the kitchen floor. What can you tell me about it?

CLIENT: The floor is vinyl and yes, it is worn in spots. It doesn't look great but it's functional.

LAWYER: I see that the only condition you noted on the form was the shared driveway.

CLIENT: I was in a rush when I prepared the form and I wasn't really sure what "defects" or "material facts" covered, so that's all I wrote down.

LAWYER: What conversation did you have with the Meridiens?

CLIENT: Not much. We talked on the phone and they said they were in a hurry to buy before school started. They knew houses in this neighborhood were selling fast. They saw my house on the FSBO—that's the "for sale by owner"—website. I e-mailed them photos of the house and they were interested. Lisa mentioned something about having her cousin Brad, who lives in Banford, come by to look at the house, but he never called me to arrange a time. Anyway, I sent the Meridiens the real property disclosure statement. Without seeing the house, they made an offer. We agreed on a price, $300,000. Pierre Meridien drafted a contract, and we signed it. Then they came to see the house in person along with their contractor. Shortly after their visit, I got the letter from their attorney.

LAWYER: Thanks. I'll review the materials you brought and I'll get back to you soon.

CLIENT: I thought we were all set for closing in two weeks, and now this! I can't believe how much money they're demanding. I really need this sale to go through because I am buying another house.

Davis, Schultz & Meyer
Attorneys at Law
3600 N. First Avenue
Banford, Franklin 33540
(555) 934-6330

July 20, 2006

Ms. Karen Larson
2016 Forsythe Street
Banford, FR 33547

Re: Sale of house at 2016 Forsythe Street

Dear Ms. Larson:

I represent Pierre and Lisa Meridien in their purchase of your property at 2016 Forsythe Street. As you are well aware, the Meridiens reside in the State of Columbia and on June 23, 2006, entered into a contract to purchase your house sight unseen. They relied on the written disclosures you made and the photos of the house and yard you e-mailed to them.

As you also know, the Meridiens recently traveled to Banford to see your house in person. They were aghast to discover the following material defects in the house and problems with the neighborhood, all of which you failed to disclose:

1. A drug rehabilitation group home scheduled to open in two months located less than three blocks from the property. This group home will significantly diminish the property values in the neighborhood and jeopardize the safety of the Meridiens' children.

2. The neighborhood recently has been designated as a historic district, severely restricting the Meridiens' plan to add a family room on the back of the house as they discussed with you.

3. Water stains on the ceiling in one bedroom upstairs, evidencing damage to the roof. While we do not yet know the extent of the damage, the cost of replacing a roof on a home of this type can exceed $30,000.

4. The Meridiens have learned from their building contractor that there is fire damage to the upstairs that affects the structural integrity of the house. His preliminary estimate to repair the damage is $12,000.

5. Severely worn vinyl floor in the kitchen. Replacement will cost $3,000.

These defects and problems should have been disclosed to the Meridiens before they entered into the contract. See Franklin Real Property Law § 350(c).

As a result of your failure to disclose these conditions, the Meridiens will be forced to spend a minimum of $45,000 in renovations on a property that is now worth significantly less because of its proximity to the drug rehabilitation group home and the restrictions on improvements under the historic district zoning classification. The Meridiens, however, are willing to settle this matter for a $60,000 reduction in the purchase price.

Please respond to this letter in two weeks. If I don't hear from you by August 10, 2006, the Meridiens will pursue all remedies available to them under Franklin law, including voiding the contract.

Sincerely,

/s/

Madeline A. Meyer
Attorney at Law

RESIDENTIAL REAL PROPERTY DISCLOSURE STATEMENT

In accordance with Franklin law, a seller of residential real property in Franklin must disclose known material facts relating to the property and its environs. (See Franklin Real Property Law § 350.)

Property address:_2016 Forsythe Street, Banford_______________State of Franklin
Building type:_Single-family residence_______________Year of construction:_1880
Zoning Class:_Residential - Historic
Seller has lived at this residence for __4__years.

1. The Property has the items checked below:
Range_X_ Oven_X_ Microwave_X_ Dishwasher_X_ Disposal
TV Antenna___ Cable TV Wiring_X_ Satellite Dish___ Ceiling Fan(s)
Attic Fan(s)___ Exhaust Fan(s)___ Central A/C___ Central Heating_X
Plumbing System: _____ Septic System _X_ Public Sewer System
Heating System: _X_ Gas ____ Electric
Water Heater: _X_ Gas ____ Electric
Water Supply: _X_ City ____ Private Well

Are you (Seller) aware of any of the above items that are not in working condition, that have known defects, or that are in need of repair? Yes_____ No _X_ If yes, explain. (Attach additional sheets if necessary.)

____

2. Are you (Seller) aware of any defects/malfunctions in any of the following? (Check any of which you are aware.)
Interior Walls___ Ceilings___ Floors___ Exterior Walls___ Doors ___ Windows
Roof___ Foundation___ Basement___ Fences___ Driveways___ Sidewalks___
Electrical System___ Lighting Fixtures___ Other Structural Components (Describe)

If the answer to any of the above is yes, explain. (Attach additional sheets if necessary.)

____

3. Are you (Seller) aware of any of the following conditions? (Check any of which you are aware.)
Termite or Wood Rot Damage_____ Previous Flooding____ Improper Drainage_____
Water Penetration________ Prior Structural/Roof Repair_______Hazardous or Toxic Materials
Asbestos Components_____ Lead-Based Paint_____ Easements_X

If the answer to any of the above is yes, explain. (Attach additional sheets if necessary.)
driveway shared with neighbor

4. Are you (Seller) aware of any other material facts relating to the Property or its environs? _____Yes _X_ No
If yes, explain. (Attach additional sheets if necessary.)

____

June 16, 2006 — Date

/s/ Karen Larson — Signature of Seller

11

Group Home Approved Despite Protests

In a controversy that has been raging for over six months, more than fifty residents and homeowners from the Terrapin Heights neighborhood spoke out yet again at last night's City Council meeting in unsuccessful opposition regarding a proposed ordinance that would allow a group home for recovering heroin addicts and other substance abusers to be located in the affluent and trendy area of Banford. The ordinance passed by a vote of 16 to 8, with council member Fred Nygard of District 15 abstaining.

The planned group home will house up to a dozen male and female residents and will be owned and run by HealthHomes International, a non-profit organization that operates more than twenty such homes across Franklin. In addition to the residential services, therapy and programs will be available on an outpatient basis. HealthHomes has already purchased the former Samuel Newell mansion at 813 Spaight Street, and expects to begin the necessary interior renovations for "Newell House" within days.

"It's not that I don't support helping people with substance abuse issues," stated resident Jack Templar. "I just don't think that Terrapin Heights is the place for a group home. It won't fit in with the character of the neighborhood." Other speakers were more candid regarding their opposition to the HealthHomes project. Emma Rigg, who has lived in Terrapin Heights for five years and has two young children, voiced concerns about an increase in crime if the group home opens as scheduled on September 18, 2006. "We've worked hard to revitalize Terrapin Heights. It was only two years ago that we cleaned up the last vacant lot on Spaight Street and created a lovely community garden there. I doubt I'll feel comfortable working in the garden with my children, knowing that twelve drug addicts live on the same block. Another thing, having the group home in the neighborhood will ruin property values."

Liz Voorhees, attorney for HealthHomes, thanked the council for allowing the plans for Newell House to proceed. She assured those who had opposed the ordinance that, based on HealthHomes' experience with its other group homes, the presence of Newell House would not be disruptive. "We are confident that the other residents of Terrapin Heights will barely notice our presence in the neighborhood," Voorhees stated. "We are not changing the exterior of Newell House, apart from a discreet sign at the front door. We do not treat individuals with a history of violence, and our staff are all highly qualified professionals in the area of substance abuse."

Mel Gerstner owns a house one street over from the site of the group home and appeared unconvinced. "I believe that HealthHomes has a good track record, but come back and ask me in a year what I think of Newell House."

LIBRARY

13

BANFORD CITY ORDINANCES

Chapter 11, Zoning

§ 11.50 Historic Districts

The following sections of the City of Banford, Franklin, are hereby designated as historic districts: Groveside, Terrapin Heights, and Sherwood. Because the Banford City Council has determined that safeguarding the historic character of these neighborhoods is integral to the quality of life and cultural heritage of Banford, no substantial changes to the exteriors of properties located within one of these designated historic districts may be made without prior approval of the Neighborhood Preservation Committee, in addition to the applicable permits from the Building and Zoning Board. This ordinance does not pertain to landscaping or the installation of satellite dishes, provided that the latter do not exceed 30" in diameter and are not placed on the side of the structure facing the street.

* * * *

FRANKLIN REAL PROPERTY LAW

§ 350 Residential Real Property – Required Disclosures

(a) Applicability. This section applies to sales of Franklin residential real estate having no less than one and no more than four dwelling units, whether or not the sale is completed with the assistance of a licensed real estate broker. This section does not apply to: eminent domain proceedings, transfers by fiduciaries as part of administering estates, sales pursuant to court orders, and bankruptcy proceedings.

(b) With respect to sales of real property under this section, the seller of the residential real property shall furnish to the buyer a disclosure statement disclosing known material facts relating to the property and its environs.

(c) The disclosure statement must be delivered to a buyer prior to entering into a real estate contract of sale.

(d) Failure by the seller to provide such a disclosure statement to a buyer does not void the purchase contract or create any defect of title. However, a seller who fails to perform any duty prescribed by any provision of this section may be liable for actual damages suffered as a result of conditions existing in the property or its environs, as of the date of the execution of the real estate purchase contract, in addition to reasonable attorney's fees and court costs.

(e) Nothing contained within this section shall prevent a buyer from pursuing any remedies at law or equity otherwise available against a seller in the event of a seller's intentional misrepresentation and/or fraudulent concealment of the condition of the subject property or its environs.

(f) This section shall take effect on March 31, 2005, and shall apply to real estate transactions entered into on or after such date.

Hernandez v. Comfrey

Franklin Supreme Court (2002)

Plaintiff Hernandez cried foul when the home he purchased from defendants proved to have a leaking basement and wood rot in its structural supports. The issue before us is whether Hernandez's claim for intentional misrepresentation raised genuine issues of triable fact. The trial court awarded summary judgment to the sellers, the Comfreys. The court of appeal affirmed that decision. For the reasons set forth below, we affirm in turn.

Hernandez argues that the Comfreys intentionally misrepresented the true condition of the property and that he would not have purchased the property but for their misrepresentations.

Hernandez viewed the house twice and states that the Comfreys told him at the time that the house was in excellent shape. Hernandez contends that he asked about the basement and the Comfreys responded that it was "fine." Five months after closing, following a torrential rain, the basement flooded, causing substantial damage. A professional inspection thereafter found that the drainage system around the house was defective and also that there was extensive wood rot in load-bearing supports. This litigation followed.

It is the buyer's responsibility to exercise due diligence by inspecting real property prior to purchase. Franklin adheres to the *caveat emptor* (buyer beware) doctrine in sales of residential real estate. Sellers have no affirmative obligation to volunteer information about defective conditions in the property being offered for sale. When, however, a seller intentionally misrepresents or fraudulently conceals material facts regarding a property's condition or its environs, a buyer is entitled to recover actual damages, and, in cases where the concealment or misrepresentation has severe financial or safety implications, punitive damages from the seller.

To prevail in an action alleging intentional misrepresentation, a plaintiff must establish the following: (1) misrepresentation of a material fact; (2) justifiable reliance; and (3) injury.[1] Materiality is an objective standard, looking to whether the purported fact would affect the decision making of the reasonable home buyer. Minor or *de minimis* defects do not qualify as material facts, even if such items may be of interest to the buyer.

It is not disputed here that the wood rot and the defective drainage system are material facts that were not disclosed to Hernandez.

1. Similarly, to prevail in an action for fraudulent concealment a plaintiff must establish: (1) concealment of a material fact with the intent to mislead; (2) justifiable reliance; and (3) injury. *See Fowles v. Hutchison* (Franklin Ct. App. 1989) (fraudulent concealment found where seller placed heavy furniture over hole in floor).

Moreover, Hernandez contends, the statements describing the property in the sales listing and the Comfreys' assurances that the house was in "excellent shape" constitute intentional misrepresentations. Therefore, Hernandez concludes, the Comfreys are liable for damages resulting from the failed drainage system and wood rot, as well as for the inconsistencies between the sales listing and the actual condition of the property.

First, we note that the Comfreys' statements that the house was in "excellent shape" are merely opinion, and will not support an intentional misrepresentation claim. A certain amount of "puffery" or sales talk is to be expected in any sales transaction. The sellers' nonspecific statements regarding the desirability of the property do not rise to the level of actionable misrepresentations.

The *caveat emptor* doctrine does not protect sellers who lie in response to a direct question about a particular feature or condition of the property. In order to demonstrate intentional misrepresentation, however, the plaintiff must show knowledge on the part of the seller. Here, there was no evidence that the Comfreys knew of material defects in the drainage system or wood supports. Because the Comfreys did not know of these structural problems with their house, they could not have intentionally misrepresented them.

Because Hernandez was concerned that the Comfreys would receive competing offers in a hot real estate market, he contends that an independent inspection was not feasible given the pressure to close on the house. He submits that he had no choice but to rely upon the Comfreys' assurances regarding the house's condition.

This rationale falls far short of a showing of justifiable reliance. It remains the buyer's responsibility, personally or through an agent, to act with due diligence and inspect the premises to his or her satisfaction. The record is devoid of any evidence that Hernandez was denied the opportunity to have the property professionally inspected before he bought it.

Although no claim of fraudulent concealment is raised by Hernandez, we note that there is nothing to suggest that the Comfreys fraudulently concealed the defects alleged in the property. Nor is this a situation where a seller's attempts to repair a problem might be interpreted as fraudulent concealment. Such cases raise factual disputes regarding the seller's intent that are not present in the record before us.

Accordingly, the order for summary judgment in favor of the Comfreys is affirmed.

Wallen v. Daniels

Franklin Court of Appeal (2006)

We address the extent of disclosure that a real estate seller must provide to a buyer. Oscar and Peg Wallen purchased a "fixer-upper" home in Verdes Canyon. Shortly after moving in, they applied for a building permit to add a second story. It was at this point that the Wallens learned that the addition had to comply with the County's strict building code for structures that, like their new home, were located in an earthquake-prone area. Consequently, the Wallens' addition would cost fifty percent more than a similar addition to a house not subject to "earthquake-proof" building codes. The Wallens sued Frank Daniels, the former owner, for failure to comply with § 350 of the Franklin Real Property Law and for fraudulent concealment in the sale of the property, alleging that Daniels had failed to inform them that, because of the house's location, improvements to the structure were not economically feasible.

The trial court granted summary judgment to the Wallens on both claims, holding that Daniels, the seller, failed to disclose a material fact affecting the property. Daniels appeals.

Until recently, Franklin followed a strict *caveat emptor* doctrine in real estate transactions. Under that doctrine, it fell to the buyer to detect any material facts regarding a property before purchasing it. The seller was prohibited only from engaging in fraudulent concealment and intentional misrepresentations. There was no affirmative duty to disclose information about the property. *Hernandez v. Comfrey* (Franklin Sup. Ct. 2002).

In 2005, however, the Franklin Legislature enacted § 350 of the Real Property Law, "Residential Real Property – Required Disclosures." Under § 350, it is now the seller's responsibility to disclose material facts known to the seller about the property itself and its environs to potential buyers. The duty to buyers created by § 350, however, does not go so far as to require that sellers inspect their properties for latent material conditions or defects to disclose.

Failure to comply with § 350 may give rise to a statutory claim for failure to disclose. For example, in *Harris v. Roth* (Franklin Ct. App. 2005), a buyer was awarded damages when the seller failed to note in the § 350 disclosure statement that the property was a half mile from a toxic waste dump that had been abandoned ten years before but was contaminating the groundwater.

Nondisclosure may result in an award for actual damages, that is, the cost to repair the property so that it conforms to its condition as represented by the seller at the time of sale with respect to those defects of which the seller had actual knowledge. When repair is not possible, damages may be measured by the difference in value between the property as represented in the disclosure statement and an independent appraisal that reflects the undisclosed material fact. *See Harris.*

In addition to liability for failure to disclose under § 350, where a seller has fraudulently concealed or intentionally misrepresented a defect, the seller remains subject to liability based on the common law.

Applying the new law, the trial court held that the increased cost of construction on properties zoned "fault area" was a material fact that § 350 obligated the seller to disclose. It awarded damages to the Wallens equal to the added cost of building in compliance with earthquake-zone construction standards. We conclude that the trial court misconstrued § 350.

The Wallens concede that before bidding on the house, Daniels provided them with a "Real Property Disclosure Statement," noting that the property was zoned as "Residential (fault area)." Nevertheless, they argue that Daniels was required to disclose that any major improvements to the house, given its location in a fault area, would be prohibitively expensive.

We conclude that § 350 does not render a seller liable for nondisclosure of facts that a buyer could have discovered with reasonable effort. A buyer has a responsibility to exercise due diligence in inspecting property before purchasing it. *See Hernandez.* Although the claim in *Hernandez* was for intentional misrepresentation, we conclude that the duty the court imposed on buyers to inspect real property prior to purchase applies equally to claims alleging failure to disclose under § 350.

We are not persuaded that the high price of remodeling according to code is a material fact. A material fact is one relating to the quality of the property which might decrease its value. While a property's classification within a particular zoning class is material, the responsibility for discovering the ramifications of the classification lies with the buyer because the relevant information is freely available and a matter of public record.

The Wallens knew when they bought the house that it was zoned "Residential (fault area)." They were therefore on notice that building codes could impact home improvement plans in the fault area. The actual impact that such ordinances would have on their plans and their pocketbook is information readily available. We will not burden the seller to research local building codes and advise a buyer as to their effect on the realty when the buyer has already been accurately informed as to the zoning.

Because it was the Wallens' responsibility to discover the legal and financial ramifications of the property's zoning, we conclude that the Wallens cannot sustain a claim for fraudulent concealment. *See Hernandez*.

Reversed.

MPT 1 - Sample Answer 1.

MEMORANDUM

To: Elaine Dreyer

From: Applicant

Date: July 25, 2006

Re: Larson Real Estate File

DISCLOSURE OBLIGATIONS

Under Franklin Real Property Law Section 350(b)-(c), sellers of residential real property are required to furnish disclosure statements providing "known material facts relating to the property and its environs" prior to entering into a contract for sale. Materiality of a fact is based on an objective standard, whether the fact "would affect the decision making of the reasonable home buyer." Hernandez, or one that would "relate to the quality of the property which might decrease its value." Wallen. It does not include facts that, while of interest, would only be considered minor by a reasonable purchaser. Hernandez.

A more recent Court of Appeals decision has interpreted the recent statute as simply disclosing known facts, but not creating an affirmative obligation on a seller to inspect their property for latent material conditions. Wallen. Furthermore, disclosure of zoning restrictions, without further explicating their impact on property values, is sufficient to discharge a seller's duties. Id.

ALLEGED DEFECTS

The Meridians' counsel reported a number of alleged defects in the property. Each will be addressed in turn.

Drug Rehabilitation Home: It is unclear whether Larson was required to disclose the rehab group home. It depends on whether it would be considered a material fact to an objective buyer. This is unclear based on the case law. Although the home was between 2-3 blocks from the Larson property, even Ms. Larson herself noted that she would have concerns. Other neighbors expressed differing responses, according to the article in the Banford Courier. Some expressed concerns over safety, although the home itself does not accept individuals with any history of violence. It is unclear whether these subjective concerns would rise to the level of material fact – i.e., affect a reasonable buyer's decision to purchase the house, or affect the property value. Prior to the opening of the rehab home, it is frankly impossible to determine the impact. Furthermore, even under the new disclosure laws, buyers maintain "responsibility to exercise due diligence in inspecting property before purchasing it," which includes facts that are commonly known. Wallen. Although the Meridiens were not from Franklin, a cousin lived in the same town, and could have disclosed the controversy to them prior to executing the contract, given the wide publicity that the home has garnered. Larson probably is not liable for failing to disclose the upcoming group home.

Zoning in the Historic District: Ms. Larson fully disclosed the fact that her home was zoned in the historic district in her disclosure statement, which was the extent of her requirement by law. The Court of Appeals spoke directly to this question in Wallen when it held that although this fact is material, "the responsibility for discovering the ramifications of the classification lies with the buyer because the relevant information is freely available and a matter of public record." Under the zoning laws, this classification only means that the Meridiens would have to obtain prior approval from the Neighborhood Preservation Committee and applicable permits to add a family room; it does not prevent them from doing so. Larson will not be liable at all on this complaint.

Water Stains Evidencing Roof Damage: Larson was obliged to disclose the roof damage, and her failure to do so is the most problematic omission from her disclosure statement. She was aware of the problem, and knew that it would cost significantly to repair. It likely amounts to the level of damage that would affect a prospective buyer's decision to purchase, or at least the price that a buyer would be willing to pay. Painting the ceiling so that the stains are less noticeable may even fall into the category of intentional misrepresentation or fraudulent concealment of a defect. Fowles. To prove a case of fraudulent misrepresentation, the purchasers must demonstrate misrepresentation, justifiable reliance, and injury. Reliance on the disclosure statement that there are no defects in the roof may be enough to make out a case for misrepresentation, which would allow much broader remedies for the Meridiens (see infra).

Fire Damage: Because Larson had no knowledge of the fire damage, she was under no obligation to disclose it under the new disclosure laws, which require only disclosure of "known material facts." S 350(b); see also Wallen. Sellers are under no obligation to inspect property for latent material conditions or defects. The Meridiens cannot recover for this.

Worn Vinyl Floor: It is questionable whether the state of the kitchen floor rises to the level of a material fact that would have to be disclosed. This appears to be the type of issue that a reasonable buyer would find interesting, but would likely rather not affect her decision to purchase. Hernandez. Common wear and tear is not considered a "defect/malfunction," which is what the disclosure statement requires sellers to disclose. Section "350 does not render a seller liable for nondisclosure of facts that a buyer could have discovered with reasonable effort. A buyer has a responsibility to exercise due diligence in inspecting property before purchasing it." The state of the flooring could easily have been discovered through a cursory inspection by the buyer's cousin. Larson faces no liability here.

RELIEF

If a seller simply fails to disclose a material fact, she will be liable for actual damages suffered as a result of that fact, along with fees and costs. Here, Larson would be liable to pay for the roof repairs, fees and costs, but the Meridiens would not be able to rescind the contract.

If, however, a seller has intentionally misrepresented or fraudulently concealed a material defect, she will be liable under all common law contract claims, up to and including rescission and even punitive damages, since the concealment has severe financial implications. The fact that Larson did not understand the import of "material" will help her case, but may not be conclusive, since she knowingly painted over the water damage. It is likely that Larson may face these penalties.

Sample Answer 2.

MEMORANDUM

To: Elaine Dreyer

From: Applicant

Date: July 25, 2006

Re: Larson Real Estate File

What disclosure obligation does a seller of residential real estate have under Franklin statutory and common law?

Prior to March 31, 2005, Franklin adhered to a caveat emptor or buyer beware doctrine in residential real estate sales. (Hernandez v. Comfrey, hereinafter "Hernandez") Under common law, seller had no affirmative obligation to volunteer information about defective conditions in the property being offered for sale. Id. A seller could not, however, intentionally misrepresent or fraudulently conceal material facts regarding a property's condition or its environs.

Presently, sellers of residential real estate are required to affirmatively disclose, through a disclosure statement, known material facts relating to the property and its environs prior to entering into a contract of sale. 350. The new legislation did not alter a seller's common law duty to not intentionally misrepresent or fraudulently conceal material facts. 350(e). Sellers do not have to go so far as inspecting their properties for latent material conditions or defects to disclose. (Wallen v. Daniels, hereinafter "Wallen")

As to each of the problems and defects cited by the Meridiens' attorney, what, if anything, was Larson required to disclose under Franklin law, and did she comply?

1. A drug rehabilitation group home scheduled to open in two months, located less than three blocks from the property.

In Harris v. Roth, cited in Wallen, the seller was required to disclose an abandoned toxic waste dump that was contaminating groundwater a half mile from the property. This case is distinguishable because the Terrapin Heights group home does not in and of itself pose a danger to the property or its occupants. There has been no history of problems associated with this group home and Health Homes, the owner, has a good track record (See article in The Banford Courier). While it may have been preferable to the buyers to know, it is doubtful that this group home was required to be disclosed.

2. The neighborhood recently has been designated as a historic district, severely restricting the Meridiens' plans to add a family room on the back of the house.

In Wallen, the Franklin Court of Appeal stated that disclosing the property as "Residential (fault area)" was sufficient to put the buyers on notice that building codes could impact home improvement plans in the fault area. Similarly, in Larson's "Residential Real Property Disclosure Statement" the zoning class is "Residential-Historic." This is likewise sufficient to put the buyers on notice that building codes could impact home improvement plans. Larson complied with the requirement.

3. Water stains on the ceiling in one bedroom upstairs, evidencing damage to the roof. Extent of damage unknown, but estimated cost of replacement is over $30,000.

Larson indicated that she knew of the leaking roof and had a roofer inspect it. The estimate was too high for Larson, so she painted the ceiling in the bedroom to make it less noticeable. Sellers are under a duty not to fraudulently conceal material facts. Materiality is judged on an objective standard, looking to whether the fact would affect the decision making in a reasonable buyer. Hernandez. A leaking roof would affect a reasonable buyer, at least to the extent of the size of his offer. It is highly doubtful that this would be a minor defect. Larson did not disclose this problem to the buyer and probably fraudulently concealed it.

Larson may argue that there was no fraudulent concealment because the buyers did not justifiably rely on the concealment. The buyers are responsible for inspecting, whether personally or through an agent, the premises. Since there was no inspection, there could be no justifiable reliance. However, the buyers will argue that this should have been on the disclosure statement and without it, it is intentional misrepresentation.

4. Fire damage to the upstairs affecting the structural integrity of the house. Preliminary damage estimate is $12,000.

As previously stated, sellers are under no duty to inspect their property for latent defects. Wallen. The fire damage was not obvious since the previous owner had covered the damage behind plaster walls. Larson would not be under a duty to inspect for the damage, and she had no reason to previously know of the problem. This, she was not required to disclose the defect.

5. Severely worn vinyl floor in the kitchen. Replacement cost of $3,000.

The worn vinyl is probably a de minimis defect (1% of purchase price), even though it would be of interest to the buyer. Many buyers replace floors upon buying a home, despite what condition they are in.

What type of relief, if any, can the Meridiens obtain against Ms. Larson under Franklin law?

Failure to provide necessary disclosures prior to the contract of sale does not void the contract nor does it create any defect to title; sellers are liable for any actual damages suffered as a result of the nondisclosure. 350(d) Actual damages are the cost to repair the property so that it conforms to its condition as represented by the seller at the time of sale with respect to those defects of which the seller had actual knowledge; if repair is not possible, damages are measured by the difference between the property as represented and an independent appraisal. Wallen. Although unlikely, if the Court determines that the zoning, the group home, the fire damage, or the worn vinyl floor were required disclosures, the Court could impose actual damages. However, the group home may present a problem for the buyers because damages would be speculative. The other items would present a definitive dollar number for the courts to impose actual damages.

Buyers may pursue both law and equity remedies in the event of a seller's intentional misrepresentation and/or fraudulent concealment. 350. Because Larson fraudulently concealed the roof damage, she is liable for the cost of repair. The buyers may be able to pursue punitive damages if they are able to prove that Larson fraudulently concealed the damage.

Sample Answer 3.

MEMORANDUM

TO: Elaine Dreyer

FROM: Applicant

DATE: July 25, 2006

RE: Larson Real Estate File—Disclosure Obligations Analysis of Claims/Relief

Disclosure obligations of seller of residential real estate under Franklin statutory and common law:

Statutory Obligations: Frank. R.P. 350(c). Under this statute, the seller of residential real estate must disclose known material defects affecting the property and environs at the time of the contract for sale. The law applies to all residential sales involving 1 to 4 units and includes sales FSBO, as is the case here. The disclosure must be delivered by the seller to the buyer before entering the contract.

The key element the requirement of disclosure for material defects. Under Franklin law (Hernandez) a defect is material if "purported fact would affect the decision making of the reasonable home buyer," based on an objective standard. Minor/de minimis defects don't amount to material defects. In Wallen (Ct. App. 2006) the court further elaborated on materiality, saying that a material fact is "one relating to the quality of the property which might decrease its value."

Therefore, under 350(c) a seller of residential real estate, including Larson, must disclose all facts known at the time of disclosure that would affect a reasonable buyer's decision about whether to purchase the property, including all facts that would materially affect the value of the property. Failure to make the disclosure results in liability for actual damages and attorney fees/court costs.

Finally, as recently interpreted in Wallen, 350(c) has not abrogated buyer's obligation to make a reasonable inspection using the due diligence and the seller is under no obligation to discover latent defects, even if they are material.

Common Law Obligations:

350(c) does not affect common law liability for intentional misrepresentation or fraudulent concealment. To establish intentional misrepresentation under Franklin common law plaintiff must establish: 1) a misrepresentation of material fact; 2) justifiable reliance; 3) injury. The elements for fraudulent concealment are the same, except for the first element, which requires plaintiff to establish intentional concealment of a material fact.

The same standard for materiality discussed above, applies here. Also, the seller must have actual knowledge of the fact. Additionally, only representations of fact are significant, while statements of opinion or mere sales puffery (e.g., "this is a great house") are not actionable.

Damages for these common law claims include actual costs of repair and if the failure to disclose involves substantial financial problems or significant problems with the property there can be punitive damages as well.

Analysis of Defects

Defects re the Neighborhood

The Group Home

Larson failed to disclose the fact that a rehab group home was planned to go into the neighborhood. It is possible that this would be considered material as a reasonable buyer might decide not to purchase because the proximity to drug addicts and potential for crime. Also, it is possible that the reasonable buyer might include one who has children, and that buyer might reasonably be concerned about this issue.

This isn't a clear win for plaintiffs, however, because disclosure is only required for facts about conditions that are actually known at the time contracting. Here, the group home wasn't yet in place and wouldn't be operating until September. So, while Larson probably had actual knowledge of the home, given all of the controversy, she didn't know at the time that the home would actually create any of the problems claimed, and there is evidence that the home will have limited impact on the neighborhood. Finally, because of the publicity, it is likely that court would conclude that a buyer exercising due diligence and making reasonable inspection would've discovered this problem.

Historic Zoning Restrictions

Larson satisfied here disclosure requirements by noting that the home was zoned "Residential-Historic" on the disclosure form. Under Wallen, the seller's disclosure of a similar zoning restriction (fault zone) on the same disclosure form used here and in the same sparse manner as Larson did here, was sufficient to satisfy the disclosure requirements of the law. It is up to the buyers to research the ramifications of the zoning law.

Defects re the House

Water Stains/Roof Leak

Larson failed to disclose roof leak and concealed the stains with paint, thereby breaching disclosure duties under 350(c) and making herself liable under fraudulent concealment theory.

It is clear that the roof leak would be considered material to an objectively reasonable buyer, because the initial estimate for repairs is as high as $30,000. Also, Larson actually knew about this problem, having had it inspected, and was aware that the costs of repair could be high (she had a high estimate). This failure to disclose a known material fact is a violation of her 350 © disclosure duties.

By painting over the stain she concealed a material fact of which she was aware and there is clearly injury, but it is unclear that the buyers relied on that "representation" because they never made an inspection of the house pre-contract. Under Hernandez, the buyer must act with due diligence. Even so the plaintiff's could have a good case here because, even if they had made an inspection they may not have noticed the problem because of concealment.

Fire Damage

Larson had no duty to disclose because she had no actual knowledge of the problem prior to the contract.

Floor

This appears to immaterial. If the damage is de minimis or minor, then it is not material and does not have to be disclosed. Also, this would clearly be seen in a diligent inspection.

Potential Relief

Given her failure to disclose the roof leak Larson is liable for the actual costs of repair. She should get an estimate to determine this amount. Based on fraudulent concealment she may also be liable for punitive damages if the problem is deemed to be substantial/significant. Finally, she will be liable for attorney fees and court costs. Damages will likely be deducted from the contract price.

INSTRUCTIONS

1. You will have 90 minutes to complete this session of the examination. This performance test is designed to evaluate your ability to handle a select number of legal authorities in the context of a factual problem involving a client.

2. The problem is set in the fictitious state of Franklin, in the fictitious Fifteenth Circuit of the United States. Columbia and Olympia are also fictitious states in the Fifteenth Circuit. In Franklin, the trial court of general jurisdiction is the District Court, the intermediate appellate court is the Court of Appeal, and the highest court is the Supreme Court.

3. You will have two kinds of materials with which to work: a File and a Library. The first document in the File is a memorandum containing the instructions for the task you are to complete. The other documents in the File contain factual information about your case and may also include some facts that are not relevant.

4. The Library contains the legal authorities needed to complete the task and may also include some authorities that are not relevant. Any cases may be real, modified, or written solely for the purpose of this examination. If the cases appear familiar to you, do not assume that they are precisely the same as you have read before. Read them thoroughly, as if they all were new to you. You should assume that the cases were decided in the jurisdictions and on the dates shown. In citing cases from the Library, you may use abbreviations and omit page references.

5. Your response must be written in the answer book provided. In answering this performance test, you should concentrate on the materials provided. What you have learned in law school and elsewhere provides the general background for analyzing the problem; the File and Library provide the specific materials with which you must work.

6. Although there are no restrictions on how you apportion your time, you should be sure to allocate ample time (about 45 minutes) to reading and digesting the materials and to organizing your answer before you begin writing it. You may make notes anywhere in the test materials; blank pages are provided at the end of the booklet. You may not tear pages from the question booklet.

7. This performance test will be graded on your responsiveness to the instructions regarding the task you are to complete, which are given to you in the first memorandum in the File, and on the content, thoroughness, and organization of your response.

Parker v. Essex Productions

FILE

LIBRARY

FILE

2

Brown Scott & Mayer
Attorneys at Law
4330 Shepard Avenue, Suite 207
New Albany, Franklin 33087
(555) 555-6578

M E M O R A N D U M

TO: Applicant

FROM: Gail Brown

RE: *Parker v. Essex Productions*

DATE: July 25, 2006

Our client, Sylvia Parker, a professional singer, has sued Essex Productions, Inc. (Essex) to recover fees owed to her under a promotional singing tour contract. Essex procures live performance engagements for musicians and other performers. Its services include promoting concert tours, finding venues, making the logistical arrangements for its performers, and collecting the fees for the performances and forwarding them to the performers after deduction of its commission and expenses.

In the complaint, we have alleged breach of contract, unjust enrichment, and violation of a state law that imposes penalties on Essex for operating without an employment agency license with respect to the tour it arranged for Ms. Parker, which was sponsored by the soft drink giant, Fizz. John Eagin, an attorney representing Essex, has filed a motion to disqualify our firm from representing Ms. Parker in this lawsuit. The trial court has scheduled a hearing on the motion for August 1, 2006.

The motion to disqualify cites a conflict based on the previous employment of one of our associates, Peter Alexander, at the law firm of Tansy & Pipe. To assist me in preparing for the hearing, please draft a persuasive memo I can use for my argument to the court, setting forth every argument we can reasonably make to show that we should not be disqualified. My experience is that disqualification cases are highly fact specific. Therefore, do not merely restate the law but argue how the facts of our case, in light of the law, support our arguments against disqualification.

STATE OF FRANKLIN

DISTRICT COURT FOR WASHINGTON COUNTY

Sylvia Parker, **Plaintiff,** v. **Essex Productions, Inc.,** **Defendant.**	))))))))	**Case No. CV-06-105**

MOTION TO DISQUALIFY LEGAL COUNSEL

Defendant Essex Productions, Inc. (Essex), by and through its attorneys, The Eagin Group, S.C., moves to disqualify the law firm of Brown Scott & Mayer from representing the plaintiff, Sylvia Parker, in this matter. In support of the motion, Essex states the following:

1. Brown Scott & Mayer recently hired Peter D. Alexander, Esq., as an associate attorney.

2. Before accepting employment at Brown Scott & Mayer, Attorney Alexander worked as an associate at the Tansy & Pipe law firm from September 2002 to June 2005.

3. During his employment at Tansy & Pipe, Attorney Alexander advised Essex on a variety of matters, including employment agency licensure issues.

4. As Essex's legal counsel, Attorney Alexander became intimately familiar with Essex and learned confidential information regarding the operation of its business.

5. Attorney Alexander advised and represented Essex on matters concerning the music industry. It was in that capacity that Attorney Alexander negotiated two contracts on behalf of Essex involving facts and circumstances substantially similar to those in the present litigation.

6. The fact that Attorney Alexander did not draft the particular contracts that are the subject of the case at bar does not preclude this Court from granting this motion. The complaint alleges that Essex was operating without an employment license. While working at Tansy & Pipe, Attorney Alexander advised Essex on employment licensure issues.

7. In light of Attorney Alexander's representation of Essex, his current position as an associate at Brown Scott & Mayer creates a conflict of interest that is imputed to the entire Brown Scott & Mayer law firm, including Carol Scott, the partner handling this matter. *See* Franklin Rules of Professional Conduct, 1.7, 1.9 & 1.10.

8. Strict enforcement of the Rules of Professional Conduct maintains the public's confidence in the legal profession. Disqualification of a law firm having a conflict of interest is a reasonable means of protecting a client's expectations of loyalty on the part of his or her legal counsel.

WHEREFORE, Essex asks this Court to grant its Motion to Disqualify the law firm of Brown Scott & Mayer from further representation of the plaintiff, Sylvia Parker, in this matter, and for any and all other appropriate relief.

Signed: ______/s/

John Eagin
The Eagin Group, S.C.
Attorney for Essex Productions, Inc.

Date: July 20, 2006

Interview of Peter Alexander, Associate, Brown Scott & Mayer
By Gail Brown, Ethics Partner, Brown Scott & Mayer

July 24, 2006

Q: (By Gail Brown) Thank you for coming in.

A: (By Peter Alexander) No problem.

Q: I won't take too much of your time. We've run into a snag on a litigation matter the firm is handling and I need to ask you some questions about your work for Essex Productions while you were at the Tansy & Pipe law firm.

A: Sure. You know, when I started here at Brown Scott & Mayer I disclosed that Essex was a former client I had represented before I joined this firm. In fact, I disclosed all my former and current clients so the firm could enter the information into our conflict check system. And then I talked to Ms. Scott when I heard that we represented Ms. Parker in a claim against Essex.

Q: Yes, I know. Unfortunately, this potential conflict, if that's what it is, did not pop up as one might have hoped. I just have to ask you about the nature of your representation. For example, all the system really tells me is that Essex is listed as a former client when you worked at Tansy & Pipe. Do you have any continuing relationship with Essex?

A: No. In January of this year, after I heard Ms. Parker was having problems with Essex and that Brown Scott & Mayer had filed a lawsuit on her behalf, I ran into Essex's president, Jim Gasso, at a concert. He asked me if I knew about this lawsuit. I told him I could not discuss it because I had left my former firm.

Q: What was his response?

A: He said he knew already. Apparently after I left, Tansy & Pipe sent him a letter saying that I was no longer with their firm and that another associate would be the point person.

Q: When was the last time you did any work for Essex?

A: Let's see. I started here in June 2005, so it must have been February 2005.

Q: Have you ever discussed the lawsuit against Essex or its business in general with Ms. Scott or anyone else in this firm?

A: Absolutely not. In fact, when I went to Ms. Scott after hearing about the lawsuit, we agreed that in the interest of avoiding an appearance of impropriety I was to have no information with respect to any issue in the Parker lawsuit and, of course, I was ethically

7

bound not to provide confidential information concerning Essex. I have not disclosed any information to Ms. Scott or to the firm and I will not do so in the future. I'm smart enough to avoid any participation in Ms. Parker's representation, and I certainly know enough not to discuss any aspect of this case with Ms. Scott or any member of Brown Scott & Mayer.

Q: Is there any ongoing communication between you and Essex? Anything that might involve confidential communication?

A: Nothing. The last communication was when I ran into Jim Gasso at the concert.

Q: Let's talk some more about your work for Essex. What kind of work did you do?

A: Tansy & Pipe was hired to do certain discrete negotiations. These were all small matters, so I was given responsibility for handling the client.

Q: Did you or your prior firm receive a retainer?

A: No. I, or technically I guess the firm, was just paid by the hour.

Q: How would you characterize the amount of work you did for them?

A: I'm not sure what you mean.

Q: Were you their primary counsel?

A: Oh, no. Essex typically uses another firm and only called Tansy & Pipe when there was a conflict. The work was pretty limited. Essex would occasionally call and need something done and I'd do it. Very small-project oriented.

Q: Did Essex call you or a partner in the firm?

A: Me.

Q: When did this start?

A: Had to be March 2003. About six months after I started at Tansy & Pipe.

Q: Did you ever represent Essex in a matter involving Ms. Parker?

A: No.

Q: Can you give me any examples of the specific kinds of work you did for Essex without revealing any confidential information?

A: Well, usually it was a simple question, something I could answer over the phone or write a letter about.

Q: Was there ever anything more complicated?

A: Well, there were two contracts I wrote.

Q: Tell me about them in general terms.

A: Let's see. In about July 2004, I negotiated a contract on behalf of Essex for a series of concerts they were promoting for another performer. In February 2005, I drafted a recording contract between Essex, a label, and a group. That was the last work I did for them.

Q: How many other concert tour contracts did you draft for Essex?

A: Well, none—that was the only one.

Q: How about management agreements? Any other contracts, including recording contracts?

A: No. These two were the only contracts I handled for Essex.

Q: Do you remember how much you billed Essex for the contracts?

A: Certainly less than 10 hours for the tour. Maybe 15 on the recording contract.

Q: How much confidential or proprietary information did you need to get from Essex?

A: You're kidding, right? I mean, as they say, this was not rocket science. Both contracts were fairly rudimentary and typical of the type of contract Essex negotiated for other, similar clients all the time. I hardly talked to anyone at Essex. They had a standard contract. The other side typically took what was offered.

Q: Did Essex ever seek your legal advice on general music industry or business matters?

A: No.

Q: How about obtaining an employment agency license? Were you ever asked and did you ever give legal advice concerning Essex's efforts to obtain a license?

A: No.

Q: How often did you meet with people from Essex?

A: Not often. Almost all communications were by telephone and fax. I visited their office only once, to drop off a demo CD for a friend's band.

Q: Did you have any contact with Ms. Parker while you worked for Essex at Tansy & Pipe?

A: No. I never even knew until I started here that she and Essex were connected.

Q: Thank you for coming in, Peter. This has been very helpful.

A: I assume you have spoken to Ms. Scott about this.

Q: She's in trial this week and then off to Chicago for a convention, so I'm going to have this typed up and given to her tonight so she can give me her thoughts on how she wants to proceed.

A: Fine. Let me know if there is anything else I can help with.

FROM: Carol Scott [CScott@BSMlaw.mpt]
TO: Gail Brown [GBrown@BSMlaw.mpt]
SENT: Monday, July 24, 2006, 8:35 p.m.
SUBJECT: Parker v. Essex Productions

Hi Gail,

Just a quick e-mail to let you know that I read the transcript of Peter Alexander's interview with you. As far as what he said about his and my communications, it's accurate.

This whole thing is bogus. This motion to disqualify is baseless. For example, even if Alexander gave Essex advice on the employment license issue (and I believe him when he says he didn't), it's a matter of public record that Essex doesn't have a license. How can it be confidential?!

As you know, Sylvia Parker has been a client of this firm for ten years, well before Alexander was out of law school, much less drafting those two contracts for Essex. Even so, we haven't handled everything for her. Our firm was not involved in Sylvia's negotiations with Essex or in negotiating agreements for her performance engagements. In this lawsuit, we're going after Essex for stacking management fees on top of promotional fees and costs, thus misrepresenting the actual amounts and making Sylvia pay twice for the expenses of the Fizz 100-city tour she recently completed.

There's no reason for the court to disqualify us. And, at this stage of the litigation, in the middle of discovery, it would be very expensive and time-consuming for new counsel to get up to speed in the case, and the $10,000 Sylvia has already invested in the case would be lost. Anyway, Sylvia wants me to be her lawyer, and she wants this matter, which Eagin has been trying to drag out, resolved.

Carol

11

Sent from my Blackberry Wireless Handheld

12

LIBRARY

Franklin Rules of Professional Conduct

RULE 1.7 Conflict of Interest: General Rule

(a) A lawyer shall not represent a client if the representation of that client will be directly adverse to another client, unless:

(1) the lawyer reasonably believes the representation will not adversely affect the relationship with the other client; and

(2) each client consents after consultation.

* * * *

RULE 1.9 Conflict of Interest: Former Client

A lawyer who has formerly represented a client in a matter shall not thereafter represent another person in the same or a substantially related matter in which that person's interests are materially adverse to the interests of the former client unless the former client consents after consultation.

RULE 1.10 Imputed Disqualification: General Rule

While lawyers are associated in a firm, none of them shall knowingly represent a client when any one of them practicing alone would be prohibited from doing so by Rules 1.7 or 1.9.

Global Financial Fund v. Omega Investments, Inc.

Franklin Court of Appeal (1992)

Plaintiff Global Financial Fund (Global) has filed a complaint against defendant Omega Investments, Inc. (Omega) alleging securities fraud.

Omega moved to disqualify Global's attorneys, the law firm of Wyant & Wheeler (the Firm) on the grounds that the Firm had a conflict of interest and its continued representation of Global in this lawsuit would violate either Rule 1.7 or Rule 1.9 of the Franklin Rules of Professional Conduct. The trial court granted Omega's motion to disqualify.

Omega's relationship with the Firm began in May 1990, when Marcy Jansen, Omega's Vice President, retained Kenneth Russell, a partner at the Firm, to draft a compliance manual for Omega's commodity futures trading operations. In October 1990, Russell sent Omega the final draft.

The Firm undertook a number of other discrete research projects for Omega, the most recent of which was in June 1991, answering commodity law questions as they came up. The record isn't clear when these services were performed or what they entailed, but the Firm billed Omega $39,149 for 214 hours of work from May 1990 to June 1991.

After June 1991, contact between the Firm and Omega continued. Omega personnel and Russell corresponded on several matters. Russell sent two billings after June 25, the last date on which the Firm performed billable work for Omega. The first billing was accompanied by a letter from Russell in which he wrote: "Please do not hesitate to contact me if you have any questions regarding the enclosed." The second request for payment lacked a similar hint of availability.

Tellingly, in August 1991, Russell telephoned Jansen and obtained Omega's consent for the Firm to represent a commodity trading advisor in negotiations with Omega. Russell assured Jansen that the matter was wholly unrelated to the work the Firm had done for Omega in the past. It was around this same time that other members of the Firm began representing Global in what was to become the present lawsuit against Omega.

At a commodities law conference in October 1991, Russell spoke with Jansen about political lobbying that Russell was performing for another client regarding proposed securities regulations. Russell attempted to enlist Omega's support for the proposed regulations both at the conference

and in two follow-up letters.
On November 4, 1991, Andrew Klein, a partner at the Firm, called Jansen, and told her that there was a potential conflict of interest problem in light of the Firm's representation of Global. He asked whether Omega would be amenable to a waiver. Jansen replied that a waiver was probable, but she never provided a written waiver.

On November 20, 1991, the Firm, on behalf of Global, filed a complaint against Omega in this action. Three weeks later, Omega filed the present motion for disqualification contending that the Firm's adverse representation of Global violates Rule 1.7 of the Franklin Rules of Professional Conduct. Rule 1.7(a) regulates an attorney's ability to undertake representation adverse to a present client.

In the alternative, Omega argues that even if its attorney-client relationship with the Firm had terminated, the Firm's participation in this lawsuit violates Rule 1.9. Rule 1.9 regulates an attorney's ability to undertake representation adverse to a former client.

We conclude that Omega was a *current* client of the Firm at the time that the Firm undertook the adverse representation and that Rule 1.7 applies. There is no question that Omega was a client of the Firm in June 1991—the last day on which the Firm performed billable work on Omega's behalf. The question is whether their attorney-client relationship ended between then and the time that the Firm undertook its adverse representation of Global.
Once established, an attorney-client relationship does not terminate easily. It is terminated only by the occurrence of one of a small set of circumstances.

First, the relationship can be terminated by the express statement of either the attorney or the client. Second, acts inconsistent with the continuation of the relationship are another means. For example, a client may become a former client by refusing to pay the attorney's bill and retaining other attorneys to do legal work which that attorney had formerly performed. Third, even without overt statements or acts by either party, the relationship may lapse over time.

None of the three terminating events is present here. First, there was no express termination by either party. Second, the parties' behavior was not inconsistent with the continuation of the relationship. Indeed, if anything, their behavior weighs very heavily in the direction of finding that the relationship was continuing. In August, about the time that the Firm began its work for Global against Omega, Russell called Jansen to obtain consent for the Firm's representation of a commodity trading advisor in negotiations with Omega. The other contacts between the Firm and Omega were uniformly conducted in the tone of a friendly, professional relationship, not at all inconsistent with the continuation of the attorney-client relationship.

Third, it cannot reasonably be stated that the relationship lapsed due to the passage of time. Within two months of finishing its last billable project for Omega on June 25, 1991, the Firm had begun its adverse representation of Global.

Because the attorney-client relationship between the Firm and Omega had not ended when the former began representing Global, the law firm has violated Rule 1.7.

Although disqualification is ordinarily the result of a violation of Rule 1.7, disqualification is not automatic. Courts must be sensitive to new complexities in the practice of law and recognize that disqualification is a blunt device that may foist substantial costs upon innocent third parties. Given the costs imposed by disqualification and the availability of other means of enforcing the disciplinary code (e.g., malpractice suits and defenses to nonpayment of legal fees), a court should look at the purpose(s) behind Rule 1.7 to determine if disqualification is a desirable sanction. A primary purpose behind Rule 1.7 is to safeguard loyalty as a feature of the attorney-client relationship.

Here, we are not persuaded that disqualification is warranted. This case is at the polar extreme from the case in which an individual has a personal relationship with a particular attorney who provides for all or substantially all of the client's legal needs. Omega has engaged a number of other outside legal counsel apart from the Firm.

Were this court to rule that disqualification was mandated by the Firm's breach of Rule 1.7, the implications would be overwhelming. Clients of enormous size and wealth, and with a large demand for legal services, should not be encouraged to parcel their business among dozens of law firms as a means of purposefully creating the potential for conflicts. The innocent client (here, Global) may suffer delay, inconvenience, and expense, and will be deprived of its choice of counsel. When disqualification is granted, sometimes the new attorney may find it difficult to master fully the legal and factual nuances of a complex case (like this one), actually impairing the adversarial process. Of course, the court may also lose the time invested in the proceedings held up to the time of disqualification. It is no secret that motions to disqualify are frequently brought as dilatory tactics intended to divert the litigation from attention to the merits.

We therefore reverse the trial court's decision to grant the motion to disqualify.

Holden v. Shop-Mart Stores, Inc.

Franklin Court of Appeal (1997)

Debra Holden filed suit against the Greene Shop-Mart store, alleging that Shop-Mart was negligent in failing to properly maintain or warn of a hole in the store's parking lot and that this negligence caused her personal injury when she fell into the hole.

The matter before the court is a motion by Shop-Mart to disqualify Holden's legal counsel, the Van Steenberg law firm, because (1) one of its partners, Fred Smith, previously represented Shop-Mart in four prior personal injury cases, and (2) another Van Steenberg attorney, Tyler Petitt, now represents a personal injury plaintiff, Holden, in the instant suit against Shop-Mart.

The district court entered an order denying Shop-Mart's motion. Shop-Mart appealed.

An in-house Shop-Mart attorney, Michelle Johnson, retained Smith to defend Shop-Mart in the four prior cases. It is agreed that in preparation for its defenses in those cases, Smith had complete access to all Shop-Mart stores in Franklin, including the Greene Shop-Mart store and its managers and staff.

While assisting Smith in preparation for Shop-Mart's defenses, Johnson revealed to Smith Shop-Mart's general defense strategy, internal policies, and the conduct of similar lawsuits in other parts of the country. In addition, Shop-Mart's regional manager for the Franklin stores gave Smith complete access to all procedure manuals, lists, and sales information. After Smith concluded his representation of Shop-Mart in the four previous cases, he was informed by Shop-Mart that neither he nor the Van Steenberg firm would represent Shop-Mart in any further matters.

Our decision relies on the Franklin Rules of Professional Conduct. Under Rule 1.9, the need for disqualification is presumptively established by proof of four elements. First, there must have been a valid attorney-client relationship between the attorney and the former client. Second, the interests of the present and former clients must be materially adverse. Third, the former client must not have consented, in an informed manner, to the new representation. Finally, the current matter and the former matter must be the same or substantially related.

Here, it is not disputed that there was a prior attorney-client relationship, that Holden's interests in this case are materially adverse to Shop-Mart's, and that Shop-Mart did not consent to Van Steenberg's representation of Holden.[1] Thus, our discussion is limited to the last element required for a violation of Rule 1.9: whether any of the previous cases in which the Van Steenberg firm defended Shop-Mart are "substantially related" to this case against Shop-Mart.

The subject matter of two cases is "substantially related" if the court determines that the unique factual and legal issues presented in both cases are so similar that there exists a genuine threat that confidential information may have been revealed in the previous case that could be used against the former client in the instant case. Then disqualification must ensue[2] unless the court believes it appropriate to be flexible in deciding the motion, given the interests in judicial economy, lawyer mobility, and client autonomy in selecting a lawyer, and acknowledging the frequent strategic use of disqualification motions. *See Global Financial Fund v. Omega Investments, Inc.* (Franklin Ct. App. 1992).

The determination of whether the matters are substantially related typically involves consideration of four factors: (1) whether the two cases raise similar factual or legal issues; (2) whether the nature of the evidence and the identity of the witnesses are similar; (3) whether, because of the length, recency, or intimacy of the prior attorney-client relationship, or because of the types of lawyering activities in the prior representation, the attorney was likely to have gained material confidential information, such as trade secrets, that would not be discoverable; and (4) whether, in the prior representation, the attorney was likely to have gained knowledge of unique, unexpected, unusual, or novel litigation strategies.

We now turn to an analysis of the factors present in this case. Of the four cases in which Van Steenberg defended Shop-Mart, the case that raises the issue of a possible conflict with the present case is *Potter v. Shop-Mart Stores, Inc.* As such, we must determine whether the *Potter* case and this case are substantially related.

---

1. Of course, the information Smith acquired through his previous defenses of Shop-Mart is imputed to the entire Van Steenberg law firm. *See* Rule 1.10.

2. In Franklin, except in cases of transferring government lawyers, paralegals, secretaries, and law student clerks, in general, we do not recognize an ethical wall as a means of avoiding conflicts of interest. An ethical wall is the screening method used to prevent participation by the "tainted" lawyer in the matter in dispute and to screen the flow of any information between the "tainted" lawyer and any other members of the lawyer's present firm.

In the instant case, Holden asserts that Shop-Mart's negligence caused her to suffer a torn knee ligament and sprained ankle when she fell into a hole in the store's parking lot.

Approximately one year after Holden was injured, but two years before Petitt entered an appearance as Holden's counsel, Van Steenberg concluded its defense of Shop-Mart in *Potter*, a lawsuit involving one of Shop-Mart's stores in Centralia, Franklin. In *Potter*, the jury found that Shop-Mart's negligence caused Potter to suffer a bulging disk, an injured elbow, headaches, and leg pain after she slipped and fell in an area inside the store that had previously been wet-mopped.

Shop-Mart asserts that these cases are substantially related because in both cases a customer was injured in a fall on Shop-Mart's premises, the complaints alleged that Shop-Mart was negligent in failing to properly maintain its premises and in failing to warn of the dangerous conditions, and Shop-Mart asserted contributory negligence and assumption of risk as defenses.

Conversely, Van Steenberg asserts that these cases are not substantially related because *Potter* involved a slip and fall on a slick surface, while the instant case involves a fall into a hole; *Potter* involved a floor, while the instant case involves a parking lot; and the accident in *Potter* happened inside the store, while the accident in the instant case happened outside the store.

Shop-Mart correctly asserts that the pleadings in these cases are similar. However, the mere fact that the pleadings are similar does not make the two cases substantially related. The differences in the factual and legal issues, where a plaintiff falls into a hole in a parking lot as opposed to where a plaintiff falls on a wet floor inside a store, are crucial and are not outweighed by the similarities.

We agree with the district court's findings that during the time Shop-Mart was represented by a Van Steenberg partner, Smith, the policies, procedures, and practices Smith was told about did not include any trade secrets or anything that was not discoverable. Courts have recognized that defense strategies are confidential information that may be factored into the disqualification decision. However, the defense strategies utilized in these types of relatively uncomplicated slip-and-fall actions are generally commonplace and routine. Shop-Mart did not assert that Van Steenberg became privy to any defense strategies that are unique, unexpected, unusual, or novel. Thus, we determine that an outside firm, with no prior association with Shop-Mart, would have the same or similar practical knowledge of how Shop-Mart would defend against this action and would have the same discovery opportunities.

Therefore, there is no genuine threat that Van Steenberg may have received confidential information from Shop-Mart that could be used against Shop-Mart in this case. The district court properly determined that the Rule 1.9 criteria for disqualification, specifically the requirement that the subject matter of the two cases be substantially related, are not met.

Affirmed.

Parker v. Essex Productions Sample Answers

<u>Sample Answer 1.</u>

ARGUMENT

Franklin Rules of Professional Conduct (FRPC) 1.7 does not apply because Essex is no longer a client of Peter Alexander.

Essex cites FRPC 1.7 as grounds to disqualify Brown Scott Meyer (BSM) from the current case against Essex due to the fact that a BSM Associate, Peter Alexander, once represented Essex on certain matters. FRPC governs conflicts of interest created when an attorney represents one client whose interests are adverse to another client. This rule would be arguably imputed to the entire firm of BSM under FRPC 1.10. The court should deny any argument based on FRPC 1.7, however, because the attorney-client relationship between Essex and Alexander terminated when Alexander left his old firm of Tansy Pipe (TP).

The case of Global Fin. Fund v. Omega Invest. Inc. addresses the issue of when an attorney-client relationship terminates. Although it is said that such a relationship does not terminate easily, there are circumstances where it does. First, an express statement of either the attorney or the client can terminate the relationship. Second, acts inconsistent with the relationship can terminate it. Finally, the relationship may terminate over time.

In the current case, Mr. Alexander was an associate of TP who did a few small jobs for Essex. However, when he left TP it was clear that the attorney-client relationship between Mr. Alexander and Essex was over. First, TP sent notice to Essex that Alexander was leaving the firm. It is clear that Essex got this notice because the President of Essex admitted knowledge of such to Mr. Alexander at a concert afterwards. Moreover, Essex was told that a new attorney would begin servicing its account, and this presumably occurred. Finally, a year and a half has gone by since Alexander has had any contact with Essex. For these reasons, it is clear that both parties considered the relationship terminated and consequently, FRPC 1.7 does not apply.

There is no conflict under FRCP 1.9 because Alexander did not represent Essex in a matter that was substantially similar to the case at hand.

The counterpart to FRCP 1.7 is FRCP 1.9, which deals with conflicts of interest regarding former clients (imputed to BSM by Rule 1.10). The need for disqualification is established by the proof of the elements. See Holden v. Shop-Mart Stores. Similar to the facts in Holden, this Court need only consider the final issue of whether the current matter is substantially related to the former matter. BSM concedes that Alexander had a valid attorney-client relationship with Essex, that the interests of Ms. Parker and Essex are adverse, and that Essex did not consent to BSM's representation.

Essex argues that BSM should be disqualified because Alexander advised Essex on a variety of matters, including employment agency licensure issues, which is the topic of one of the claims in the current case. Moreover, Alexander represented Essex on matters concerning the music industry including the negotiation of two contracts, which they argue are substantially similar to those in the present litigation.

Despite Essex's arguments, the matters that Alexander represented Essex in and the current matter are not substantially similar. Holden suggests four factors that the representation of Essex involved simple transactional work. He had no involvement in anything to do with litigation work and had no opportunity to learn anything that could be used against Essex in this case.

Disqualification is not appropriate in this case.

Even if the Court were to somehow find that FRCP 1.7 or 1.9 apply, disqualification is not automatic. Global Finance addresses the problems that disqualification can often cause. Disqualification can cause the innocent client to suffer delay, inconvenience and expense. Such would be the case here. Ms. Parker has already spent $10,000 on this case and we are currently in the middle of discovery. Moreover, a new attorney would have a hard time catching up with where we are in this case, which would only cause greater delays and expense. Of course, this Court will also lose precious time it has invested thus far in the proceedings. Finally, Ms. Parker, who has been a client of BSM for ten years, would lose her autonomy in selecting her attorney.

It is the belief of this firm that the Eagin Group's motion to disqualify is little more than a strategic move to get this court off of the facts and should therefore be denied.

Sample Answer 2.

Response to Motion to Disqualify Legal Counsel

I. Attorney Alexander is not disqualified from representing the plaintiff because Defendant Essex is neither a current client nor a former client with adverse interests:

Franklin Rules of Professional Conduct will not prohibit attorney Peter D. Alexander ("Alexander") from representing plaintiff Sylvia Parker ("Parker") and thus the firm of Brown Scott Mayer ("Brown") shall not be disqualified pursuant to Rule 1.10. An attorney's disqualification imputes to all attorneys that he is associated with regardless of whether ethical walls are in place to avoid conflicts. See Holden. Thus, the court must examine the disqualification for Alexander since there is no dispute that Essex cannot be a client of Brown without Alexander.

II. Defendant is not a current client of Alexander and/or the firm of Brown and thus Rule 1.7(a) is inapplicable:

Defendant is not a current client of Alexander and/or Brown as the representation was terminated in February of 2005 – four months before Alexander began to work for Brown. Franklin Rules of Professional Conduct 1.7 (a) regulates an attorney's ability to undertake representation adverse to a present client. See Global.

Because the attorney-client relationship cannot be terminated easily, the Franklin courts have established three ways to terminate the relationship, all three of which occurred in regard to Essex. First, the relationship was terminated by the express statement of Alexander's old firm, Tansy Pipe, by letter after Alexander's employment ended. Second, Alexander and Essex both acted inconsistently with the continuation of the relationship when Alexander informed the Gasso, Essex's president, that he could not discuss any legal matters when they randomly saw each other at a concert. Finally, the relationship was terminated by lapse of time as Alexander's very minimal work for Essex was complete in February of 2005. Thus, there should be no dispute that Essex has not been a client of Alexander since February.

III. The subject matter of the current litigation and Alexander's prior representation of Essex is not substantially related:

Although Essex is considered to be a former client of Alexander, and therefore Brown, the Franklin Rules of Professional Conduct Rule 1.9 will not require disqualification because the subject matter of the current litigation and that of Alexander's prior representation are not substantially related.

Under Rule 1.9, the need for disqualification is met once the plaintiff has established four elements – only one of which is disputed here. First, there must have been a valid attorney-client relationship between Alexander and Essex. Second, the interests of Essex and Parker must be materially adverse. Third, Essex must not have consented to the representation of Parker. These three elements are not disputed- leaving only the element of substantial similarity to be examined.

The subject matter of the current litigation and Alexander's past representation is not substantially related because there are no unique factual and legal issues presented in both cases that are so similar that there is a genuine threat that confidential information may have been revealed to Alexander in his previous dealing with Essex that can be used against Essex in the current litigation. To determine if the cases are substantially similar, the court must consider the four factors established by the court in Holden.

First, the two cases do not raise similar factual or legal issues. Alexander's only substantial representation of Essex involved negotiating a concert contract and a recording contract. He never drafted any management contracts. The two contracts which Alexander spent only 10 to 15 hours on each did not involve any claim similar to Parker's claims for stacking management fees and misrepresentation. The only possible argument for their similarity is that they involve contracts for performance in the music industry. However, the mere fact that pleadings are similar does not make the two cases substantially related. See Holden.

Second, the nature of the evidence and the identity of the witnesses are not similar. Parker was not a party to either of the contracts that Alexander drafted for Essex. Neither Alexander nor Brown were not involved in Parker's negotiations with Essex or in negotiating agreements for her performance.

Third, the nature of the attorney-client relationship did not give Alexander access to confidential information. Alexander was only hired to do limited small matters for Essex when Essex had a conflict with another firm. It was small-project oriented hourly employment, usually only requiring a letter or a telephone call to resolve the matter. In fact, Alexander only visited Essex's office once and even that was for a personal matter. Moreover, the fact that Essex does not have an employment agency license is a matter of public record and obviously is not a confidential matter.

Finally, Alexander did not gain knowledge of unique, unexpected, unusual or novel litigation strategies when he represented Essex. Not only did Alexander have limited contact with Essex, but the contracts that he did draft were rudimentary and typical contracts. Such general commonplace and routine matters do not rise to the level of substantial relatedness. See Holden.

IV. Even if the court should find that Essex is a client, disqualification is not the appropriate remedy:

If the court should find that Essex is, in fact, a former client of Alexander the court should still decline to enforce disqualification for its harsh results. Disqualification is not automatic and the court must look at several other factors before granting disqualification, including interests of judicial economy, lawyer mobility, client autonomy in selecting a lawyer, while acknowledging the frequent strategic use of and hardship resulting from disqualification motions. See Global.

Disqualification would impose a tremendous hardship on Parker as she will suffer delay, inconvenience, and expense, and will be deprived of her choice of counsel. She has already invested $10,000 in pursuing this case with Brown and the parties are in the middle of discovery. Thus, it would be very expensive and time consuming to find Parker new counsel who is available to give the case the attention that it deserves.

Sample Answer 3.

MEMORANDUM

To: Gail Brown

From: Applicant

Date: July 25, 2006

Re: Parker v. Essex Productions motion in response to motion to disqualify

Facts: Brown Scott Mayer represents Sylvia Parker in a dispute against Essex Productions, Inc. to recover excessive management and promotional fees that it charged to Ms. Parker after a recent tour she did in which Essex handled the promoting, the venue, collecting fees, and the like. Essex has filed a motion to disqualify Brown Scott Mayer ("Brown") for certain conflicts it claims based on a few discrete contracts the a Brown associate wrote for Essex. Essex motion is clearly unfounded and Brown has violated no Rules of Conduct.

Legal Argument:

Brown Scott Mayer should not be disqualified from representing Sylvia Parker in her suit against Essex Productions, Inc., despite the previous employment of one of its associates, Peter Alexander. Although Rule 1.10 would impute Alexander's disqualification to the firm because Franklin Rule 1.9 does not accept as a defense that attorneys at a firm can be screened as a means to avoid conflict, Alexander would not be individually disqualified either.

I. Rule 1.7, which applies to current clients, is not implicated by Brown's litigation against

A. Essex is not a current client of either Brown or Alexander, thus Brown has not violated Rule 1.7. Alexander's relationship with Essex had already terminated prior to the current litigation with Ms. Parker. Modes of termination are express statement of attorney or client, acts inconsistent with the continuing relationship, or lapse over time. Here, although Alexander did not expressly communicate the terminated relationship, his firm clearly did when it mailed Essex a letter stating that Alexander had left and a different associate would be representing them. Additionally, the President of Essex personally stated that he was aware Alexander no longer worked for Tansy Pipe. Even without express termination, Alexander's leaving Tansy Pipe and moving to another law firm in addition to his statement to Essex President Gasso that he could not discuss the case are acts inconsistent with a continuing relationship. Lastly, the relationship would have lapsed over time because Alexander's last project for Essex was in February 2005 and this dispute did not arise until July 2006.

B. The fairness factors of Rule 1.7, which is not mandatory, weigh in favor of Brown continuing to represent Ms. Parker. Additionally, Rule 1.7 is not a mandatory rule, but is discretionary and must take into consideration the added costs imposed on the current client, including delay, costs, and inconvenience. Here, Ms. Parker has already invested $10,000 into the case with Brown and would suffer unnecessary delay because this case is already in the middle of discovery. The purpose of 1.7 is to safeguard loyalty, which is not a problem implicated here where Essex is a large corporation that rarely did business with Tansy Pipe and because Alexander's interactions with Essex were discrete projects on rudimentary, impersonal matters. Loyalty weighs in favor of Brown remaining with Parker, who was a client of ten years. The court has even found no disqualification when a current relationship had not terminated between law firm and former client.

Brown is not disqualified under Rule 1.9, which applies to former clients, because Essex has not proven a prima facie case of substantial similarity.

A prima facie case for conflict with a former client under Rule 1.9 requires 1) a previous valid attorney client relationship with the former client, 2) the interests of the current and former client are materially adverse, 3) the former client has not consented, and 4) the current and former matters must be the same or substantially related. Here, the first three elements are met because Alexander and Essex had an attorney client relationship, Ms. Parker's interests are materially adverse to Essex now, and Essex has not consented. However, the last element is not met because Ms. Parker's current suit against Essex to recover for excessive fees she was charged are not the same or substantially similar to the contracts that Alexander wrote for Essex in the previous job. The court must disqualify a firm under Rule 1.9 unless the judge finds it appropriate to weigh other fairness factors such as the interests of judicial economy, client autonomy, or other hardship.

Four factors for determining substantial similarity are: 1) if the cases raise similar factual/legal issues; 2) if nature of evidence or witnesses are the same; 3) if the attorney gained confidential, undiscoverable information, and 4) the attorney gained information about unique or novel litigation strategies. Essentially, cases are "substantially similar" when the factual or legal issues are so "unique" that there is a real threat the confidential information could be disclosed to the new client.

Here, the cases do not raise the same legal issues because Alexander drafted routine form language contracts for Essex, whereas the current litigation is a dispute over recovery for excessive fees on a music singer's touring contract. Second, the evidence and witnesses would not be the same because the contracts Alexander wrote were with different parties and had nothing to do with Parkers claims that Essex was not licensed. Alexander didn't even know that Essex and Parker had worked together until this current litigation. Third, because Alexander worked only on a couple of discrete projects for Essex, which were standard form contracts, he rarely had any personal contact with Essex (they communicated by fax and email mostly) and had no opportunity to obtain confidential information from them. He only billed them a total of 25 hours worth of work, which is hardly enough time to obtain secret information. Lastly, the lack of intimate representation could not have led to disclosure to Alexander of Essex's novel litigation strategies. Courts have not disqualified law firms in situations in which a partner of the law firm actually had complete access to a former client's stores, business documents, and litigation strategy, and an associate at that firm was still not disqualified.

Conclusion: Brown is not disqualified under either Rule 1.7 or 1.9

FILE

LIBRARY

FILE

Anderson, Simmons Bayrd, LLP
Attorneys at Law
2000 Highland Avenue
Lawton, Franklin 33623

Memorandum

To: Applicant
From: Michael Simmons
Date: February 27, 2007
Re: *George Glickman v. Phoenix Cycles, Inc.*

Our client, George Glickman, believes that he was wrongfully demoted by his employer, Phoenix Cycles, Inc., after he took leave from work under the federal Family and Medical Leave Act (FMLA). Before his FMLA leave, Glickman was *Vice President* of Bicycle Marketing; when he returned to work, he was given the position of *Coordinator* of Bicycle Marketing.

Ideally, Glickman would like to get his former job back without going to court. However, if the matter cannot be resolved short of litigation, he wants us to pursue whatever relief he can get.

After interviewing Glickman and getting his approval, I called Phoenix's general counsel, Regina Snow, and told her that we have been retained by Glickman regarding this employment matter. Snow asserted that Phoenix fully complied with the FMLA by granting Glickman's leave request. Snow acknowledged that there had been some changes to his employment, but claimed that none of the changes in his position was substantial. In any event, she said that Phoenix had legitimate business reasons for making the changes. She also asserted that the FMLA permits an employer not to reinstate an executive like Glickman to his former position.

Please draft a letter to Snow to persuade her that Phoenix has violated Glickman's FMLA rights, and refute her assertions to the contrary. In addition, you should argue that if Glickman is not restored to his former position (or its equivalent), and the matter is litigated, Phoenix will be responsible for all potential relief available under the FMLA, which you should identify and explain. Be sure to present the law and the facts in the light most favorable to Glickman's position. However, contrary authority should be explained and distinguished. Because Snow is familiar with the situation, your letter need not include a separate fact section; however, because FMLA cases are very fact-dependent, be sure to explain how the facts fit into the relevant legal standard.

Transcript of Client Interview: George Glickman

February 19, 2007

Attorney: George, good to see you! I gather from your message that you'd like to talk about some issues with your position at Phoenix Cycles.

Glickman: My *former* position. I've been demoted.

Attorney: I'm sorry to hear that. Tell me what happened. Let's start with your history at Phoenix Cycles.

Glickman: I knew John Pearsall from competitive cycling in college. He owned a bike shop and hired me as a bike mechanic. Two years later John patented his bike frame modification and started manufacturing his own bikes under the name Phoenix Cycles.

Attorney: I didn't know the company had started as such a small outfit. Tell me more about how Phoenix is organized.

Glickman: For the last few years, Phoenix has had about 80 employees, all here at the company headquarters in Lawton, Franklin. I was one of six division vice presidents—my area was bicycle marketing. The marketing of helmets, clothing, etc., was headed by Sue Cowen in the Bicycle Accessories Division. There are four other divisions: Engineering, Production, Legal, and Accounting. At the top is the Executive Board, composed of John Pearsall, his wife, the comptroller, and two finance people.

Attorney: How did you become a vice president at Phoenix Cycles?

Glickman: I started out as a bike mechanic 15 years ago, but I really enjoyed sales, too, especially putting together sales campaigns and contributing ideas about how we could broaden our customer base. When we began to manufacture our own bikes, I continued to work in marketing. I even started working on an MBA by taking some night courses. Eventually, I became Vice President of Marketing for the Bicycle Division.

Attorney: What did that job entail?

Glickman: I was in charge of a number of marketing projects: supervising market research, monitoring Phoenix Cycles retailers, and developing new product ideas and presenting them to Engineering. I also coordinated product reviews, dealer education seminars, and industry trade shows. I had two marketing assistants working with me as well as support staff.

Attorney: Okay, when did problems develop?

Glickman: Approximately four months ago when I started having migraines. On November 15, 2006, the day before my appointment with a neurologist, I was at my desk when I got an excruciating headache and passed out. When I came to in the hospital, I was told that I'd had a stroke. My left arm and the left side of my face were numb. I spent the next five weeks recovering.

Attorney: But I must say, you look fine now.

Glickman: Yeah, I was amazingly lucky. I feel pretty good and I'm back to my usual activities, including biking.

Attorney: Were there repercussions at Phoenix after your stroke?

Glickman: At first everyone seemed really supportive. John helped me find a top physical therapist, and I was looking forward to returning to work.

Attorney: So, what changed?

Glickman: You know how everything always has to happen at once? My wife Lauren and I had been on a list to adopt a baby for two years. Well, in the second week of December, I was getting ready to return to work when we were notified that a baby girl was available for adoption immediately. We were told that we had a week to prepare for her.

Right away I called John at Phoenix and told him that, although I'd planned to return to work in a week, I needed another four weeks to be home to help Lauren with the baby. John seemed happy for us, but I could tell he was disappointed that I needed more time off. He suggested that I let Lauren manage the baby.

Initially, John offered to extend my leave for two more weeks. When I insisted on four weeks, he agreed, but he noted that the work was really piling up. John pointed out that my absence would create stress at the company. In the weeks before my stroke, I'd been leading a new project—a line of retro-styled bikes that were my idea. Engineering had created a prototype, and I was overseeing its testing and the marketing campaign. The project was on hold while I was recuperating, and I knew that John was anxious to get the final design to Production.

John's whole life is Phoenix Cycles, and I think he just couldn't comprehend why I would want to be gone during this time. Even though I was really excited about the new bike line, my family was my top priority.

Attorney: What was the atmosphere like when you returned to work at Phoenix?

Glickman: I was gone a total of nine weeks—five weeks for the stroke and four weeks with the baby. My recovery was 100 percent but I wasn't willing to work 70–hour weeks any more because I wanted to be with the baby. Life's too short. Anyway, shortly after I returned to work, on January 18, I learned that a marketing assistant and a member of my support staff had been transferred to the Accessories Division.

Attorney: Did John tell you why?

Glickman: John told me that while I'd been on leave, he'd discovered that my division was overstaffed, and so he'd ordered the transfers. He also said that he was making several changes that our management consultants, Hutchison Consulting, had recommended, including combining the bicycle and accessories marketing divisions for increased profitability. He said that my salary and benefits wouldn't change, but I would no longer be Vice President of Bicycle Marketing. Instead, I would be Coordinator of Bicycle Marketing, and would report to Sue Cowen, who had been promoted to Marketing Director of the new combined division. Sue's very capable, but I'd been at Phoenix a lot longer, and I know the industry better. If anyone had the ability to lead the unified marketing division, it was me.

Attorney: What are your job responsibilities now as Coordinator of Bicycle Marketing?

Glickman: I have the same salary but I am no longer a vice president. I've lost my support staff and I have to report to Sue Cowen, my former peer. Sue is overseeing all the marketing plans that I used to make alone.

Attorney: What's happened to the retro bike line?

Glickman: John said that he'd had to "put in several days on the project to cover the bases" when I was on leave and so he was "letting the chips fall where they may." After all the work I did, Sue's now in charge of the retro bike line and it is likely that she will receive the $25,000 bonus that John promised me months ago.

Attorney: Why do you think you were demoted?

Glickman: I'm not entirely sure, but the more I think about it, I'm certain that John is mad because I took time off for the baby. It just doesn't make sense to have Sue in charge of all marketing without more help. In fact, she confided to me that she was stressed by her added duties. And I don't believe that John was being up front with me when he said that he was just implementing the changes recommended by the management consultants—that report was completed over eighteen months ago and this is the first time I've heard of any of Hutchison's suggestions being followed. And on top of that, I wasn't even given a chance to interview for the new marketing position that Sue was given.

Ideally, I'd like to get my old job back. I love the company and the work that I used to do. If I can't get my job back, I think I'm entitled to damages or something for being demoted without cause.

Attorney: Did Phoenix Cycles give you any information about your rights and benefits when you began your leave, either at the time of your stroke or with the baby?

Glickman: They sent me a letter about reinstatement when John approved the last four weeks of leave. I'll get that to you tomorrow along with a copy of the Hutchison Consulting report and an article from the *Franklin Business News* about the bike I designed.

Attorney: I think that you have a claim under the federal Family and Medical Leave Act. I happen to know the general counsel at Phoenix. I'd like to talk to her about your potential claim under the FMLA. Is that okay?

Glickman: Yes, anything to help me get my old job back.

FRANKLIN BUSINESS NEWS

November 24, 2006

PHOENIX CYCLES GEARING UP NEW PRODUCT LINE

LAWTON, FRANKLIN – Phoenix Cycles, Inc., announced today that it will soon begin production of its latest bicycling innovation, the Retro RoadMaster. Phoenix, a relative newcomer to the biking world, is now widely recognized as one of the industry's premier manufacturers, having built a reputation for cutting-edge design backed by superior technology and a true commitment to quality. A locally owned company, Phoenix now sells bicycles and accessories nationwide and in over 30 countries. The Retro RoadMaster is expected to make its first appearance at the Franklin Bike Expo this summer, and the bikes will be shipped to Phoenix's worldwide dealers a few months later.

"Everyone at Phoenix is really thrilled with our creation of 'The Retro,'" enthused John Pearsall, Phoenix's founder and CEO. "This line embodies our passion for bicycling and our continuing desire to improve performance while giving us the chance to celebrate some of the design features that made classic bikes of the 1960s and '70s so special." Pearsall added that the engineering division at Phoenix had done outstanding work in developing the new bicycles, but "the real credit for initiating this project goes to George Glickman, one of our marketing executives. He really has a talent for knowing what will appeal to our customers, and his contribution to creating 'The Retro' has been invaluable. Unfortunately, George is on leave due to a sudden illness, but I'm looking forward to his full recovery and I'm counting on him to be a significant part of the product launch for this new model."

When asked about rumors that Phoenix might become a publicly traded company, Pearsall denied that such a move was in the works. "Our current organization has enabled us to become one of the leaders of the industry. Being a privately held company allows me to put my employees and our bicycles first, without worrying about how the numbers will spin for Wall Street."

Phoenix has received many design awards, including "Best Racing Cycle of the Year" from Cycling World magazine. The company also sponsors the Tour de Franklin, a bicycle race that attracts world-class athletes.

Phoenix Cycles, Inc.
Your Ride to the Future of Bicycling!
2300 LeMond Parkway
Lawton, Franklin 33623

December 19, 2006

Mr. George Glickman
2842 Trevayne Court
Lawton, Franklin 33606

Re: Request for additional FMLA leave

Dear George:

I have approved your request, arising from the adoption of your new daughter, for four weeks' Family and Medical Leave Act (FMLA) leave from your position as Vice President of Bicycle Marketing at Phoenix Cycles, Inc., effective from December 19, 2006, through January 15, 2007. This leave is in addition to the five weeks of FMLA leave you used for your illness.

Unfortunately, we cannot guarantee that restoration to your pre-leave position will be available at the end of the four weeks. You are part of the highest-paid 10 percent of Phoenix Cycles' salaried employees; thus, you are a "highly compensated employee" under the FMLA and employment restoration is not required under the FMLA for such employees. *See* 29 U.S.C. § 2614(b). If we determine that restoration after your leave is not feasible, we will telephone you at that time to discuss the matter.

Please direct any other questions regarding your benefits to Jill Carr in our Human Resources Department.

Yours truly,

John Pearsall, CEO

cc: Jill Carr, HR Dept.

Hutchison Consulting, LLC

Organizational Analysis Prepared for Phoenix Cycles, Inc.
Executive Summary
June 15, 2005

Objective

To evaluate the organizational structure at Phoenix Cycles, Inc., identify areas in need of streamlining, increase cost effectiveness, improve communication, and enhance teamwork, so that Phoenix Cycles can meet the evermore competitive demands of the bicycling marketplace.

Process

Our assessment consisted of four phases: review of Phoenix's financials for the last four quarters; interviews with key managers; observation of corporate culture; and firm-wide employee surveys.

Preliminary Conclusions

Phoenix has done tremendous work in maintaining its focus on manufacturing a high-quality product despite the pressures caused by rapid growth in the last few years. Our concern is that Phoenix's past performance may encourage complacency—something that no company can afford in today's global economy. However, small changes in organization can have a huge impact. The following recommendations are intended to help Phoenix differentiate between operations that are critical to success and those that are expendable.

Recommendations

- Create collaborative relationships with suppliers to avoid their problems becoming Phoenix's problems.
- Invest in state-of-the-art inventory tracking to make Phoenix a more responsive organization.
- Schedule annual corporate retreats to facilitate communication and foster strong working relationships between divisions and individual managers.
- Although Phoenix's profits are above average for the industry, and its six divisions currently operate at or below budget targets, the present scheme of two marketing divisions poses significant risks of unnecessary duplicative efforts. One centralized marketing division could maximize communication between the Bicycle and Accessories groups, thereby ensuring that Phoenix projects a consistent brand image across product lines. Such a restructuring would first require that Phoenix identify a manager with the experience and creativity to lead the new division.
- Reallocate all support staff positions in Marketing, Legal, and Accounting. With such a redesign, Phoenix's corporate work could be done with an 8 percent smaller workforce.
- Consider redefining the functions and composition of the Executive Board

LIBRARY

Family and Medical Leave Act
29 U.S.C. § 2601 *et seq.*

§ 2612. Leave requirement

(a) In general.

(1) Entitlement to leave. An eligible employee shall be entitled to a total of 12 workweeks of leave during any 12-month period for one or more of the following:

(A) Because of the birth of a son or daughter of the employee and in order to care for such son or daughter.

(B) Because of the placement of a son or daughter with the employee for adoption or foster care.

* * * *

(D) Because of a serious health condition that makes the employee unable to perform the functions of the position of such employee.

* * * *

§ 2614. Employment and benefits protection

(a) Restoration to position.

(1) In general. Except as provided in subsection (b), any eligible employee who takes leave under this Act . . . shall be entitled, on return from such leave—

(A) to be restored by the employer to the position of employment held by the employee when the leave commenced; or

(B) to be restored to an equivalent position with equivalent employment benefits, pay, and other terms and conditions of employment.

(2) Loss of benefits. The taking of leave . . . shall not result in the loss of any employment benefit accrued prior to the date on which the leave commenced.

(3) Limitations. Nothing in this section shall be construed to entitle any restored employee to–

(A) the accrual of any seniority or employment benefits during any period of leave; or

(B) any right, benefit, or position of employment other than any right, benefit, or position to which the employee would have been entitled had the employee not taken the leave.

* * * *

(b) Exemption concerning certain highly compensated employees.

(1) Denial of restoration. An employer may deny restoration under subsection (a) to any eligible employee . . . if—

(A) such denial is necessary to prevent substantial and grievous economic injury to the operations of the employer; [and]

(B) the employer notifies the employee of the intent of the employer to deny restoration on such basis at the time the employer determines that such injury would occur . . . .

* * * *

(2) Affected employees. An eligible employee described in paragraph (1) is a salaried eligible employee who is among the highest paid 10 percent of the employees employed by the employer. . . .

§ 2615. Prohibited acts

(a) Interference with rights.

(1) Exercise of rights. It shall be unlawful for any employer to interfere with, restrain, or deny the exercise of or the attempt to exercise, any right provided under this Act.

* * * *

§ 2617. Enforcement

(a) Civil action by employees.

(1) Liability. Any employer who violates this Act shall be liable to any eligible employee affected [for damages equal to the amount of]—

(i) any wages, salary, employment benefits, or other compensation denied or lost to such employee by reason of the violation; [and]

* * * *

(iii) an additional amount as liquidated damages equal to the sum of the amount described in clause (i) . . . and . . . such equitable relief as may be appropriate, including employment, reinstatement, and promotion.

* * * *

Ridley v. Santacroce General Hospital

United States Court of Appeals (15th Cir. 2001)

At issue is whether Santacroce General Hospital (SGH) violated the Family and Medical Leave Act (FMLA), 29 U.S.C. § 2601 *et seq.*, when it failed to restore Lena Ridley to her former position upon her return from maternity leave and later terminated her employment. The district court granted summary judgment to SGH, and Ridley appeals.

Ridley worked full time as nursing supervisor of SGH's surgical unit. In March 1996, Ridley began 12 weeks of paid FMLA leave for her son's birth. When she returned to work, her salary and benefits were unchanged but she was now scheduled for the evening shift every two weeks. Pre-leave, Ridley worked days only. Further, her duties as nursing supervisor had now been split between two other nurses. When she complained about the evening shifts and reduction in responsibilities, SGH offered to transfer her to pediatrics or to a per diem home health nurse position. Ridley declined the transfer to pediatrics, as there was no guarantee of a day shift and it was not a supervisory position. She also rejected the home health nurse job, because while her hourly wage would be higher, her health insurance costs would increase.

One month after her return from leave, SGH notified Ridley that, due to falling patient admissions, staffing levels were being cut and Ridley's surgical unit position was being eliminated. SGH informed Ridley that at this time the only nursing position available was for a home health nurse. For a second time, Ridley refused this option and her position at SGH was terminated. A month after her job at SGH ended, she found work at Valley View Medical Center.

Ridley filed this action alleging that SGH violated her rights under the FMLA. She is seeking reinstatement to her position as nursing supervisor of the surgical unit or its equivalent, and damages for lost wages and benefits.

The district court held that SGH had complied with the FMLA and that Ridley had not brought forth evidence to dispute SGH's claim that the changes in her position and its subsequent elimination were caused by anything other than legitimate business reasons.

The FMLA entitles an eligible employee to up to 12 weeks of leave for the birth of a child. To make out a prima facie claim for a violation of FMLA rights, a plaintiff must establish that (1) she was entitled to FMLA leave; (2) she suffered an adverse employment decision; and (3) there was a causal connection between the employee's FMLA leave and the adverse employment action. An employer who interferes with FMLA rights is liable for damages and/or appropriate equitable relief. *See* 29 U.S.C. § 2617(a)(1). The amount of lost wages or other monetary losses may be doubled (the additional portion called "liquidated damages") unless the employer can prove that the violation was in good faith and that it reasonably believed that the act or omission did not violate the FMLA. While there is a strong presumption in favor of liquidated damages, the FMLA does not authorize punitive damages.

Ridley's eligibility for FMLA leave is not disputed. At issue are whether SGH restored Ridley to her pre-leave employment (or its equivalent) and whether any changes to her position were due to legitimate business reasons.

An equivalent position is one that is equal or substantially similar in the conditions of employment. *See* § 2614(a)(1)(B). The fact-finder considers whether the duties and essential functions of the new position are materially different from the pre-leave position. If the undisputed facts show that, as a matter of law, the employer offered the employee an equivalent position upon her return, summary judgment in favor of the employer is appropriate.

To be equivalent, an employee's new position must be virtually identical to the employee's former position in terms of pay, benefits, and working conditions, including privileges, perquisites, and status. It must involve the same or substantially similar duties and responsibilities, which must entail substantially equivalent skill, effort, responsibility, and authority. It must also have similar opportunities for promotion and salary increase. For example, there was no FMLA violation in *Mills v. Telco, Inc.* (15th Cir. 1998) where the employee returning from FMLA leave was given a new position not involving statewide travel as in her pre-leave auditing position, but rather auditing from a central office. Apart from the travel, the nature of the work and the pay and benefits remained the same.

That Ridley was not restored to her pre-leave position is not seriously questioned. While SGH argues that Ridley's salary remained the same, SGH concedes that eliminating her duties as a supervisor rendered her a manager in name only. The terms of her employment also changed when, after her leave, Ridley was scheduled for evening shifts. These changes, notably removing her managerial duties, were not *de minimis*, but, in contrast to the facts in *Mills*, affected the essential functions of Ridley's pre-leave employment. Nor were the other jobs SGH offered Ridley equivalent in status and duties to her previous position.

SGH asserts that the changes in Ridley's employment were necessitated by legitimate business reasons. The FMLA does not give an employee an absolute right to reinstatement. It does not confer "any right, benefit, or position of employment other than any right, benefit, or position to which the employee would have been entitled had the employee not taken the leave." 29 U.S.C. § 2614(a)(3)(B). Thus, if, as SGH claims here, Ridley's employment was already slated for reduced hours or termination for legitimate business reasons, it has not violated the Act because the adverse employment action was not causally connected to the employee's taking FMLA leave. *See, e.g., Floyd v. Cullen Mfg.* (15th Cir. 1995) (no violation of FMLA where one month after returning from leave, employee was fired for excessive tardiness and insubordination). Alternatively, an employer is not required to reinstate an employee who has exceeded the amount of leave permitted under the statute.

Here, SGH relied on testimony from its human resources manager, Ann Levine, who stated that SGH's accounting office projected lower patient admissions for the second half of 1996 and that such projections required the staff reduction in Ridley's unit. Levine noted that Ridley was not the most senior nurse in her unit and that SGH had been working on staff restructuring prior to Ridley's leave.

SGH, however, does not dispute the fact that Ridley was the only surgical staff member in six years to take a full 12 weeks of maternity leave. Nor does it dispute that hers was the only nursing position eliminated among all of SGH's medical departments. SGH also concedes that six months after Ridley's termination, the surgical unit resumed previous staffing levels.

The relatively brief interval between Ridley's return from leave and her termination is problematic, as is the fact that she was the only member of the surgical unit to use the full amount of maternity leave in several years. Most telling, SGH does not dispute that it returned to full staffing levels a few months after it eliminated Ridley's position. Thus, summary judgment in favor of SGH on Ridley's FMLA claims was improper as there is a genuine issue of material fact regarding whether SGH's actions were the result of a legitimate business decision and not in response to Ridley's having taken 12 weeks of FMLA leave.

Reversed and remanded.

Jones v. Oakton School District

United States Court of Appeals (15th Cir. 2004)

This case arises from plaintiff Greg Jones's use of Family and Medical Leave Act (FMLA) leave. Jones, an employee of the defendant Oakton School District, appeals from the lower court's ruling that the district could lawfully refuse to reinstate him under the FMLA.

Jones worked for the district as principal of Taft Elementary School. In March 2002, Jones requested, and was granted, 12 weeks of FMLA leave for back surgery. This meant that Jones would be absent during budget planning for the next school year as well as during the preparation period for a new test required by Franklin law, the Elementary Skills Assessment. Eligibility for certain educational grants depended upon how Taft students performed on the assessment.

Concerned that Jones would be unavailable during this time, the district hired Anne Rios to take over as principal at Taft. Rios, an experienced school administrator, would not fill the position on a temporary basis, so the district hired her as a permanent replacement for Jones. Further, because Taft had had substantial staff turnover in the preceding two years, the district decided that a permanent replacement was preferable to an interim principal.

In late May, Jones asked to return to work, but the district refused to dismiss Rios. Nor did it offer Jones employment as principal of another school, as all such positions were filled. Jones then commenced this action against the district.

Jones's right to take 12 weeks of FMLA leave for his serious medical condition is not contested. The question is whether the district may deny restoration to Jones under the FMLA's exception for highly compensated employees, 29 U.S.C. § 2614(b). If an employer can show that reinstatement of the employee would result in "substantial and grievous economic injury," the FMLA permits an employer to elect not to reinstate that employee. We note that the requisite economic injury is not that caused by the employee's *absence*, but the injury that will result from *restoring* the employee to his prior position or its equivalent. It is not disputed here that Jones received the required notice under § 2614(b)(1)(B).

Jones argues that the district failed to meet the "substantial and grievous" standard as a matter of law. We disagree.

There is no precise test that identifies the extent of economic injury that an employer must show to take advantage of the FMLA's key employee exception. The pertinent regulation defines "substantial and grievous economic injury" as follows:

> If the reinstatement of a "key employee" threatens the economic viability of the employer, that would constitute "substantial and grievous economic injury." A lesser injury which causes substantial, long-term economic injury would also be sufficient. Minor inconveniences and costs that the employer would experience in the normal course of doing business would certainly not constitute "substantial and grievous economic injury." 29 C.F.R. § 825.218(c).

When assessing economic impact, the employer may consider the cost of reinstating the employee to an equivalent position if hiring a permanent replacement for the employee on leave was unavoidable. *Id.*

Here, the district had no reasonable alternative but to hire a permanent replacement for Jones. Restoring Jones to his prior position would require the district to breach its employment contract with Rios. Further, we are satisfied that placing Jones in a position equivalent to school principal would create substantial economic hardship.

Jones is among the highest paid 10 percent of the district's salaried employees. The district provided ample evidence that there were no funds available to pay for another position. Indeed, part of the budget planning that occurred during Jones's leave involved selecting programs to cut in the face of declining tax revenue and increasing enrollments. Because of the district's financial constraints, restoring Jones after contracting with Rios would create more than a minor inconvenience—the added stress of his salary would force cuts in other areas and the repercussions would be felt for years to come. As a public entity, the district cannot raise its prices to make up for the shortfall. We conclude that, as a matter of law, the district met the threshold for "substantial and grievous economic injury," and that therefore Jones's FMLA rights were not violated.

Affirmed.

1. You will have 90 minutes to complete this session of the examination. This performance test is designed to evaluate your ability to handle a select number of legal authorities in the context of a factual problem involving a client.

2. The problem is set in the fictitious state of Franklin, in the fictitious Fifteenth Circuit of the United States. Columbia and Olympia are also fictitious states in the Fifteenth Circuit. In Franklin, the trial court of general jurisdiction is the District Court, the intermediate appellate court is the Court of Appeal, and the highest court is the Supreme Court.

3. You will have two kinds of materials with which to work: a File and a Library. The first document in the File is a memorandum containing the instructions for the task you are to complete. The other documents in the File contain factual information about your case and may also include some facts that are not relevant.

4. The Library contains the legal authorities needed to complete the task and may also include some authorities that are not relevant. Any cases may be real, modified, or written solely for the purpose of this examination. If the cases appear familiar to you, do not assume that they are precisely the same as you have read before. Read them thoroughly, as if they all were new to you. You should assume that the cases were decided in the jurisdictions and on the dates shown. In citing cases from the Library, you may use abbreviations and omit page references.

5. Your response must be written in the answer book provided. In answering this performance test, you should concentrate on the materials provided. What you have learned in law school and elsewhere provides the general background for analyzing the problem; the File and Library provide the specific materials with which you must work.

6. Although there are no restrictions on how you apportion your time, you should be sure to allocate ample time (about 45 minutes) to reading and digesting the materials and to organizing your answer before you begin writing it. You may make notes anywhere in the test materials; blank pages are provided at the end of the booklet. You may not tear pages from the question booklet.

7. This performance test will be graded on your responsiveness to the instructions regarding the task you are to complete, which are given to you in the first memorandum in the File, and on the content thoroughness, and organization of your response.

DRAFTERS' POINT SHEET

In this performance test item applicants' law firm represents George Glickman, who was demoted from his vice president position at Phoenix Cycles, Inc. Glickman recently returned to work after taking nine weeks' leave to recover from a stroke and to care for his newly adopted baby daughter. It appears that his demotion is connected to his leave from work; if so, Phoenix's actions violate Glickman's rights under the Family and Medical Leave Act (FMLA), 29 U.S.C.

§ 2601 *et seq*., specifically, the right to be restored to pre-leave employment or an equivalent position. The supervising partner has already spoken to Phoenix's in-house counsel, Regina Snow, in an attempt to resolve Glickman's claims without resorting to litigation. Applicants' task is to draft a follow-up letter to Ms. Snow persuasively setting forth the basis for Glickman's claim under the FMLA and explaining why none of the exceptions in the Act applies. The letter should discuss the specific FMLA provisions that Phoenix has violated and demonstrate that Glickman has a right to relief under the statute. In addition, applicants are to respond to the potential defenses raised by Phoenix's in-house counsel in her conversation with the managing partner.

The File consists of the task memo describing the assignment, the transcript of the client interview, a newspaper article about Phoenix's new bike design, a letter to Glickman regarding his FMLA leave, and a management consulting firm's report on Phoenix.

The Library contains provisions of the FMLA that may or may not be relevant and two cases from the United States Court of Appeals for the Fifteenth Circuit.

The following discussion covers all of the points the drafters intended to raise in the problem. Applicants need not cover them all to receive passing or even excellent grades. Grading decisions are entirely within the discretion of the user jurisdictions.

I. Overview and Format

Applicants' work product should resemble legal correspondence (including citations to the relevant legal authority) and be persuasive in tone. Because this is a fact-intensive item and the analysis will require applicants to apply the facts to the legal standards, no separate statement of facts is necessary, and applicants are so informed in the task memorandum. (However, some applicants may begin with an introductory paragraph briefly describing the nature of the matter and noting that this is a follow-up letter to the previous telephone conversation between the supervising partner and Phoenix's in-house counsel.)

There are four issues that applicants should identify and discuss:

- Whether Phoenix restored Glickman to the same or an equivalent position upon his return from FMLA leave.
- Assuming Glickman was demoted, whether Phoenix acted in furtherance of legitimate business reasons in failing to restore Glickman to the same or equivalent position.
- Whether Phoenix properly denied Glickman reinstatement based on the "key employee" exemption under the FMLA.
- What potential remedies Glickman would be entitled to under the FMLA.

These headings are suggestions only. Likewise, applicants need not discuss these issues in any particular order, although some forms of organization may be more persuasive to opposing counsel than others. It is left to the user jurisdictions to decide whether the organization of applicants' papers is a basis for grading distinctions. All issues require applicants to examine the facts of the case in light of the relevant FMLA provisions and case law.

II. Argument: Phoenix Violated Glickman's FMLA Rights.

The FMLA entitles eligible employees to take up to 12 weeks of leave from work for a serious medical condition, or for the birth or adoption of a child. 29 U.S.C. § 2612(a)(1). Upon returning from FMLA leave, an employee is entitled to his or her pre-leave position or its equivalent. It is unlawful "for any employer to interfere with, restrain, or deny the exercise of or the attempt to exercise, any right provided under this Act." § 2615. Employees may pursue a private right of action against an employer who interferes with the rights conferred by the statute. *See* § 2617. Employers violate the FMLA when they deny an employee the benefits provided by the statute (e.g., deny requests for leave, refuse to return employee to pre-leave employment) or when they take negative action against an employee who has taken FMLA leave (e.g., demotion, termination).

As an employee claiming that his employer has violated the FMLA, Glickman has the initial burden to establish a prima facie case that his leave from work is protected by the statute. *Ridley v. Santacroce Gen. Hosp.* (15th Cir. 2001). A plaintiff must establish (1) that she was entitled to FMLA leave; (2) that she suffered an adverse employment decision; and (3) that there was a causal connection between the employee's FMLA leave and the adverse employment action. *Id.*

Although it appears that Phoenix does not challenge the first component, that Glickman had the right to take FMLA leave, thorough applicants may briefly note the basis for Glickman's entitlement to leave:

- Both Glickman's stroke (a serious medical condition) and the adoption of his child are valid reasons for FMLA leave. 29 U.S.C. § 2612(a)(1)(B) (D).
- The length of his leave, a total of nine weeks, is well within the 12 weeks allowed by the FMLA. 29 U.S.C. § 2612(a)(1).

A. Phoenix Did Not Restore Glickman to His Pre-Leave Employment or Its Equivalent.

To establish that Phoenix denied Glickman the rights accorded by the FMLA, applicants should argue that Glickman was not restored to his pre-leave position or its equivalent, referencing the applicable FMLA section and the court's discussion in *Ridley*. Such a discussion should include the following points:

- Employees returning from FMLA leave are entitled to restoration of their previous position or to an equivalent position. 29 U.S.C. § 2614(a).
- "Equivalent position" is defined by the FMLA as employment with equivalent benefits, pay, and "other terms and conditions of employment." 29 U.S.C.
- § 2614(a)(1)(B).
- An equivalent position "must be virtually identical to the employee's former position in terms of pay, benefits, and working conditions, including privileges, perquisites, and status. It must involve the same or substantially similar duties and responsibilities, which must entail substantially equivalent skill, effort, responsibility, and authority. It must also have similar opportunities for promotion and salary increase." *Ridley.*
- Thus the focus in the "equivalent position" inquiry is "whether the duties and essential functions of the new position are materially different from the pre-leave position." *Id.* In *Ridley*, the combination of changing the plaintiff's

work hours and greatly decreasing her job responsibilities rendered her employment materially different from her pre-FMLA leave position.

- However, *de minimis* changes to employment will not contravene the FMLA. *See Mills v. Telco, Inc.* (15th Cir. 1998) (no FMLA violation where post-leave employment differed from pre-leave position only in that employee now worked from central office and no longer traveled to branch offices) (cited in *Ridley*).
- Applicants should compare Glickman's pre- and post-leave employment, noting the changes in his responsibilities and status.
- Before taking FMLA leave, Glickman was Vice President of Bicycle Marketing, one of six division heads working under the guidance of Phoenix's CEO and Executive Board. He had two marketing assistants and support staff working for him. His duties included supervising market research, monitoring retailers, developing new product concepts and presenting them to Engineering, coordinating product reviews, overseeing dealer education, and preparing for industry trade shows.
- After returning from nine weeks of FMLA leave, Glickman's job title was changed to Coordinator of Bicycle Marketing, although his salary and benefits remained the same. Other changes to his employment included:
- Glickman supervised fewer people; two of his marketing assistants were transferred to another division.
- Glickman now reports to Sue Cowen, his former counterpart in Bicycle Accessories, who was promoted over him to run the new consolidated marketing division.
- Glickman said that after returning to work, "Sue is overseeing all the marketing plans that I used to make alone."
- Although Glickman initiated the idea for the Retro bike line, Sue Cowen is now in charge of that project and will likely receive the $25,000 bonus for it that John Pearsall, Phoenix's CEO, promised Glickman.
- Glickman has effectively been demoted, in that there is now a new layer of management between his position and the Executive Board.
- Analogizing to *Ridley*, applicants should argue that Phoenix failed to restore Glickman to a position that was equivalent to his pre-leave employment as Vice President of Bicycle Marketing. Glickman's responsibilities and status within the company were reduced substantially; thus the changes are not *de minimis* but in fact deprive Glickman of his right to job restoration under the FMLA.

B. Phoenix Did Not Have Legitimate Business Reasons for Failing to Restore Glickman to Pre-leave Employment or Its Equivalent.

The third element of establishing a violation of FMLA rights is that the plaintiff employee must demonstrate a nexus between the adverse employment action and taking FMLA leave. *Ridley.* Applicants should recognize that under § 2614 the right to job reinstatement under the FMLA is not absolute, and employees taking leave are not entitled to "any right, benefit, or position of employment other than any right, benefit, or position to which the employee would have been entitled had the employee not taken the leave." In *Ridley*, the court noted that the FMLA is not violated if the employee's position "was already slated for reduced hours or termination for legitimate business reasons."

When viewed overall, the facts suggest that Glickman's demotion was very likely a negative response to his taking FMLA leave (particularly the additional four weeks to care for his newly adopted daughter) rather than the result of legitimate business reasons. Facts supporting this allegation include:

- As in *Ridley*, the temporal proximity between taking FMLA leave and the negative employment action supports an inference that the employer's action is not simply the result of a business decision. Glickman learned that his bicycle-marketing division was being subsumed into a larger marketing department only three days after returning from leave.
- Nothing was communicated to Glickman during his leave to indicate that such changes were imminent or even under consideration.
- Glickman was not afforded an opportunity to apply for the position that was ultimately handed to Sue Cowen.
- Such substantial changes in company structure on such short notice would seem inconsistent with a planned, deliberate reorganization.
- John Pearsall tried to dissuade Glickman from taking four weeks' leave for the adoption of Glickman's daughter.
- Pearsall told Glickman that he'd had to put in time on the Retro bike project because Glickman was on leave—a possible reason for Pearsall's resenting the extra four weeks for the adoption. Indeed, Pearsall remarked to Glickman that he was "letting the chips fall where they may."
- This statement is in stark contrast to the *Franklin Business News* article about Phoenix, dated November 24, 2006, just before Glickman requested additional FMLA leave for the adoption, in which Pearsall praises Glickman's contributions to the new bike line and his performance as a marketing executive.
- Also in the news article, John Pearsall denies that an IPO is in the works and observes that, "Our current organization has enabled us to become one of the leaders of the industry." This remark underscores the last-minute character of the changes in Glickman's position.
- Statements in the Hutchison Consulting report conclude that the company is profitable with its current (i.e., pre-FMLA leave) organization.
- According to Glickman's comments at the client interview, Sue Cowen is feeling stressed with all the added responsibilities of her promotion to Marketing Director. In his interview, Glickman suggests that he was better qualified for the new Marketing Director position.

Nevertheless, there is some support for Phoenix to assert that legitimate business reasons justify the changes in Glickman's employment:

- The Hutchison Consulting report expressly recommends consolidating the marketing divisions, stating that "the present scheme of two marketing divisions poses significant risks of unnecessary duplicative efforts."
  - However, the Hutchison report was completed approximately 18 months ago and the changes in Glickman's employment were the first he'd heard of any of the consultant's recommendations being implemented.
- It is only Glickman's opinion that he was better qualified to head the new division.
- Glickman indicates that, because of his new family responsibilities, he is no longer willing to work the long hours that he did before taking FMLA leave. Phoenix may argue that Glickman is not available to carry the workload of having sole responsibility for bicycle and accessories marketing.

C. Phoenix Cannot Deny Glickman Reinstatement Based on the FMLA's "Key Employee" Exemption.

According to the task memorandum, Phoenix intends to deny any FMLA claim by Glickman on the basis that "the FMLA permits an employer not to reinstate an executive like Glickman to his former position." Thus, applicants should address and refute application of the FMLA's "key employee" exemption.

Under 29 U.S.C. § 2614(b), employers may deny job restoration to "certain highly compensated employees." This exemption applies to salaried employees that are among the highest-paid 10 percent of the employer's workforce. § 2614(b)(2). Such workers are also known as "key employees." *See Jones v. Oakton School District* (15th Cir. 2004).

To successfully use the "key employee" exemption an employer must show that

1. denying restoration was necessary in order "to prevent substantial and grievous economic injury to the operations of the employer," and
2. upon determining that such an injury would occur, the employer notified the affected employee that he or she would not be restored to pre-FMLA leave employment.

Jones provides guidance as to what constitutes "substantial and grievous economic injury." The FMLA does not require job restoration when doing so "threatens the economic viability of the employer." *Id.* A lesser harm, but one that causes "substantial, long-term economic injury," may be sufficient for an employer to deny job restoration without running afoul of the FMLA. Minor inconveniences and costs imposed on the employer, however, do not meet the "substantial and grievous" standard. *Id.*

When discussing whether Phoenix could rely on the FMLA's key employee exemption as justification for not restoring Glickman to his pre-leave employment, pertinent facts are:

- Phoenix informed Glickman, when granting the additional four weeks of leave, that he is among the highest-paid 10 percent of Phoenix employees, and that restoration to his pre-leave position was not guaranteed.
- However, the letter indicates that Phoenix has not yet determined whether Glickman's job will be available at the end of his leave—"If we determine that restoration after your leave is not feasible, we will telephone you at that time to discuss the matter." It is unclear when Phoenix made that determination and/or explicitly conveyed such information to Glickman. Presumably, the conversation in which Pearsall told Glickman that Phoenix was implementing the management consultant's recommen-dations constituted the required notice.
    - The fact that Phoenix did not notify Glickman of its intention to invoke the highly compensated employee exemption until he requested the additional leave to care for his new daughter casts further doubt on whether the change in Glickman's position was the result of a legitimate business reason. (*See* section B, *infra*).
- Applicants should focus on whether Phoenix could prevail on a claim that restoring Glickman would cause substantial and grievous economic harm.
    - Upon returning to work, Glickman's salary and benefits were the same; only his job description and title changed. The inference is that continuing to employ Glickman in a position equivalent to his pre-leave position would not cause Phoenix significant financial hardship.
    - Unlike the situation in *Jones*, Phoenix did not have to hire a permanent replacement (or even a temporary replacement) while Glickman was on FMLA leave, despite the fact that Pearsall took on some of his responsibilities during that time.
- The notification to Glickman that he was considered a "key employee" came only when he requested four weeks leave to care for his daughter—not when he first took FMLA leave to recuperate from his stroke.

Note: In *Jones*, the court emphasized that the pertinent harm is not that caused by the employee *taking* leave, but the harm resulting from *restoring* the employee to the pre-leave position. Thus, applicants who focus on Pearsall's comments to Glickman that he (Pearsall) had worked hard to "cover the bases" while Glickman was on leave (indicating that Glickman's absence from the company during the production of the Retro RoadMaster created a hardship) have missed the point on the question of whether Glickman may be denied job restoration because of his key employee status.

D. Potential Damages and Other Relief

Section 2617 of the FMLA provides that an employer who violates an employee's rights under the statute is liable for damages equal to wages, salary, benefits, and/or other compensation lost by the employee because of the employer's actions. The FMLA also allows for double damages: an employee can recover liquidated damages equal to the award of lost wages or other compensation. There is a presumption in favor of such damages, but the court has discretion to deny an award of liquidated damages if the employer can show it had a good faith belief that its actions were not in violation of the FMLA. *See Ridley*. Finally, a wronged employee may receive "such equitable relief as may be appropriate, including employment, reinstatement, and promotion." § 2617(a)(1)(iii).

Thus, the letter to Phoenix's counsel should state that if Glickman is forced to sue, he will seek damages in the amount of other compensation lost since he was demoted, liquidated damages, and a return to his pre-leave position at the company.

- Because Glickman's current position as Coordinator of Bicycle Marketing is not equivalent to his pre-leave employment as Vice President of Bicycle Marketing, a court may award equitable relief in the form of reinstatement.
- Although Glickman's salary and benefits have not changed, it appears likely that he will lose out on a $25,000 bonus that he would have received had he not taken FMLA leave.
  - The lost bonus would qualify as "other compensation" under the FMLA, as it is not part of his normal wages or salary.
- Given the description of Pearsall's comments when Glickman requested four weeks' additional leave to care for his new daughter, it is doubtful that Phoenix could successfully argue that it had a good faith belief that its failure to reinstate Glickman to his pre-leave employment was consistent with its obligations under the FMLA.
- Thus it is likely that a court would award another $25,000 in liquidated damages.

The key point is that applicants recognize that Glickman's remedies are not restricted to compensatory monetary damages; the FMLA explicitly allows plaintiffs to receive double damages and reinstatement as forms of relief.

Sample Answer 1.

Dear Ms. Snow,

Glickman's FMLA rights were violated by Phoenix when he returned from his 9 week leave by being demoted from vice president of bicycle marketing to coordinator of bicycle marketing. If this case is litigated, Phoenix will be held liable for violation of Glickman's FMLA rights for damages and for equitable relief. 29 VSC §2617(a)(1). The amount of lost wages or monetary loss may be doubled unless Phoenix can prove violation was in good faith and believed the act didn't violate FMLA. (Ridley v. Sgh 2001) Here, Phoenix will fail to prove it acted in good faith and didn't violate the rights of Glickman under FMLA.

Glickman was not returned to his equivalent position upon his return. Equivalent position is one equal or substantially similar in conditions of employment 2614(a)(1)(b). The new position must be virtually identical to employee's former position in terms of pay, benefits, working conditions and involve substantially same duties and responsibilities with equivalent skill, effort and authority. Ridley v. Sgn 2001. In Mills v. Teleglne (1998) there was no FMLA violation when employee returned, his new position was the same besides not involving statewide travel and rather just working from central office. In contrast, in Ridley, the court held that the employee wasn't given job equivalent in status duties to previous position. In Ridley, employee went from days shifts, to return scheduled to evening shifts, and removed managerial duties, which affected the essential functions of employee's status and duties to previous position.

Similarly to Riley, Glickman returned to a position which was not equivalent in status and duties to previous position. Glickman left as a vice president and when he returned was offered position as a coordinator. Just like in Riley, Glickman's salary and benefits didn't change but his duties did. Glickman had to now report to Sue Cohen, his former peer, that was director of another division. Phoenix got rid of Glickman's department completely upon his return. Sue oversees marketing plant he used to make on his own. Sue took over the project he started and all the work he did on the retro bike line and Sue probably will receive the $25,000 bonus Glickman was promised from Phoenix. If this should go to trial, we will seek damages for the bonus not received and given to Sue for Glickman's work on retro bike line. Glickman was vice president in marketing and now as coordinator must report to Sue who was head of accessories division. Obviously, Glickman's return position is not equivalent in his duties and status and is in violation of FMLA.

Phoenix asserts it had a legitimate business reason for making the changes. FMLA doesn't give employee absolute right to reinstatement but it confers the right, benefit or position to which employee would've been entitled had he not taken the leave. 2614(a)(3)(b). For legitimate reasons for changing in employment is shown where the month after returning from leave, employee is fired for excessive tardiness and insubordination. Floyd v. Cullen Mfg. 1995. However, in Riley, the relatively brief interval between employee's return from leave and her termination was problematic and didn't result from taking the leave. Riley court held that if employee's employment was "already slated for reduced hours or termination for legitimate business reasons, it's not violated FMLA because adverse employment action is not causally connected to employee taking FMLA leave. Therefore, for a FMLA violation there needs to be that causal connection.

Glickman's demotion to coordinator and report to only Sue whereas before hand he didn't report to anyone. The facts show that only Glickman's division was eliminated and the other five divisions of vice presidents are still there. There is reason to believe that Phoenix took away Glickman's division due to frustration that the new line would be put on hold. Phoenix is quoted in Franklin News on November 24, 2006 before Glickman asked for the additional leave for the baby as "Glickman's contribution is invaluable to creating the Retro and the credit goes to him because of his talent." However, since the article and Phoenix found out about extra leave Phoenix has demonstrated by demoting Glickman to coordinator and to be under Sue for his project which is contrary to the article published. Therefore, Glickman can show that there is a causal connection because the adverse employment decision and his FMLA leave to show his rights are violated.

Phoenix will not be able to show any legitimate business purpose for the demotion because it took away his superior skill and talent and changes in Glickman's position were substantial.

Phoenix also can't rely on FMLA's provision which permits an employer not to reinstate an executive to his former position who is among the highest 10% of employees paid by employer. 2614(b)(2). If employer can show that reinstatement of employee would result in "substantial and grievous economic injury, FMLA permits employer not to reinstate that employee. 2614(b). The key employee exception assess economic impact by considering cost of reinstatement of employee to equivalent position if hiring permanent replacement or leave was unavailable. 29 C.F.R.§825.218(c).

In Jones, employee was absent during budget planning for next year and eligibility of school grants depending on student tests. The school hired a permanent replacement for Jones because substantial staff turnover in preceding 2 years and permanent replacement was preferable. The court looked at the injury that results when restoring Jones to his prior position or equivalent. Jones was among highest 10% paid employees and school proved no funds were available to pay for another position which occurred during budget plan when Jones was gone. Because of school's financial constraints it couldn't restore him to his position because it would create more than minor inconvenience.

However, Phoenix claims Glickman's division was overstaffed and was making changes that management consultants recommended to combine bicycle and accessories marketing divisions for increased profit. In contrast to Jones, this organizational analysis was done 18 months ago and not while Glickman was on leave and it was the first time the consultants suggestions were being followed. In addition, one person is in charge of marketing with a new line coming out. Sue even stated that she was stressed with the added duties. Also, this summer the new line is expected to make its first appearance at the Franklin Bike Expo and bikes will be shipped to Phoenix's dealers worldwide. Phoenix has not shown any financial conditions that show it had to cut back positions due to budget and the line needed a permanent employee to take over while he was gone. Glickman's position was eliminated because of a report from 18 months ago and not during his 9 week leave. Putting Glickman back in a position equivalent to marketing executive would not create a substantial economic hardship to Phoenix. Therefore, Glickman's demotion constitutes a minor inconvenience and costs by Phoenix that Phoenix would experience in the normal course of doing business and doesn't constitute a substantial and grievous economic injury.

Phoenix has violated Glickman's FMLA rights by not having legitimate business reasons for a substantial change in his position and there was no evidence that Phoenix reinstating Glickman would cause substantial and grievous economic injury.

If Glickman is not restored to vice president of bicycle marketing or its equivalent and this matter is litigated, Phoenix will be responsible for wages, salary, benefits, and the $25,000 bonus denied which was promised because he lost it to Sue from the violation of FMLA. Also, an additional amount as liquidated damages to equal sum stated above under 2617, which will include Glickman's employment, reinstatement and promotion.

Sincerely, Applicant

- Sample Answer 2.

MEMO

To: Regina Snow

From: Applicant

Subject: George Glickman v. Phoenix Cycles, Inc.

Dear Ms. Snow,

As you are aware, we have been hired by Mr. Glickman with regard to the above matter. It is clear to our firm that your client, Phoenix Cycles, Inc. has violated Mr. Glickman's FMLA rights by demoting him while on FMLA leave. It is also clear that Phoenix Cycles will be liable for certain damages, including but not limited to, any lost wages, monetary compensation, and liquidated damages. In addition, Phoenix Cycles will be liable, in equity, for the promotion of Mr. Glickman.

The FMLA provides that workers are allowed up to 12 work weeks for placement of adoption and for serious health conditions. FMLA §2612(a)(1). Additionally, Ridley held that an employee makes a case for violation of FMLA rights when he/she establishes (1) he was entitled to FMLA leave, (2) she suffered an adverse employment decision, and (3) there is a caused connection between the leave and the adverse employment action. All of these elements are clearly established.

First, Glickman was initially on leave due to a stroke. This would easily satisfy the "serious health condition" element of the FMLA. The last four weeks (totally 9 weeks - well below the allowed 12 weeks) of leave was due to an adoption proceeding. This proceeding is clearly provided for in FMLA §2612(a)(1)(b). This clearly establishes that Mr. Glickman, an employee of Phoenix Cycles, was entitled to take FMLA leave.

Secondly, we can clearly establish that Mr. Glickman suffered an adverse employment decision. Mr. Glickman's pre-leave duties included being in charge of several marketing projects, supervising market research, monitoring retailers, developing (on his own) new product ideas and conducting product reviews, dealer services and trade shows. Additionally, he had a supervisory role over the marketing assistants. Upon his return, his product line has been given to a less competent employee, he has no subordinates, and he has to run all of his previously genius ideas past a newly promoted peer! See Franklin Business News.

Phoenix Cycles will no doubt cit Mills and claim that Glickman has not been subject to a negative decision because he has the same salary with de minimus changed duties. However, in that case, the only change was mere travel. Here, although the salary has remained the same, his supervisory role, development role, title, and overall position - the essential function of the job - has changed. Ridley. Mills is not a sufficient defense for your client's violation.

Additionally, Phoenix Cycles might claim that they had the right to not hire Mr. Glickman back to his old position because he was in the top 10% of salaried employees. They also will claim that the consultant's recommendation called for the type of consolidation completed. Jones However, Mr. Glickman was not notified of his demotion (as specified in Phoenix Cycles' 12/19/06 letter) when the decision was made [a condition necessary under FMLA §2614(b)(1)(b)]. Additionally, the consultant recommendation came well before Mr. Glickman's leave, which leads one to believe the decision was made due to his leave. Finally, due to these turn of events, Mr. Glickman will likely miss out on the $25,000 bonus promised by John. Due to the above reasons, we see no issues in proving that Mr. Glickman has been a victim of an adverse employment decision.

Lastly, Mr. Glickman can show a causal connection between his leave and the employment decision. John expressed his severe displeasure when Mr. Glickman requested additional time off for the adoption ("let your wife handle it" and "work is piling up"). As stated previously, the consultant recommendation vastly pre-dated Mr. Glickman's leave. This report is simply being used as a gauge to demote our client. Mr. Glickman was one of the, if not the most, senior executives prior to his leave. There is no other explanation for Mr. Glickman's demotion - his FMLA rights have been violated. Additionally, Phoenix Cycles has no claim under Floyd because our client has not been tardy or insubordinate, and has taken less that the time allotted.

Phoenix also has no claim that Mr. Glickman causes a substantial and grievous burden on the company. . .he was re-hired at his old salary. Phoenix Cycles simply saw fit to demote our client, take his title, reduce his responsibilities, embarrass him by making him report to less competent peers, and generally making his work-life-balance miserable in hopes of his resignation. All of this because our client wanted to adopt a child.

Due to his FMLA rights being violated, Mr. Glickman has both damages and equitable relief. Although there doesn't seem to be any lost wages, Mr. Glickman did/will lose the opportunity of monetary benefit. . .the $225,000 bonus he was promised. Section 2617(a)(1)(I) provides for lost "other compensation." Additionally, §2617(a)(1)(iii) provides for doubling that amount as liquidated damages. Therefore, Mr. Glickman will be able to collect $50,000 for your client's violations. In addition, §2617(a)(1)(iii) provides for the equitable relief of "promotion." The facts illustrate that Mr. Glickman is really the brains behind the bike. The Franklin Business News articles hale him as "God-like." He should and will be given Sue's job once litigation is completed. Please discuss with your client and convey our thoughts.

- Sample Answer 3.

Dear Ms. Snow,

This letter is concerning the violation of Mr. Glickman's FMLA rights. It has become apparent that after Mr. Glickman returned to work after his nine week FMLA, his job or an equivalent one was not restored. We have determined that you have violated his FMLA rights and we demand reinstatement at an equivalent position or suit will be brought. If suit is brought, Phoenix Bikes will be held liable for damages.

Under FMLA, an employee is entitled to restoration of his original job or an equivalent one after his leave is up. We only have to prove that Mr. Glickman was entitled to his leave, he suffered an adverse employment decision and some causal connection between the two. (Ridley v. Santacroce). This isn't very hard to prove given the situation. As admit is a letter to Mr. Glickman by John Pearsall, CEO of Phoenix Cycles, Mr. Glickman was entitled to leave both for the recovery of his stroke, 29 U.S.C. §2612(a)(d) and for the adoption of his daughter, 29 U.S.C. §2612(a)(b). Furthermore, upon returning to work after such life changing events, Mr. Glickman was demoted from vice president of bicycle marketing to coordinator of bicycle marketing. Courts have determined that an "equivalent position" must be equal or substantially similar in the conditions of employment. This is determined by looking at the duties, essential functions, and are required to be virtually identical (Ridley). Mr. Glickman's new job of coordinator does not fit as an equivalent. While he may be getting paid similar wages, he has lost some of his privileges, benefits and status, including his authority, responsibility and opportunities for benefits. These are all factors that courts can consider. (Ridley) Before his leave, Mr. Glickman was in charge of a division, he was vice president and had people report to him and stood to get a $25,000 bonus for the launch of a line of bikes that were his creation. Now he is among many in a division, reports to people and has lost his promised bonus. These are far from equivalent positions. Lastly, a causal connection is easily proven. Pearsall, by his own choice, proclaimed to Franklin Business News how wonderful of an employee Mr. Glickman was, and how his talents are important to the company. Further in the same article, Pearsall spoke about Mr. Glickman's return to Phoenix after his recovery and how he is going to be a significant part of the new line. (Nov. 24, 2006) Then after hearing that Mr. Glickman needed another four weeks off for his daughter, Mr. Pearsall's tone change and he was no longer going to be a significant part of the line.

Phoenix has claimed that this has nothing to do with Mr. Glickman's leave, and instead is part of a "legitimate business change." But the "legitimate business change" is nothing more than a facade. It is hard to believe that 18 months after an organizational analysis a company only implemented a few portions of it directly affecting Mr. Glickman and without giving him a chance for an equal position is legitimate especially when he is more qualified to hold it than the person currently. This is clearly not a legitimate business change. Furthermore, hiding behind the highest paid 10% exception will not save Phoenix from this action.

Highly compensated individuals do not have to be reinstated IF their reinstatement would cause "substantial and grievous economic injury." As discussed in the case of Jones v. Oakton School District, while there is no specific test the harm cannot be minor. It is hard to even place an economic injury here, considering that from November 15 to January 18, no permanent replacement was hired, and Mr. Glickman was hired at the same salary rate. An example of a substantial grievous economic injury is having to hire a permanent replacement as in Jones but no replacement was hired here and no economic injury has occurred. Since there is no economic injury to Phoenix, Mr. Glickman was improperly demoted after returning from his FLMA leaves.

Since Mr. Glickman was improperly demoted, if this issue is litigated, under FLMA, Phoenix can be held liable for double Mr. Glickman's monetary loses. Considering that Mr. Glickman was promised a $25,000 bonus before his leave and now that Sue Cowen stands to receive that bonus, Mr. Glickman is entitled to $50,000 liquidated damages minimum, and reinstatement.

Mr. Glickman is willing to accept reinstatement of his old job or one substantially similar, but if he isn't reinstated, we are comfortable litigating this issue.

Applicant

FILE

NATIONAL CONFERENCE OF BAR EXAMINERS

Allender, Levine Chu LLP
Attorneys at Law
3020 Hayden Square, Suite 700
Victoria, Franklin 33117
(608)555-9412

M E M O R A N D U M

TO: Applicant
FROM: Laura Levine
DATE: February 27, 2007
RE: Tamara Shea

Our client Tamara Shea, a real estate broker, seeks legal advice concerning her entitlement to payment for services rendered in connection with a real estate transaction. When the property was first listed for sale, Shea and the seller, Ann Remick, entered into a written "listing agreement," which is a contract between a real estate broker and a property owner setting forth the terms of the broker's services, the rights and duties of the parties, and the broker's right to compensation. Typically, the seller pays the broker a commission, expressed as a percentage of the agreed-upon sale price, when the property is sold with the broker's assistance.

Remick sold the property a few weeks ago. Shea believes that the purchaser, Dan Anderson, convinced Remick to sell the property to him directly at a reduced price, thereby avoiding payment of Shea's commission. To date, Shea has not received any compensation in connection with the sale of the property. I want to know what legal recourse she may have.

Please draft a memorandum analyzing the following:

(1) Whether Shea can maintain a breach of contract claim against Remick; and

(2) Whether Shea can maintain a claim for interference with contractual relations and/or interference with prospective economic advantage against Anderson.

You need not include a separate statement of facts, but in each part of your memorandum be sure to incorporate the relevant facts, analyze the applicable legal authorities, and explain how the facts and law affect your analysis. Another associate is researching whether Shea can recover under the doctrine of promissory estoppel, so you need not address that issue.

TRANSCRIPT OF CLIENT INTERVIEW: Tamara Shea

February 26, 2007

Levine: I'm glad we could meet on such short notice. In your phone message, you mentioned something about a real estate deal that fell through. What's going on?

Shea: Well, I'm pretty upset—I've been cheated out of a commission.

Levine: Why don't you start at the beginning and walk me through what happened?

Shea: Okay. In early November, I was approached by Ann Remick, who owned a 20-acre undeveloped parcel of land in the Briarwood Township in Cleveland County. Remick told me she had been referred to me by a friend and said that she wanted my assistance in selling the property. After I met with her and inspected the property, we signed a 60-day listing agreement setting forth the terms of our relationship as broker and client.

Levine: I'm familiar with the Briarwood area. It's really beautiful country out there, but a little off the beaten track. Did you bring a copy of the listing agreement with you?

Shea: Yes. As you'll see, the agreement clearly states that I was to be paid a 10 percent commission if I found a buyer for the property during the listing period.

Levine: What happened after you put the property on the market?

Shea: I was confident the property would sell within a couple of months, because properties of that size in Briarwood are hard to come by. It was just a matter of finding the right buyer, someone seeking country living less than two hours outside of town. I did everything from listing the property in local newspapers and on the Multiple Listing Service, to circulating flyers to other real estate agents and showing the property to potential buyers. Before the listing agreement expired, I'd already received inquiries from more than a dozen people and had shown the property to three individuals who expressed serious interest in it. Because none of these prospects had panned out, and because more than one potential buyer had expressed concern about the listing price, Remick agreed in writing to reduce her asking price from $225,000 to $200,000. She seemed very motivated to sell and I could tell she was getting frustrated, even after I told her that the holiday season was historically a slow time for real estate sales. Nevertheless, I was certain that we'd be receiving at least one offer within the next several days, based on the efforts I'd made to market the property, the price reduction, and my discussions with potential buyers.

Levine: I'm somewhat familiar with the Multiple Listing Service, but can you tell me a little more about it?

Shea: Sure. The Multiple Listing Service, or MLS, maintains a computer database of all the property listings in a particular area. It's available to real estate brokers as well as the general public, who can access MLS listings online. This is a copy of the MLS listing for the Remick property.

Levine: Thanks. You mentioned earlier that the property has been sold. What happened?

Shea: On January 10, I got a call from a guy named Dan Anderson. He said he'd seen the MLS listing for the property and he wanted to schedule a tour as soon as possible. I knew that my listing agreement with Remick had expired. Although I wasn't worried at the time about Remick agreeing to extend the agreement, I felt I could not show the property without her express authority, so I tried to contact her to see how she wanted to handle the situation.

Levine: Were you able to reach her?

Shea: Not directly. I left her a voicemail message indicating that Anderson was interested in seeing the property and that I wanted to show it to him, but that because our listing agreement had expired, I needed to know how she wanted to proceed. She left me a reply voicemail stating she was out of town due to a family emergency and wasn't sure how long she'd be gone. She said she would extend the listing agreement as soon as she got back in town and that I should go ahead and continue showing the property in the meantime. I sent her a confirmation letter for her signature that she never returned. Here's a copy of what I sent.

Levine: Thanks. By the way, other than the listing agreement and the letter you sent Remick, were there any other written communications between the two of you?

Shea: Only Remick's written authorization to reduce the price.

Levine: Did you ever end up showing the property to Anderson?

Shea: Yes, we met as planned the morning of January 13, 2007. When he saw the land, he was really excited and said it was exactly what he was looking for. He wanted to submit an offer that day, so I helped him put one together and he signed it in my office.

Levine: What were the terms of the offer?

Shea: Anderson offered to buy the property for $185,000. I told him I didn't think Remick would accept the offer, because she had already reduced her asking price from $225,000 to $200,000, and that the reduced asking price—which worked out to only $10,000 an acre—was already at the lower end of the market. Anderson said he couldn't go any higher than $185,000. I should point out that if Remick had accepted Anderson's $185,000 offer, I would have received a commission of $18,500 and Remick would have netted $166,500 from the sale before her closing costs. Anyway, that evening, I left Remick a voicemail message informing her of the offer. I also faxed the offer to her so she'd have it when she got back in town.

Levine: Did she accept the offer?

Shea: No. She called a few days later to say Anderson's offer was too low and that she wasn't interested in making a counteroffer or considering any other offers because she had decided not to sell the property after all. When I called Anderson to deliver the bad news, he didn't act surprised or seem particularly disappointed. Then I learned that Remick went ahead and sold the property directly to Anderson, and now she's refusing to pay my commission!

Levine: I can understand your concerns, and I agree that this doesn't pass the smell test. How did you find out about the sale, anyway?

Shea: About a week ago, a broker friend of mine heard that the property had sold. He remembered that I'd been involved with the property, and he called to congratulate me on the sale. I was blown away when I found out what had happened. I did some checking and confirmed that the sale closed on February 2, and the property sold for $180,000. Since then, I've tried to reach Anderson and Remick. Anderson hasn't returned my calls. Remick finally called back the other night after business hours and left a message stating that Anderson had told her that realtors couldn't be trusted because all we wanted were quick sales to get our commissions with as little work as possible. Remick said Anderson also told her that if she dealt directly with him she wouldn't owe me any commission. When I heard this, I decided I needed a lawyer and called you for advice.

Levine: Did you and Anderson ever discuss the subject of your commission?

Shea: As a matter of fact, we did. When we were putting together his offer, he asked who would be responsible for paying my commission if his offer were accepted. I explained that because I had a listing agreement with Remick and she was the seller, she would be responsible for the commission, as long as he didn't default prior to the closing. He wanted to know what my commission would be. I told him that it was customary for brokers to receive 10 percent of the agreed-upon purchase price where, as here, the sale involved unimproved land. At the time, I thought the conversation was a little odd, but now I think I know why he was asking all those questions about my commission!

Levine: I can understand why you're so upset. Let me look into this. I should be able to get back to you within the next couple of days.

Shea: That would be great. Thanks for your help.

LISTING AGREEMENT

This Listing Agreement (Agreement) is entered into between Ann Remick (Seller) and Tamara Shea (Broker) and concerns the following property (Property):

> The parcel consisting of 20 acres located in the Briarwood Township of Cleveland County, Franklin, and legally described by the Deed dated September 5, 1987, and recorded in the Cleveland County Records, in Record Book 725 at page 317, and Plat Book 50 at page 72.

In consideration of the mutual promises contained herein, Seller gives Broker the exclusive right to sell the Property at the listing price of two hundred twenty-five thousand dollars ($225,000) cash or such other terms and conditions as Seller may agree to in writing.

The period of this Agreement shall be sixty (60) days, from the date hereof up to and including January 8, 2007.

Broker agrees to use reasonable efforts to procure a ready, willing, and able buyer for the Property in accordance with the terms and conditions of this Agreement. Broker is granted the sole authority to undertake any one or more of the following actions: advertise the Property; post "For Sale" signs on the Property; . . . and disclose, print, or publish information that is obtained during the listing period to prospective buyers and other brokers.

Seller will pay Broker a brokerage commission of 10 percent of the agreed-upon sale price if, prior to the expiration of this Agreement, Broker procures a buyer ready, willing, and able to purchase the property, in accordance with the price, terms, and conditions of this Agreement, or on such other price, terms, and conditions as shall be acceptable to Seller.

Seller agrees to refer all inquiries and offers made for the purchase of the Property to Broker, to cooperate with Broker in every reasonable way, and to maintain and insure the Property.

* * * *

Seller represents that she is the owner of the Property, and that the information contained in this Agreement is true and accurate. Receipt of a copy of this Agreement is hereby acknowledged. This Agreement shall be interpreted in accordance with the laws of the State of Franklin.

This Agreement can be extended, cancelled, or revoked only if Seller and Broker agree in writing.

IN WITNESS WHEREOF, the parties have executed this Agreement as of the date set forth below.

Seller: ______________________________ Date: November 10, 2006
Ann Remick

Broker: ______________________________ Date: November 10, 2006
Tamara Shea
Shea Realty

Shea Realty
Victoria's Premier Real Estate Company
420 Tenth Street
Victoria, FR 33117
333.555.0602
www.SheaRealty.com

14014 Memorial Crossing
Lakewood Park, Franklin 33017

January 10, 2007

Ms. Ann Remick
5632 Birdie Lane
Diamond Springs, Franklin 33017

Re: Briarwood Parcel

Dear Ann:

This will confirm that our Listing Agreement dated November 10, 2006, is extended for a period of 30 days, effective as of January 9, 2007, through and including February 7, 2007.

I look forward to continuing to assist you in selling your Briarwood property. Please countersign and return this letter to me at your earliest convenience.

Sincerely,

Tamara Shea
Licensed Real Estate Broker

I hereby consent to the Listing Agreement extension set forth above.

Seller: ______________________ Date: ________________
Ann Remick

Shea Realty	
No Photo Available	**MLS# 07046619** Contact: Tamara at Shea Realty Tamara@SheaRealty.com (333) 555-0602

Location, Location, Location!!! A new listing available exclusively from Shea Realty! If you're looking for that special setting off the beaten path, don't miss out on this rare 20-acre tract of undeveloped land in the Briarwood Township, Cleveland County. Very private location at the end of a rural county road with Victoria Creek running through the property. Close to the Carmel Hills with magnificent views to the east. Lots of wooded acreage with abundant wildlife, including mule deer, whitetails, and turkeys. Also contains a small crop of alfalfa. Accessible to town. Power is available.

OFFER FOR THE PURCHASE OF REAL PROPERTY

To: Ann Remick, Seller

The undersigned hereby offers One Hundred Eighty-Five Thousand Dollars ($185,000) for the purchase of the following real estate:

> A 20-acre parcel located in the Briarwood Township of Cleveland County, Franklin, and legally described by the Deed dated September 5, 1987, and recorded in the Cleveland County Records, in Record Book 725 at page 317, and Plat Book 50 at page 72.

This offer to purchase is contingent on the following terms:

1. An earnest money deposit of five thousand dollars ($5,000) as part of the purchase price shall be paid to Seller upon acceptance of this offer and placed in escrow pending execution of a deed, real estate contract, or other conveyance, with the remaining balance of $180,000 to be paid by cash, cashier's check, or certified check at closing.

2. Taxes, insurance, and other applicable expenses shall be prorated as of the closing date.

3. Seller shall deliver the property free and clear of all liens, restrictions, and encumbrances and shall furnish a policy of title insurance. Title shall be conveyed by warranty deed.

If purchaser defaults following acceptance of this offer, the earnest money deposit shall be forfeited and applied to payment of the broker's commission and any expenses incurred, with the balance paid to seller.

This offer is withdrawn if not accepted within 10 days.

____________________________ January 13, 2007____________

Dan Anderson Date
219 South Figueroa
Lakewood Park, Franklin 33020

ACCEPTANCE

I accept the above offer for the purchase of the described real property.

____________________________ ____________________________

Ann Remick, Seller Date

LIBRARY

§ 1500. Agreements required to be in writing.

The following agreements are unenforceable, unless they, or some note or memorandum thereof, are in writing and subscribed by the party to be charged:

(a) An agreement that by its terms is not to be performed within a year from the making thereof;

(b) A special promise to answer for the debt, default, or miscarriage of another;

(c) An agreement for the leasing of real property for a longer period than one year, or for the sale of real property or of an interest therein;

(d) An agreement that authorizes or employs a broker, for compensation or a commission:

1. To procure a purchaser or seller of real estate; or
2. To procure a lessee or lessor of real estate where the lease is for longer than one year; or

(e) An agreement that by its terms is not to be performed during the lifetime of the promisor.

Mather v. Bowen
Franklin Court of Appeal (1997)

This is an action to recover a broker's commission allegedly due plaintiff Karen Mather for her services in procuring defendant Crown Research Corporation (CRC) as a tenant for defendant William Bowen's commercial real property.

Mather's complaint alleged the following: Mather is a licensed real estate broker and Bowen is the owner of the property. In June 1995, Mather attended an open house conducted by Bowen at the property site for the purpose of soliciting real estate brokers to procure tenants for the property on a 10-year lease. At the open house, Bowen distributed an offering brochure stating that brokers and prospective tenants would be registered and including a schedule of brokers' commissions.

Mather further alleged that in December 1995, she advised Bowen by telephone that she wished to bring a prospective tenant, defendant CRC, to view the property. In the phone call, Bowen acknowledged that Mather would be entitled to a broker's commission if and when CRC leased the premises. Mather then brought a CRC representative to view the property and completed Bowen's client-broker registration form, identifying herself as the broker and CRC as the prospective lessee, with Bowen signing the form identifying himself as lessor. Two weeks later, CRC submitted a written lease offer that identified Mather as broker and CRC as prospective lessee, and which further provided that "Lessor agrees to pay all commissions due Broker arising out of or in connection with Lessee's offer to lease." Bowen rejected the lease offer. However, in March 1996, Bowen and CRC executed a written lease for the property at a lower cost, without Mather's knowledge.

After finding out about the lease and receiving no commission, Mather brought this action against Bowen and CRC. Mather's first cause of action was directed against Bowen for breach of contract, and alleged that the brochure and client-broker registration form collectively constituted a written agreement under which Bowen owed Mather a commission. Mather's second cause of action alleged that CRC interfered with her economic and contractual relationship with Bowen. The defendants' motions to dismiss the complaint were granted without allowing Mather leave to amend her complaint.

The function of a motion to dismiss is to test the sufficiency of a plaintiff's pleading by raising questions of law. The allegations in the complaint must be regarded as true and are to be liberally construed. On appeal, the court is not concerned with a party's possible difficulty or inability in *proving* the allegations of the complaint, but only that the party *may* be entitled to some relief. We apply these principles in reviewing the complaint.

1. The writings satisfy the statute of frauds and support the claim against Bowen for breach of contract.

The Franklin statute of frauds provides that an agreement to pay a commission to a real estate broker to procure a buyer or seller of real property, or to procure a lessee or lessor of property for a period of more than a year, must be in writing. Franklin Civil Code § 1500(d). The purpose of the statute of frauds is to protect real estate sellers and purchasers from false claims by brokers for commissions. As such, § 1500(d) is designed to protect consumers, and is strictly enforced.

For a writing to satisfy the statute of frauds, it need not contain all the terms of the contract. The principal requirements for a broker to satisfy the statute of frauds are: (1) the writing shows the authority of the broker to act for the party to be charged, and (2) the writing is subscribed (signed) by or on behalf of the party to be charged. When these requirements are met, the other terms, including the amount of the commission, and even the agreement to pay the commission, may be shown by extrinsic evidence. Such evidence may also show the circumstances that attended the writing's making, or explain ambiguities on the writing's face. Finally, where a plaintiff relies on multiple writings, the court must determine whether the writings as a whole constitute an enforceable agreement.

Bowen maintains the writings are insufficient because they do not show on their face the fact of Mather's employment as Bowen's real estate broker. We disagree. The brochure and registration form appear to be related to each other. Both were prepared by Bowen, and he signed the registration form. The registration form containing the reference to broker commissions did not appear in a vacuum, but supplemented the initial brochure, which set forth the amount of commission to be paid and further provided that "brokers will be protected." Moreover, Bowen's signature on the registration form is sufficient to satisfy the subscription requirement as to this set of writings.

Together, these documents show that Bowen, in writing, actively solicited and engaged the cooperation of real estate brokers *en masse* in an effort to lease the property, with assurances that the brokers would be protected and compensated. Relying on these written representations, Mather brought CRC as a prospective tenant, and registered herself and CRC on Bowen's registration form, in accordance with Bowen's advertised procedure, with Bowen himself subscribing the document. As no other conceivable purpose could be served by Bowen's having Mather register CRC as a prospective tenant, the writings warrant the inference that Bowen authorized Mather to procure CRC as a tenant for the property.[2] 1"/> Therefore, Mather properly alleged a cause of action against Bowen for breach of contract.

Bowen's reliance on *Phillip v. Carter Industries* (Franklin Ct. App. 1991) is misplaced. There, the broker sued his client for breach of contract, alleging that an exchange of letters between the broker and client showed that the client had retained the broker to act on its behalf and had agreed to pay the broker's commission. However, the only writings that related to the broker's commission were *from the broker to the client,* not from the client to the broker. Thus, the writings did not satisfy the statute of frauds, as they were not subscribed by the party to be charged.

2. Mather's interference claims against CRC also withstand a motion to dismiss.

Mather pleaded one cause of action against CRC, labeling it "interference with economic advantage and contract." As such, Mather inartfully combined two distinct torts, interference with prospective economic advantage and interference with contractual relations, into one claim. Although these two torts are closely related and share many of the same elements, liability for interference with contractual relations requires an *existing valid and enforceable* contract. In contrast, a cause of action for interference with prospective economic advantage necessarily assumes that a contract has not yet been formulated (e.g., where the relationship is based on pending negotiations) or that the contract involved is unenforceable (e.g., due to lack of consideration or violation of the statute of frauds). The two torts, however, involve basically the same conduct on the part of the tortfeasor. In one case, the interference takes place when a valid contract is already in existence, in the other, when either a contract likely would have been consummated but for the conduct of the tortfeasor or where the plaintiff would otherwise have received an economic benefit but for the defendant's interference.

We note initially that even though these two torts are distinct, some plaintiffs may be able to state causes of action for both torts. Thus, a plaintiff who believes that she has a contract but who recognizes that the trier of fact might conclude otherwise, might bring claims for both torts so that, in the event of a finding of no contract, the plaintiff might prevail on a claim for interference with prospective economic advantage. Where the exact nature of the facts is in doubt, or where the exact legal nature of plaintiff's rights and defendant's liability depends on facts not known by the plaintiff, the pleading may properly state alternative theories in separate, inconsistent causes of action. However, where there is no existing enforceable contract for whatever reason, only a claim for interference with prospective economic advantage may be maintained.

We conclude that Mather pleaded both theories in the alternative, and will consider each claim against CRC in turn. The elements of the tort of interference with prospective economic advantage are: (1) an economic relationship between the plaintiff and a third party containing the probability of future economic benefit to the plaintiff, (2) the defendant's knowledge of the existence of the relationship, (3) intentional *and* improper acts on the part of the defendant designed to disrupt the relationship, (4) actual disruption of the relationship, and (5) economic harm to the plaintiff proximately caused by the defendant's acts.

As stated above, the tort of interference with prospective economic advantage is not dependent on compliance with the statute of frauds. The wrong complained of in this cause of action is that CRC interfered in Mather's advantageous relationship with Bowen. Specifically, Mather alleged that she had an economic relationship with Bowen containing the probability of future economic benefit (i.e., payment of her broker's commission); that CRC had knowledge of the relationship, as evidenced by the commission provision contained in CRC's lease offer; that CRC intentionally excluded Mather from the lease negotiations, knowing and intending that such conduct would disrupt the relationship

---

[2] 1"/>1 Because the writings satisfy the statute of frauds, evidence of the December 1995 telephone conversation between Bowen and Mather (in which Bowen allegedly confirmed that Mather would receive a commission if CRC leased the property) may be admitted to explain any ambiguity in the registration form's purpose or function, as well as to show the circumstances that attended its making.

between Mather and Bowen; that CRC secured the lease at a lower price than it would have if Mather's commission had been paid; and that Mather was therefore damaged in an amount at least equal to the commission. These allegations are sufficient to state a cause of action for interference with prospective economic advantage. *See, e.g.*, *Howard v. Youngman* (Franklin Ct. App. 1985) (defendant real estate broker's economic interest in getting a higher commission if seller sold home to a different buyer did not give broker legal right to interfere with ongoing negotiations for sale of home).

Turning to Mather's second claim against CRC, to state a cause of action for interference with contractual relations, a plaintiff must allege: (1) a valid and enforceable contract between the plaintiff and a third party, (2) the defendant's knowledge of the existence of the contractual relationship, (3) intentional *and* improper acts on the part of the defendant designed to disrupt the relationship, (4) actual disruption of the relationship, (5) economic harm to the plaintiff proximately caused by the defendant's acts.

CRC moved to dismiss this cause of action solely on the ground that there was no valid and existing contract between Mather and Bowen. Because the brochure and registration form were sufficient to satisfy the statute of frauds, we hold that Mather properly pleaded a claim for interference with contractual relations against CRC.

Accordingly, the trial court's judgment of dismissal is reversed and the case is remanded for further proceedings.

Downey Co. v. Sierra Growers
Franklin Court of Appeal (2000)

Plaintiff Downey Co. (Downey) appeals from the trial court's judgment dismissing its action against defendant Sierra Growers (Sierra). The facts stated in Downey's complaint reveal that commencing in 1990, Downey entered into a series of contracts with Margaret Livingston, the sole proprietor of Villa D'Oro Olive Oil Company, an olive oil processing plant located in Butte County, Franklin. The Downey-Livingston contracts, which are incorporated into the complaint, provided for the sale of certain olive products to Downey.

Following execution of the contracts, a legal dispute arose between Downey and Livingston. As a result, in September 1993, Livingston advised Downey in writing that she intended to rescind and cancel the contracts on grounds of material breach and fraudulent misrepresentation by Downey. Downey filed an action in Cleveland County seeking declaratory and related relief against Livingston. While the Cleveland County action was pending, Livingston sold the Villa D'Oro processing plant to Sierra. Thereupon, Downey brought the present action against Sierra, purporting to state causes of action on the dual tort theories of interference with contractual relations and interference with prospective economic advantage. The district court granted Sierra's motion to dismiss the complaint and entered judgment against Downey. We affirm.

The gist of Downey's grievance is that, by buying the processing plant from Livingston, Sierra improperly interfered with and induced the breach of the Downey-Livingston contracts and also interfered with Downey's prospective economic advantage. It is well established that one who intentionally and improperly interferes with the contractual relations between the plaintiff and a third party is liable to the plaintiff for the harm caused thereby. It is likewise settled that the elements of the torts of interference with contractual relations and interference with prospective economic advantage are identical except that the former requires the existence of a legally binding agreement. Both torts require a showing of the defendant's knowledge of the existence of the plaintiff's relationship with a third party, intentional and improper acts by the defendant designed to disrupt the relationship, actual disruption of the relationship, and resulting economic harm to the plaintiff.

When tested against the foregoing standards, the challenged causes of action are facially deficient. Downey's complaint alleges that Sierra acquired knowledge of the Downey-Livingston contracts the day *after* it purchased the processing plant from Livingston. It is elementary that interference with contractual relations and interference with prospective economic advantage are intentional torts. The interference is intentional if the actor desires to bring it about or if he knows that the interference is certain or substantially certain to occur as a result of his action. Intent may be established by inference as well as by direct proof. In addition, a plaintiff must show either that the defendant had actual knowledge of the existence of the relationship or knowledge of facts and circumstances that would lead a reasonable person to believe in the existence of the relationship and plaintiff's interest in it. If the defendant had no knowledge of the existence of the relationship or if his actions were not intended to interfere with the relationship, he cannot be held liable even if an actual breach results from his acts.

Downey's complaint not only fails to allege that Sierra intentionally interfered with Downey's relationship with Livingston, but also fails to allege that at the time of purchasing the plant Sierra was even aware of the existence of the Downey-Livingston contracts, rendering Downey's claims against Sierra fatally defective. Liability will not be imposed for unforeseeable or unknown harm, since a plaintiff must prove that the defendant knew that the consequences were substantially certain to occur.

Similarly, Downey has failed to allege that Sierra's conduct was improper. Impropriety can be established by showing the defendant's bad motive or bad conduct. Absent such motive or conduct, a defendant's acts will not be deemed improper. Downey's novel proposition that Sierra acted improperly by failing to rescind or cancel its contract to purchase the plant after learning about the Downey-Livingston contracts is supported by neither reason nor law. While the law rightly prohibits an intentional interference with contractual rights or economic relations existing between others, there is no equivalent duty to rescind a contract lawfully entered into on the ground that it might offend the legal rights of others. To the contrary, no impropriety exists where, as here, the defendant's conduct consists of something that it had an absolute right to do. As such, this case stands in stark contrast to those cases finding the defendant's actions improper.

A plaintiff seeking to hold a defendant liable for improperly inducing another to breach a contract must allege that the contract would otherwise have been performed and that it was breached by reason of the defendant's conduct. Here, performance of the Downey-Livingston contracts had been abandoned by Livingston several months prior to Sierra's acquisition of the plant. Under these circumstances, proximate causation, a vital element of both causes of action, was lacking as a matter of law. Thus, Downey failed to allege a valid cause of action under either tort.

Affirmed.

In Re Tamara Shea Point Sheet

DRAFTERS' POINT SHEET

In this performance test item, the client, Tamara Shea, is a real estate broker who handled the listing for a 20-acre undeveloped parcel owned by seller Ann Remick. Shea and Remick entered into a 60-day listing agreement under which Remick retained Shea to serve as her broker and agreed to list the property at $225,000. Pursuant to the express terms of the agreement, Shea was to be paid a commission of 10 percent of the purchase price if she procured a buyer for the property. Shortly after the listing agreement lapsed, Shea was contacted by Dan Anderson, a potential buyer. Shea then contacted Remick, who confirmed, in a telephone message, her intention to extend the listing agreement, and instructed Shea to show the property. Shea showed Anderson the property and he made an offer on it. Remick, however, rejected the offer, claiming it was too low. Shea subsequently discovered that following expiration of the listing agreement, Remick sold the property directly to Anderson for $180,000 ($5,000 less than Anderson's previous offer and $20,000 less than the reduced listing price of $200,000). Remick is now refusing to pay Shea any commission on the sale, claiming that she need not compensate Shea because she sold the property directly to Anderson. Shea seeks advice from applicants' firm on whether she has any legal recourse against Remick and/or Anderson.

Applicants' task is to draft an objective memo to the supervising attorney analyzing whether Shea can maintain claims against Remick for breach of contract and against Anderson for interference with contractual relations and/or interference with prospective economic advantage.

The File contains the task memorandum, a transcript of an interview between the supervising attorney and Shea, the listing agreement, a letter from Shea confirming the extension of the listing agreement, the property's MLS listing, and Anderson's initial offer to purchase the property for $185,000. The Library contains the Franklin statute of frauds and two cases.

The following discussion covers all of the points the drafters intended to raise in the problem. Applicants need not cover them all to receive passing or even excellent grades. Grading is entirely within the discretion of the user jurisdictions.

I. Format and Overview

Applicants' work product should resemble a memorandum from one attorney to another. They are told that the discussion of each issue in the memorandum should set out the relevant facts, analyze the legal authorities, and explain how the facts and law affect their analyses.

- Applicants are instructed that they need not write a separate statement of facts, but must use the facts in the File to support their analyses.
- Better applicants will use headings to identify the issues.
  - The headings set forth below are examples only and are not to be taken by graders as the prescribed headings.
- Applicants must first determine whether Shea can maintain a claim for breach of contract against Remick.
  - Because commission agreements between real estate brokers and clients are subject to the statute of frauds (Franklin Civil Code § 1500(d)), applicants must analyze whether the communications between Shea and Remick satisfy the statute of frauds.
- Applicants should note that the listing agreement had expired and conclude that Remick's oral consent to extend the agreement is not enforceable.
  - Moreover, Shea's confirming letter dated January 10, 2007, does not cure the deficiency, as it was not signed (subscribed) by Remick.
- Consequently, Shea cannot maintain a claim against Remick for breach of contract.
- To state a claim for interference with contractual relations against Anderson, there must be an existing valid and enforceable contract between Shea and Remick. This threshold issue is dispositive. Because there is no contract between Shea and Remick, Shea cannot maintain a cause of action against Anderson for interference with contractual relations.
- Applicants should reach the opposite conclusion regarding a claim for interference with prospective economic advantage against Anderson.
  - The facts show that Shea and Remick had an existing economic relationship, that Anderson knew of their relationship, that he intentionally contacted Remick for the improper purpose of eliminating Shea's commission so that he could buy the property at a lower price, that Anderson actually disrupted Shea's relationship with Remick by so doing, and that Shea lost a prospective economic advantage—the commission she would have earned but for Anderson's acts.

II. Detailed Analysis

A. Shea Cannot Maintain a Breach of Contract Claim Against Remick Because the Communications Between Them Do Not Satisfy the Franklin Statute of Frauds.

The Franklin statute of frauds requires that an agreement to pay a broker a commission for procuring a buyer for real property must be in writing to be enforceable. Fr. Civil Code § 1500(d)1.

- For a writing to satisfy the statute of frauds in a real estate brokerage situation, it must meet two requirements: (1) it must show the authority of the broker to act for the party to be charged, and (2) it must be subscribed (signed) by or on behalf of the party to be charged. *Mather v. Bowen.*

- Where, as here, the plaintiff relies on multiple writings to satisfy the statute of frauds, the court must examine the writings to determine whether, as a whole, they constitute an enforceable contract. *Id.*

- As a preliminary matter, applicants should discuss the initial contractual relationship between Shea and Remick, which forms the backdrop for analysis of their relationship at the time Shea showed the property to Anderson.

- The initial 60-day listing agreement (in effect from November 10, 2006, through January 8, 2007) was valid under the statute of frauds because Remick signed it and it showed that she had retained Shea to serve as her broker.

  - Shea showed the property to Anderson on January 13 and assisted him in preparing an offer to purchase. These events occurred *after* the listing agreement had expired on January 9, but within the period that would have been covered by the letter confirming Remick's oral consent to extend the listing, had she signed it as Shea requested. Anderson's purchase of the property was also within this attempted extension (the sale closed on February 2, 2007). Thus, if Shea could establish that she had an existing listing agreement when she showed the property to Anderson, she would be able to state a claim for breach of contract against Remick. However, there would have to be an additional writing signed by Remick to show a continued contractual relationship following expiration of the listing agreement.

  - No such writing exists. Shea's January 10, 2007, letter to Remick confirming receipt of Remick's voicemail message and attempting to extend the listing agreement through February 7, 2007, does not comply with the statute of frauds. Although the writing purports to show Shea's authority to act for Remick, the letter is not "subscribed" (signed) by or on behalf of the party to be charged (Remick). *See Phillip v. Carter Ind.* (cited in *Mather*) (writings from broker to client did not satisfy statute of frauds where client was party to be charged).

- Because the statute of frauds has not been complied with, extrinsic evidence (such as the phone message from Remick authorizing Shea to continue serving as her broker) is not admissible to show the circumstances surrounding the letter. *Mather*.

- Thus, unlike the plaintiff in *Mather*, who was able to demonstrate that a series of writings collectively established an existing valid and enforceable contract between the broker and her client and could then introduce extrinsic evidence to establish the circumstances surrounding the agreement and to resolve ambiguities, Shea cannot satisfy the statute of frauds.

- Applicants who discuss in depth how the doctrine of promissory estoppel could be asserted to circumvent the requirements of the statute of frauds are not following the directions in the task memorandum, which explicitly instructs them that another associate is researching that issue, so they need not address it.

B. Shea *Cannot* Maintain a Claim for Interference with Contractual Relations Against Anderson Because She Did Not Have an Existing Valid and Enforceable Contract With Remick at the Time Her Claim Arose.

A claim for interference with contractual relations requires: (1) a valid existing contract between the plaintiff and a third party, (2) knowledge by the defendant of the existence of the contractual relationship, (3) intentional and improper acts on the part of the defendant designed to disrupt the relationship, (4) actual disruption of the relationship, and (5) damages to the plaintiff proximately caused by the acts of the defendant. *Mather*.

- As discussed above, Shea cannot maintain a breach of contract action against Remick for violation of the listing agreement because it was not validly extended by Shea's letter of January 10, 2007, or any other writing. Thus, at the time of Anderson's actions, there was no existing contractual relationship between Shea and Remick. It follows, then, that Shea is precluded from bringing a claim against Anderson for interference with contractual relations.

- There is no need to discuss the additional elements of this tort since the threshold requirement cannot be satisfied.

    - Better applicants should begin and end an analysis of the contract interference claim by referencing their conclusion that Shea has no potential contract action against Remick, since this threshold inquiry determines whether the claim is even available. Applicants who analyze the remaining requirements for a contract interference claim will simply be duplicating the analysis they will have to set out on the potential claim for interference with prospective economic advantage, as the remaining elements of both torts are virtually identical.

  NOTE: It is up to the user jurisdictions to determine whether such duplicative analysis constitutes a basis for making grading distinctions.

- On a related note, *Mather* indicates that in some cases a plaintiff may state alternative claims under both interference tort theories where the exact nature of the facts is in doubt or where the exact legal nature of the plaintiff's rights and the defendant's liabilities depends on facts not known by the plaintiff. However, *Mather* also cautions that "where there is no existing enforceable contract for whatever reason, only a claim for interference with prospective economic advantage may be maintained."

    - Here it is clear from the client interview that there are no additional writings between Shea and Remick that could affect the analysis of whether they had an existing valid and enforceable contract. Moreover, the statute of frauds is a consumer protection device to be strictly enforced. *Mather*. Consequently, answers stating that the tort claims should be pled in the alternative may be considered less responsive to the call of the question and therefore may provide a basis to make grading distinctions.

C. Shea *Can* Maintain a Claim for Interference with Prospective Economic Advantage Against Anderson.

The tort of interference with prospective economic advantage is closely related to the tort of interference with contractual relations in that they involve basically the same conduct on the part of the tortfeasor. However, the former assumes that a contract has not yet been formed (e.g., where the relationship is based on pending negotiations), or that a contract is unenforceable (e.g., lack of consideration or violation of the statute of frauds). By contrast, the latter requires an existing valid and enforceable contract. *See Mather*; and Sections II A B, above.

- The tort of intentional interference with prospective economic advantage is not dependent on the existence of a contract; thus, there is no need for applicants to discuss compliance with the statute of frauds. The necessary elements are: (1) an economic relationship between the plaintiff and a third party containing the probability of future economic benefit to the plaintiff, (2) the defendant's knowledge of the existence of the relationship, (3) intentional *and* improper acts on the part of the defendant designed to disrupt the relationship, (4) actual disruption of the relationship, and (5) economic harm to the plaintiff proximately caused by the acts of the defendant. *Mather.*

- Here, the facts and case law show that these elements can be met, at least for purposes of proceeding with a claim under this theory.

    - Better applicants may cite to the standard articulated in *Mather* for the necessary pleading requirements and may recognize that the primary concern at this stage is whether such a claim can be asserted, not whether it can be proven; in other words, whether Shea *may* be entitled to some relief. ("The allegations in the complaint must be regarded as true and are to be liberally construed." *Mather*.)

(1) The existence of a protected economic relationship:

- The facts in the File indicate that Shea and Remick had an economic relationship with the probability of future economic benefit to Shea, in that they had previously entered into a listing agreement which, by all indications, would have been extended but for Anderson's interference. Pursuant to this arrangement, Shea was to receive 10 percent of the purchase price of Remick's property, which clearly constitutes an economic benefit to Shea.

- Although one could argue that there was no guarantee that Shea would find a buyer for the property and thus earn her commission, the facts suggest a likely sale. According to the interview transcript, Shea had received more than a dozen inquiries concerning the property and had shown the property to several potential buyers. Indeed, Anderson himself initially offered to buy the property for $185,000—$5,000 more than the eventual sale price.

(2) The defendant's knowledge of that relationship:

- A plaintiff must show that the defendant had either actual knowledge of the existence of the relationship between the plaintiff and the third party, or knowledge of such facts and circumstances that would lead a reasonable person to believe in the existence of the relationship and the plaintiff's interest in it. If the defendant had no knowledge of the existence of the relationship, there will be no liability even if an actual breach results from the defendant's acts, because liability will not be imposed for unforeseeable or unknown harm. *Downey Co. v. Sierra Growers.*

- Anderson knew about Shea and Remick's economic relationship.

  - Not only did he specifically ask about Shea's commission while she helped him prepare an offer, his own written offer made reference to the commission, stating that in the event of default, "the earnest money deposit shall be forfeited and applied to *payment of the broker's commission* and any expenses incurred . . . ." (Emphasis added)

  - Anderson's knowledge can also be inferred from the MLS listing and from the fact that he contacted Shea to view the property and enlisted her help in preparing his initial offer, thereby evidencing his understanding that Shea was the broker handling the listing.

- The facts here parallel those in *Mather*, where the defendant's written lease offer referred to the plaintiff's commission. This is not a situation where the defendant first learned of the existence of the underlying relationship between the plaintiff and the third party after the defendant had engaged in the alleged tortious acts, as was the case in *Downey*. As such, *Downey* is distinguishable.

(3) The defendant's intentional and improper acts:

- ***(a) Intentional:*** The interference with another's prospective economic advantage is intentional if the actor desires to bring it about or if he knows that the interference is certain or substantially certain to occur as a result of his action. *Downey.*

  - Because interference with prospective economic advantage is an intentional tort, an action will lie only if the defendant *purposely* interfered with the plaintiff's economic relationship with a third party. *Id.*

  - Intent may be established by inference as well as by direct proof. *Id.*

- Here, the facts and inferences to be drawn conclusively demonstrate the purposefulness of Anderson's acts. After questioning Shea about the amount of her commission, Anderson approached Remick to engineer a deal behind Shea's back, knowing full well that Shea was the listing broker for the property and that she was supposed to receive a 10 percent commission if her efforts found a buyer, thus evidencing an intent to achieve precisely the result that followed (i.e., sale of the property at a reduced price, cutting out Shea's commission).

- ***(b) Improper:*** Typically, the wrongfulness of a defendant's act may be shown by demonstrating bad motive or bad conduct. Absent a motive or purpose to injure the plaintiff, or to appropriate an economic advantage belonging to the plaintiff, or some other aggravating circumstance, a defendant's acts will not be deemed tortious. *Downey*.

  - Every reasonable inference to be drawn from the facts suggests that Anderson's interference was improper. He took advantage of Shea's efforts in marketing the property, made disparaging comments about real estate brokers to Remick, and also told Remick that if she dealt directly with him, she wouldn't owe Shea a commission. In this way, Anderson persuaded Remick to exclude Shea from the negotiations and induced Remick to accept a lower price. Shea was thus deprived of the commission to which she would otherwise have been entitled. Such conduct has been found improper in similar circumstances and held to be tortious. *See Mather*; *Howard v. Youngman* (cited in *Mather*) (broker's personal interest in obtaining higher commission did not give him legal right to interfere with ongoing negotiations for sale of home).

(4) Actual disruption of the relationship:

- To maintain a claim for interference with prospective economic advantage, a plaintiff must demonstrate that the prospective relationship with the third party would have come to fruition but for the defendant's wrongful acts—in other words, that the defendant's acts were the proximate cause of the plaintiff's injuries. *Downey*.

- Although it is unclear from the File exactly when Remick was contacted by Anderson, it can be inferred that this occurred sometime after Anderson submitted his initial offer of $185,000 and before Remick declined the offer. Prior to that point, Remick appeared willing to extend the listing agreement. She also appeared motivated to sell the property, having reduced the price and reconfirmed with Shea that she wanted to sell. Remick's sudden disinterest in making a counteroffer and Anderson's apparent lack of surprise or disappointment upon learning that his offer had been rejected suggest that Remick and Anderson were already negotiating at that point. This inference is bolstered by the fact that Remick's outright rejection of Anderson's $185,000 offer was quickly followed by her sale of the property to him for $180,000.

- This is not a situation where the disputed relationship had been abandoned and discontinued months prior to the defendant's alleged interference, as was the case in *Downey* (in which the olive oil plant owner had notified the plaintiff of her intent to rescind the contract months before the defendant bought the plant, the latter action having given rise to the plaintiff's unsuccessful claims for tortious interference with contractual relations and interference with prospective economic advantage). Here, Anderson's interference was likely the direct cause of Remick's change in position.

- Nor was this a situation where the alleged prospective economic relationship was too speculative to support the interference claim; that is, Anderson could not successfully assert that Shea would have been unable to sell the property at the higher price that included her commission. On the contrary, the listing at a higher price that *included* Shea's commission had generated substantial interest to date (including Anderson's own initial offer of $185,000).

(5) Economic harm to the plaintiff proximately caused by the defendant's acts:

- Shea suffered economic harm as a result of Anderson's actions.
- Shea's 10 percent commission ($20,000 had the property sold for $200,000, $18,500 had Remick accepted Anderson's initial $185,000 offer) is itself an undeniable economic benefit. Thus, there is a nexus between Anderson's acts and Shea's damages. While it is not a *certainty* that the property would have sold for $185,000 or more, there is evidence to support such a conclusion.

- In *Mather*, the court upheld a claim for interference with prospective economic advantage on facts substantially similar to those presented here. In *Mather*, the measure of the plaintiff's loss was the commission she would have received but for the defendant's wrongful actions.
- Thus, a court would likely conclude that Shea can maintain a claim against Anderson
- for interference with prospective economic advantage.

In Re Tamara Shea Sample Answers

- Sample Answer 1.

Memo to Ms. Levine:

You asked me to research potential causes of action against Ann Remick Don Anderson. This memorandum summarizes my findings:

1. Breach of contract Claim Against Ann Remick

The Franklin Civil Code requires that agreements authorizing brokers for compensation or commission for the purchase of sale of real estate are unenforceable unless they are (1) in writing and (2) signed by the party charged. In this case, the initial listing agreement was executed on November 10, 2006 and terminated on January 8, 2007. Both Ann Remick and Tamara Shea were aware of this. Ms. Shea encountered a potential buyer January 10, 2007, but knew that her contract with Ms. Remick had expired. Thus, she contacted Ms. Remick in an attempt to extend the contract for a longer period. Ms. Remick orally agreed to extend the contract and Ms. Shea sent a confirmation letter on January 10, 2007. The letter extended the contract to February 7, 2007. This writing satisfies the first element under the Statute of Frauds.

Unfortunately, for Ms. Shea, Ms. Remick (the party charged) never executed the agreement. Thus, it fails the second requirement to satisfy the Statute of Frauds. These facts are very similar to those in Phillips. In Phillips, a real estate broker sued his client for breach of contract alleging that an exchange of letters comprised a written agreement for commission. The court, however, held that since the letters were only from the broker to the client and not the client to the broker that they were not "signed" by the charged party. Therefore, under those facts it is very unlikely that Ms. Shea could sustain an action against Ms. Remick for breach of contract.

2. Tortious Interference Claims

In Mather, the court noted that a plaintiff who believes that she has a contract but who recognizes that the trier of fact might conclude otherwise, might bring two separate tort actions: (1) Interference with economic advantage and (2) Interference with contractual relations.

2(a). Interference with Contractual Relations Against Don Anderson

A claim for interference with contractual relations requires that a plaintiff allege: (1) a valid and enforceable contract, (2) the defendant's knowledge of the existing contract, (3) intentional and improper acts on the part of the defendant to disrupt the contact, (4) actual disruption of the relationship, and (5) economic harm to the plaintiff proximately caused by the defendant's acts. The crux of this cause of action against Mr. Anderson relies on whether or not there is a valid and enforceable contract. As discussed in Section 1 of this memo, there is not a valid and enforceable agreement because it fails to satisfy the statute of frauds as required by Franklin Civil Code 1500. Therefore, a cause of action against Mr. Anderson cannot be sustained. (Mather)

2(b). Interference with Economic Advantage Against Don Anderson

In contrast to a claim for interference with contractual relations, the cause of action for interference with economic advantage assumes that a contract has not yet been formed. Mather For example, it applies in cases in which a relationship is based on pending negotiations or in which a contract is unenforceable because it does not satisfy the statute of frauds. Mather In Mather, the Franklin Court of Appeal set forth the elements required to establish such a claim: (1) an economic relationship between the plaintiff and a third party containing the probability of future economic benefit to the plaintiff, (2) the defendant's knowledge of the existence of the relationship, (3) intentional interference and improper acts on the part of the defendant to disrupt the relationship, (4) actual disruption of the relationship, and (5) economic harm to the plaintiff proximately caused by the defendant's acts.

The most promising aspect of this action is that no written contract need exist. Under the first element, Don Anderson knew that Ms. Shea Ms. Remick had an economic relationship that would result in a 10% commission benefit to Ms. Shea if the sale had gone through as originally offered. This is evidenced by the fact that Mr. Anderson asked Ms. Shea specifically about her compensation on the sale. Mr. Anderson knew of the relationship between Ms. Shea Ms. Remick as Mr. Anderson submitted the offer and received the reduction via Ms. Shea.

Furthermore, Mr. Anderson intentionally and improperly interfered with the relationship between Ms. Shea Ms. Remick by advising Ms. Remick that Ms. Shea was untrustworthy and that they could "cut her out" of the deal and eliminate the commission. This also is in compliance with the intentional and improper requirements of Downey. This is because Mr. Anderson knew that his actions to a degree of substantial certainty would harm Ms. Shea economically. Moreover, he knew that the contract would have been otherwise performed absent his action. For example, when he received the reduction he was neither surprised nor upset. Downey

His actions also satisfy the fourth element in that his conduct disrupted the relationship (in fact it ended it) between Ms. Shea and Ms. Remick. And finally, his actions were the proximate cause of Ms. Shea losing out on her commission. This is evident that Ms. Remick decided to deal directly with Mr. Anderson as a result of his actions. Thus, it is very likely that we can establish a case for interference with economic advantage against Mr. Anderson.

In conclusion, I recommend filing a cause of action against Mr. Anderson for interference with economic advantage. However, we should not file the breach of contract claim against Ms. Remick or the other interference claim against Mr. Anderson.

- Sample Answer 2.

Although Shea probably cannot maintain a cause of action against Remick for breach of contract, she can probably maintain a cause of action against Anderson for intentional interference with prospective economic advantage.

I. Shea probably cannot maintain a cause of action against Remick for breach of contract because the writing extending the Listing Agreement was not subscribed by Remick.

Section 1500 of the Franklin Civil Code requires that an agreement that authorizes or employs a broker, for compensation or a commission, to procure a purchaser or seller of real estate must be in writing and subscribed by the party to be charged. In Mathers v. Bowen, the Franklin Court of Appeal held that his requirement embodies two separate principal requirements: (1) the writing shows the authority of the broker to act for the party to be charged; and (2) the writing is subscribed (signed) by or on behalf of the party to be charged. Once these two requirements are met, extrinsic evidence is admissible to provide additional terms or to explain any ambiguities or the circumstances at the time the contract was made. Mathers

The original Listing Agreement between Shea and Remick satisfied these requirements. The agreement was in writing and stated that Shea had exclusive authority to sell Remick's property at the listing price of $225,000 and that her authority was to last for 60 days, up to and including, January 8, 2007. Furthermore, the agreement was signed by Remick, the party to be charged.

The subsequent agreement in which Remick agreed to reduce the sale prince contained in the Listing Agreement to $200,000 was also in writing and signed by Remick. However, the agreement in which Remick purportedly agreed to extend Shea's authority for another 30 days, up to and including February 7, 2007, was not signed by Remick. This agreement seeks to change the authority granted to Shea by the original Listing Agreement. It does more than provide additional terms or explain ambiguities or the circumstances at the time of contracting. Therefore, it was probably required under the Franklin Civil Code to be in writing and to be signed by Remick. Because it was not signed by Remick, it is probably invalid and cannot extend the Listing Agreement period. In addition, the voicemail from Remick agreeing to extend the Listing Agreement period is probably not admissible because it is extrinsic evidence being used to contradict an essential term of the original Listing Agreement. The agreement was not ambiguous as to the duration of Shea's authority - it specifically stated that her authority would only last until January 8, 2007. The extension agreement and the voicemail from Remick also do not explain the circumstances surrounding the making of the contract - both attempt to explain circumstances more than two months after the making of the contract.

Therefore, since Shea's authority under the Listing Agreement expired on January 8, 2007, she no longer had the exclusive right to sell Remick's property and receive a commission. Thus, by accepting Anderson's offer, Remick did not breach the contract because the contractual relationship had ended.

II. Shea can probably maintain a cause of action against Anderson for interference with a prospective economic advantage because Anderson knew about her relationship with Remick and took steps to intentionally and improperly interfere with that relationship.

In Mathers, the court noted the difference between the torts of "intentional interference with a prospective economic advantage" and "intentional interference with contractual relation." The latter requires the existence of a valid and enforceable contract, whereas the former does not. Even though these torts are separate, the court explained, they both may be brought by a plaintiff who "believes that she has a contract but who recognizes that the trier of fact might conclude otherwise." Thus, Shea could bring causes of action against Anderson for both torts, but, if the court determines that no contract existed between her and Remick, she can only collect damages for intentional interference with a prospective economic advantage.

In Mathers, the court identified the following elements of the tort of intentional interference with a prospective economic advantage: (1) an economic relationship between the plaintiff and a 3rd party containing the probability of future economic benefit to the plaintiff; (2) the defendant's knowledge of the existence of the relationship; (3) intentional and improper acts on the part of the defendant designed to disrupt the relationship; (4) actual disruption of the relationship; and (5) economic harm to the plaintiff proximately caused by the defendant's acts.

The court in Downey Co. v. Sierra Growers held that a defendant has knowledge of an economic relationship when he had actual knowledge of the existence of the relationship or knowledge of the facts and circumstances that would lead a reasonable person to believe in the existence of the relationship. The court also defined intentional interference as that interference occurring when the actor desires to bring it about or knows that it is certain or substantially certain to occur as a result of his action. Finally, the court defined improper conduct as showing bad motive or bad conduct.

There was clearly an economic relationship between Shea and Remick in which Shea expected to benefit. Furthermore, Anderson knew about this relationship, as evidenced by his conversations with Shea. By entering a contract with Remick without the participation of Shea, he intended to act in a way that would deprive Shea of her commission and sought to achieve a lower purchasing price for himself. This last fact is evidence of his improper conduct. Because his actions caused a disruption of the relationship between Shea and Remick and because Shea was harmed by this disruption, Shea probably has a cause of action against Anderson for intentional interference with a prospective economic advantage.

Shea probably does not have a cause of action against Anderson for intentional interference with a contractual relationship because there was no longer a valid contract between her and Remick. Should the trier of fact find otherwise, however, the elements of this tort are the same as those for intentional interference with a prospective economic advantage, with the exception of the first element.

Sample Answer 3.

1. To determine whether Shea can maintain a breach of contract claim against Remick, one must determine if there was a valid contract (K) between Shea and Remick. Under Franklin Civil Code §1500, an agreement that authorizes or employs a broker for compensation or a commission to procure a purchaser or seller of real estate is unenforceable if not in writing and subscribed by the party to be charged. Shea had a written agreement signed by both Shea and Remick for 60 days, up until the 8th of January 2007. When this offer to buy the property occurred, it was after January 8th. In fact the buyer, Anderson, did not contact Shea until after the 8th of January, on January 10th. While Shea did get verbal agreement from Remick to extend their listing agreement, there was no writing signed by Remick, the person to be charged. Shea sent a letter to Remick, but it was only signed by Shea, never by Remick. Thus, there was no written agreement satisfying the Franklin statute for an enforceable agreement. Additionally, the court in Mather v. Bowen (Bowen) said there had to be a writing and it must be subscribed by the party to be charged. The court was discussing the same statute and section as in the instant issue. The court said extrinsic evidence could be brought in to explain ambiguities but only if the two previous requirements were met. While the phone call to Remick could be used as extrinsic evidence, it could only be used if the writing requirements were first met, according to the court in Bowen. Thus, Shea probably cannot maintain a breach of contract action against Remick.

2. To show whether Shea can maintain a claim for interference with contractual relations, there must be a valid existing and enforceable contract, as stated by the court in Bowen. As stated earlier, it will be difficult for Shea to prove there was a valid existing enforceable K with Remick. Their first existing valid and enforceable K ended on January 8th and this interference that is alleged happened after that date. The alleged K between Shea and Remick after January 8th was in writing but not signed by the party to be charged, Remick. However, Shea could still bring this action along with an action for interference with prospective economic advantage against Anderson, if Shea believes she has a K but the trier of fact might conclude otherwise. (Bowen) This can be done if there are facts in doubt and Shea's exact legal rights are no completely known by Shea or Anderson. The court in Bowen said inconsistent causes of action may be plead. But, if there is no existing enforceable K, then only a claim for interference with prospective economic advantage may be maintained.

3. The elements to prove either interference with contractual relations or interference with prospective economic advantage are identical, except to prove the former requires an existing legally binding agreement. This is what the court stated in Downey Co. v. Sierra Growers (Sierra). To determine whether Shea can maintain a claim for interference with prospective economic advantage (IPEA) against Anderson, she must show: (1) an economic relationship between the plaintiff and a third party containing the probability of future economic benefit, (2) the defendant's knowledge of the existence of the relationship, (3) intentional and improper acts on the part of the defendant designed to disrupt the relationship, (4) actual disruption, and (5) economic harm to the plaintiff proximately caused by defendant's acts. (Bowen) No K has to be formed here. (Bowen) There was an economic relationship between Shea and Remick that contained the probability of future economic benefit to Shea. They had a prior agreement in writing, MLS listings by Shea for Remick's property, an oral agreement and a confirmation letter. Through Remick's actions, she consented to Shea showing the property to Anderson, as well. Anderson had knowledge of the relationship, as well. According to Shea she showed Remick's property to Anderson on the morning of January 13th and helped put together the offer. Anderson said he saw the MLS listing, too. Remick also told Shea that Anderson said to bypass Shea. The court in Sierra said that if defendant had actual knowledge of the existence of the relationship or knowledge of facts and circumstances that would lead a reasonable person to believe existence of a relationship and plaintiff's interest, there is knowledge. This element is satisfied. Anderson also had intent and improper acts to disrupt the relationship. Sierra said intent can be shown if the actor desires to bring it about or knows interference is substantially certain to occur.

Remick's statement to Shea shows that Anderson had this intent. Sierra also said impropriety can be established by bad motive or conduct. Anderson's motive was bad, wanting to avoid the commission to buy the house at a lower price. There was an actual disruption, since Remick did not use Shea nor pay Shea which then caused economic harm to Shea proximately caused by Anderson's acts. Thus, it appears that Shea could win against Anderson on a claim for IDEA. All five elements are most likely met and there is no requirement for a valid enforceable contract.

FILE

Peterson, Michaels Williams
Attorneys at Law
1530 Lakeside Way
Franklin City, Franklin 33033

M E M O R A N D U M

To:	Applicant
From:	Conrad Williams
Date:	July 24, 2007
Re:	*Black Hawk et al. v. Acme Resources, Inc.* (Black Eagle Tribal Court); *Acme Resources, Inc. v. Black Hawk et al.* (U.S. Dist. Ct. for the Dist. of Franklin)

We represent Robert Black Hawk and seven other members of the Black Eagle Indian Tribe (the Tribe) in an action in Black Eagle Tribal Court (Tribal Court) against Acme Resources, Inc. (Acme). Acme's mining activities, specifically the extraction of coal bed methane, have caused our clients' water wells to begin to run dry. In the Tribal Court action we are seeking damages and an injunction ordering Acme to cease its operations on the Black Eagle Indian Reservation.

The coal bed methane underlies private land on the Reservation owned in fee simple by Patrick Mulroney, who is not a member of the Tribe. While Mulroney owns the surface of the land, the underlying minerals are owned by the Tribe. The Tribe granted Acme the right to extract the methane from under Mulroney's land in exchange for a royalty. At the same time, Mulroney granted Acme the right to use his land to build the infrastructure that is necessary for mining.

In response to our complaint in Tribal Court, Acme filed an answer denying liability and also denying the jurisdiction of the Tribal Court. No further proceedings have occurred in Tribal Court. Instead, Acme filed a separate federal action in U.S. District Court for the District of Franklin seeking both a declaratory judgment that the Tribal Court lacks jurisdiction in this matter and an injunction against prosecution of our Tribal Court action. (See attached complaint.)

I plan to respond to Acme's complaint by filing a motion with the federal court: (1) for summary judgment on the ground that the Tribal Court has jurisdiction; or, in the alternative (2) to stay or dismiss Acme's federal action on the ground that the Tribal Court should be permitted to consider its jurisdiction over the matter. (See attached draft motion and affidavits of Robert Black Hawk and Jesse Bellingham, Ph.D.)

Please draft the argument sections of the brief in support of both points. Each distinct point in the argument should be preceded by a subject heading that encapsulates the argument it covers and succinctly summarizes the reasons the court should take the position you are advocating. A heading should be a specific application of a rule of law to the facts of the case and not a bare legal or factual statement of an abstract principle. For example, improper: The Police Did Not Have Probable Cause to Arrest Defendant. Proper: The Fact That Defendant Was Walking Alone in a High-Crime Area at Night Without Photo Identification Was Insufficient to Establish Probable Cause for His Arrest.

The argument under each heading should analyze applicable legal authority and state persuasively how the facts and the law support our clients' position. Authority supporting our clients' position should be emphasized, but contrary authority should also generally be cited, addressed, and explained or distinguished. Be sure to address the grounds asserted in Acme's complaint; do not reserve arguments for reply or supplemental briefs. No statement of facts is necessary, but be sure to incorporate the relevant facts into your argument.

Transcript of Interview with Robert Black Hawk

May 18, 2007

Williams: Good afternoon, Mr. Black Hawk. What can I do for you?

Black Hawk: My neighbors and I are at the end of our ropes. We are all members of the Black Eagle Tribe and we are in bad shape. Our wells are running dry.

Williams: Do you know why?

Black Hawk: You bet we do. Two years ago, Acme Resources came onto our Reservation with promises of jobs and riches. Acme wanted to develop a huge coal bed methane field under the Reservation. The easiest access to the field is by way of Patrick Mulroney's land. None of us tribal members wanted it because we had heard of water problems associated with the development of coal bed methane.

Williams: I know that methane is a primary source of natural gas and that coal bed methane is simply methane found underground in coal seams. How does developing coal bed methane affect your water wells?

Black Hawk: Well, I read up on this. Both groundwater and methane flow through fractures in the coal seams—in fact, coal seams are often aquifers. To extract the methane, water is pumped out of the coal seam. As the water pressure decreases, the methane separates from the groundwater and can be piped out. Developing coal bed methane involves extracting huge quantities of groundwater to reduce the water pressure enough to release the methane gas in the coal seam. Since my neighbors and I all farm and ranch on land surrounding Mulroney's place, we were worried about our wells running dry because of the drop in water pressure.

Williams: And your worries came true.

Black Hawk: No kidding. We're running out of water for our livestock and our crops. We're going to go broke because our land just won't support us without water. A geologist who looked at it says that all wells on the Reservation are likely to be affected eventually. We tried to tell the Tribal Council before it voted on the Acme agreement, but the promises of easy money from Acme carried the day. Under the deal, the Tribe is getting a 20 percent royalty on all methane production.

Williams: So you want to see what we can do for you?

Black Hawk: Yes. We really are in a tough spot. Word about the water problem has spread around the Reservation and we believe the vast majority of our fellow tribal members have second thoughts about what the Tribal Council did. We have a Tribal Court and the judge is a fair man. He knows the history of our Tribe and tribal ways. We think that if he and a tribal jury could hear about our problems caused by Acme's extraction of the coal bed methane, we could win.

Williams: Well, I've litigated some in Tribal Court. I know there is no federal statute or treaty addressing the Tribal Court's civil jurisdiction. Your Tribe's constitution and code have some provisions in them about protecting the environment. Maybe that could be a hook for us. I'm somewhat worried about the Tribal Council approving the deal. Can you tell me what your losses have been?

Black Hawk: We neighbors got together with a farm finance guy from Franklin City. He estimates our losses to date to be $1.5 million, and they aren't done yet.

Williams: What about this Patrick Mulroney?

Black Hawk: Well, he's a non-Indian—not a member of our Tribe. Mulroney owns fee land within the Reservation that his family bought from Tribe members about a hundred years ago. Anyway, I'm surprised he went along with the

Acme deal because he must be losing his water, too. But he's getting a lot of money from Acme and he's been talking for years about selling and moving somewhere warmer. With the money from the deal, he may not care anymore.

Williams: Okay. Let's get your neighbors in to discuss filing an action in Tribal Court to see what we can do.

Black Hawk: Great. I'll get in touch with everybody and call you.

IN THE UNITED STATES DISTRICT COURT
FOR THE DISTRICT OF FRANKLIN

Acme Resources, Inc., **Plaintiff,**	))	**Case No. CV 103-07**
v.	)))	**COMPLAINT**
Robert Black Hawk, Stewart Marsh, Irene Martin, James Davis, Mary Gray, Katherine White Horse, Lester Stewart, and James Black Hawk, **Defendants.**	))))	

Plaintiff Acme Resources, Inc., alleges:

1. This action involves the federal question of whether the Black Eagle Tribal Court can exercise jurisdiction over Acme Resources, Inc. (Acme), in an action brought by members of the Black Eagle Indian Tribe arising out of a controversy involving the development of coal bed methane underlying fee land owned by Patrick Mulroney, who is not a member of the Tribe.
2. This court has jurisdiction under 28 U.S.C. § 1331.
3. Defendants are all members of the Black Eagle Indian Tribe and brought an action against Acme in Black Eagle Tribal Court seeking damages and an injunction to stop Acme from developing the coal bed methane underlying Mulroney's land.
4. The Black Eagle Tribal Court lacks jurisdiction over Acme in the tribal court action because Acme is not a member of the Tribe. *Montana v. United States* (U.S. 1981).

Wherefore, Acme Resources, Inc., prays the Court enter judgment:

1. Declaring that the Black Eagle Tribal Court lacks jurisdiction over Acme in the tribal court action;
2. Enjoining the defendants from prosecuting the tribal court action; and,
3. Awarding Acme its costs and any other appropriate relief.

Dated: July 9, 2007

Respectfully submitted,

Frank Johnson
Frank Johnson
Franklin Bar #1012
Counsel for Acme Resources, Inc.

Draft

IN THE UNITED STATES DISTRICT COURT
FOR THE DISTRICT OF FRANKLIN

Acme Resources, Inc.,) **Case No. CV 103-07**
Plaintiff,)
) **MOTION FOR SUMMARY JUDGMENT, OR TO STAY OR DISMISS**
v.)
)
Robert Black Hawk, Stewart Marsh, Irene Martin,)
James Davis, Mary Gray, Katherine White Horse,)
Lester Stewart, and James Black Hawk,)
Defendants.)

The above-named defendants move the Court as follows:

1. To grant the above-named defendants summary judgment on the ground that there exists no genuine issue of material fact that the Black Eagle Tribal Court has jurisdiction over plaintiff Acme Resources, Inc., and the action pending before it under *Montana v. United States* (U.S. 1981), and that the defendants are entitled to judgment as a matter of law; or, in the alternative,
2. To dismiss or stay this action on the ground that Acme has failed to exhaust its remedies in the Black Eagle Tribal Court as required by *National Farmers Union Ins. Cos. v. Crow Tribe* (U.S. 1985).

This motion is supported by the affidavits of Robert Black Hawk and Jesse Bellingham, the pleadings on file, and a brief filed contemporaneously herewith.

Dated: July ____, 2007

Respectfully submitted,

____
Conrad Williams
Franklin Bar # 1779
Counsel for Defendants

IN THE UNITED STATES DISTRICT COURT
FOR THE DISTRICT OF FRANKLIN

Acme Resources, Inc., **Plaintiff,** **v.** **Robert Black Hawk, Stewart Marsh, Irene Martin, James Davis, Mary Gray, Katherine White Horse, Lester Stewart, and James Black Hawk,** **Defendants.**	)	**Case No. CV 103-07** **AFFIDAVIT OF ROBERT BLACK HAWK IN SUPPORT OF DEFENDANTS' MOTION FOR SUMMARY JUDGMENT, OR TO STAY OR DISMISS**

County of Custer)
) ss:
State of Franklin)

Upon first being duly sworn, Robert Black Hawk says:

1. I am a member of the Black Eagle Tribe, a federally recognized Indian tribe.
2. I farm and ranch a 3,000-acre tract of land on the Black Eagle Reservation.
3. My land abuts land owned in fee simple by Patrick Mulroney. All of Patrick Mulroney's land is within the Black Eagle Reservation. Two years ago, Mulroney granted Acme Resources, Inc., permission to use his land to explore for and develop coal bed methane.
4. The Black Eagle Tribe leased the minerals under Mulroney's land to Acme, and Acme began developing the coal bed methane.
5. Within six months of the commencement of Acme's coal bed methane operation under Mulroney's land, the water wells on my land began to run dry. My neighbors have told me that their wells are also running dry.
6. I cannot economically use my land to grow crops and feed my cattle without water, and there is no other source of water reasonably available to me.

Dated: July 23, 2007

Robert Black Hawk

____
Robert Black Hawk

Signed before me this 23rd day of July, 2007
Jane Mirren

____
Jane Mirren
Notary Public

IN THE UNITED STATES DISTRICT COURT
FOR THE DISTRICT OF FRANKLIN

Acme Resources, Inc., **Plaintiff,** v. **Robert Black Hawk, Stewart Marsh, Irene Martin, James Davis, Mary Gray, Katherine White Horse, Lester Stewart, and James Black Hawk,** **Defendants.**	)	**Case No. CV 103-07** **AFFIDAVIT OF JESSE BELLINGHAM, Ph.D., IN SUPPORT OF DEFENDANTS' MOTION FOR SUMMARY JUDGMENT, OR TO STAY OR DISMISS**

County of Custer)
) ss:
State of Franklin)

Upon first being duly sworn, Jesse Bellingham says:

1. I am a geologist and have a Ph.D. in geology from the University of Franklin.
2. I was employed by Beta Resources in its mineral exploration department for twenty years before I began my own forensic geology firm, Bellingham Geologic Consulting.
3. I was engaged by the defendants to conduct a study to determine the cause of the water wells running dry on the Black Eagle Reservation and have completed my study.
4. Coal bed methane development requires the extraction of huge quantities of water from the land. Based on my investigation of (a) the records of the water produced from the defendants' land over the last ten years, (b) geological studies of the area, and (c) my knowledge and experience with coal bed methane development, it is my professional opinion that coal bed methane development activity by Acme Resources, Inc., is causing the defendants' wells to run dry.
5. Due to the nature of the groundwater system underlying the Black Eagle Reservation, my professional opinion is that it is likely all wells on the Reservation will run dry over the next five years if Acme's coal bed methane development continues.

Dated: July 23, 2007

Jesse Billingham

____
Jesse Bellingham, Ph.D.

Signed before me this 23rd day of July, 2007
Jane Mirren
Jane Mirren
Notary Public

LIBRARY

Article IV, Black Eagle Tribal Constitution

Section 1

The land forms part of the soul of the Black Eagle Tribe. The land of the Black Eagle Reservation shall be preserved in a clean and healthful environment for the benefit of the Tribe and future generations. The Tribal Council shall have power to enforce, by appropriate legislation, the provisions of this section.

Black Eagle Tribal Code

§ 23-5 Protection of Reservation Environment

(1) Recognizing that a clean and healthful environment is vital to the economic security of the Black Eagle Tribe, no person shall pollute or otherwise degrade the environment of the Black Eagle Reservation.

(2) Any person harmed by a violation of subsection (1) may bring a civil action in Black Eagle Tribal Court for damages and other appropriate relief against the person responsible for the violation.

AO Architects v. Red Fox et al.

United States Court of Appeals (15th Cir. 2005)

The question in this appeal is whether a tribal court may exercise civil jurisdiction over a nonmember of the tribe in a wrongful death action arising from injuries on nonmember fee land.[3]1"/>

The Church of Good Hope, composed of tribal members, owns a parcel of land in fee simple on the Red River Indian Reservation in the State of Columbia. The Church built a meeting hall designed by AO Architects, a firm with offices in Columbia City, Columbia. The Church acted as its own general contractor for the project. AO was not asked to, and did not, supervise the construction. The meeting hall served the Church. However, from time to time the Red River Tribe leased the hall for general tribal meetings in which tribal leaders were elected and other tribe business was conducted.

After a very heavy snowfall in January 2003, the meeting hall's roof collapsed during a general tribal meeting. Five tribe members were killed and many more were injured. The families of those killed brought wrongful death actions in tribal court against AO Architects alleging negligence in the design of the meeting hall roof. Before responding to the complaint filed in tribal court, AO filed a complaint in federal district court claiming that the tribal court did not have jurisdiction over it or the action pending in tribal court. The district court granted a preliminary injunction to AO Architects against further proceedings in the tribal court. The tribe members appealed. For the reasons set forth below, we vacate the preliminary injunction and remand for further proceedings consistent with this opinion.

Standard of Review

Whether a tribal court may exercise civil jurisdiction over a nonmember of the tribe is a federal question. *National Farmers Union Ins. Cos. v. Crow Tribe* (U.S. 1985). We review questions of tribal court jurisdiction and exhaustion of tribal court remedies *de novo*. A district court's order regarding preliminary injunctive relief is reviewed for abuse of discretion.

Governing Law

Analysis of Indian tribal court civil jurisdiction begins with *Montana v. United States* (U.S. 1981). In *Montana*, the United States Supreme Court held that, although the tribe retained power to limit or forbid hunting or fishing by nonmembers on land still owned by or held in trust for the tribe, an Indian tribe could not regulate hunting and fishing by non-Indians on non-Indian- owned fee land within the reservation. In what is often referred to as *Montana*'s "main rule," the Court stated that, absent express authorization by federal statute or treaty, the inherent sovereign powers of an Indian tribe do not, as a general proposition, extend to the activities of nonmembers of the tribe.

The Court acknowledged, however, that "Indian tribes retain inherent sovereign power to exercise some forms of civil jurisdiction over non-Indians on their reservations, even on non-Indian fee lands." *Id.* The Court set out two instances in which tribes could exercise such sovereignty: (1) "A tribe may regulate, through taxation, licensing, or other means, the activities of nonmembers who enter consensual relationships with the tribe or its members, through commercial dealings, contracts, leases, or other arrangements"; and (2) "A tribe may also retain inherent power to exercise civil authority over the conduct of non-Indians on fee lands within its reservation when that conduct threatens or has some direct effect on the political integrity, the economic security, or the health and welfare of the tribe." *Id.*

In *Strate v. A-1 Contractors* (U.S. 1997), the Court held that a tribal court had no jurisdiction to hear a personal injury lawsuit between non-tribal members arising from a car accident that occurred on a state highway running through a reservation. The road upon which the accident took place, although on tribal land, was subject to a right-of-way held by the State of North Dakota. The Court determined that this right-of-way rendered the stretch of road "equivalent, for nonmember governance purposes, to alienated, non-Indian land." The Court declined to comment on the proper forum when an accident occurs on a tribal road within a reservation.

Strate also considered whether either of the two *Montana* exceptions conferring tribal court jurisdiction applied. In determining that the case was not closely related to any

---

3 1"/>1The terms "nonmember fee land" and "non-Indian fee lands" refer to reservation land acquired in fee simple by persons who are not members of the tribe.

consensual relationship between a nonmember and the tribe or a tribe member, the Court noted that the event at issue was a commonplace state highway accident between two non-Indians. Therefore, even though it occurred on a stretch of highway running through the reservation, it was "distinctly non-tribal in nature." *(Cf. Franklin Motor Credit Co. v. Funmaker* (15th Cir. 2005), also finding no consensual relationship under *Montana* because there was no "direct nexus" between the lease entered into by Franklin Motor Credit and the tribe and the subsequent products liability claim against Franklin Motor Credit by a tribe member injured while driving one of the leased vehicles.)

Turning to the second *Montana* exception for activities that directly affect the tribe's political integrity, economic security, or health and welfare, the Court in *Strate* also concluded that the facts did not establish tribal civil jurisdiction. The Court recognized that careless driving on public highways running through the reservation would threaten the safety of tribal members. However, if the assertion of such broad public safety interests were all that *Montana* required for jurisdiction, the exception would swallow the rule. Instead, the exception must be interpreted with its purpose in mind, which was to protect tribal self-government and control of internal relations. "Neither regulatory nor adjudicatory authority over the state highway accident at issue is needed to preserve 'the right of reservation Indians to make their own laws and be ruled by them.'" *Strate* (quoting *Montana*).

Exhaustion of Tribal Remedies

In *National Farmers*, the Supreme Court applied a tribal exhaustion doctrine requiring that a party exhaust its remedies in tribal court before seeking relief in federal court. This doctrine is based on a "policy of supporting tribal self-government and self-determination," and thus a federal court should ordinarily stay its hand "until after the tribal court has had a full opportunity to determine its own jurisdiction." *Id.* In other words, the tribal court should be given the first opportunity to address its jurisdiction and explain the basis (or lack thereof) to the parties. In such cases, the proceedings in federal court are stayed (or dismissed without prejudice) while the tribal court determines whether it has jurisdiction over the matter.

The Supreme Court has emphasized that the exhaustion doctrine is based on comity. The comity doctrine reflects a practice of deference to another court and is not a jurisdictional prerequisite. Thus, where it is clear that a tribal court lacks jurisdiction, the exhaustion doctrine gives way for it would serve no purpose other than delay. *See Strate*. In the present case, tribe members allege that there has been no exhaustion of tribal remedies because AO Architects commenced this federal action without affording the tribal court the opportunity to consider the jurisdictional issues.

Disposition

Here, the accident occurred on nonmember fee land, and AO Architects is not a member of the tribe. This would suggest under *Montana*'s main rule that the tribal court would lack jurisdiction. Moreover, on the record before us, it appears that AO Architects did not perform any services on the reservation, and that its contract was with a nonmember of the tribe, the Church of Good Hope.

Yet AO Architects must have known that it was designing a building for use of large gatherings on the reservation, and it may well have known that the facility would be used by the tribe for general meetings involving governance functions. The consequences of AO Architects' actions in designing the building would certainly be felt on the reservation. We are mindful of the two exceptions to *Montana*'s general rule against extending a tribe's civil jurisdiction to nonmembers of the tribe in the absence of express Congressional authorization or any treaty provision granting a tribe jurisdiction.[42"/>] As discussed above, those exceptions are that a tribe may have jurisdiction over (1) nonmembers who enter into consensual relationships with the tribe or its members, or (2) activities that directly affect the tribe's political integrity, economic security, or health and welfare. Either or both of the exceptions may have application here.

The record comes to us on appeal from a preliminary injunction. The proceedings were abbreviated, and we are uncertain on the record before us whether the tribal court would have jurisdiction under either of the *Montana* exceptions and whether AO Architects must first exhaust its tribal court remedies before seeking relief in federal court.

Therefore, we vacate the preliminary injunction and remand to the district court to develop a record and reach a reasoned conclusion on these issues of jurisdiction and exhaustion. We express no opinion on these questions.

42"/>2The parties concede that no federal statute or treaty bears on the question before us.

Vacated and remanded.

DRAFTERS' POINT SHEET

This performance test requires applicants, as associates in a law firm, to draft a persuasive brief in a federal court action contesting whether an Indian tribal court may exercise civil jurisdiction over a nonmember of the tribe.

Applicants' law firm represents Robert Black Hawk and seven other members of the Black Eagle Indian Tribe (collectively, "tribe members" or "Black Hawk et al."). The tribe members have filed a lawsuit in tribal court against a mining company, Acme Resources, Inc. (Acme), for damages caused by Acme's extraction of coal bed methane from under reservation land. The process used to develop the coal bed methane has depleted the water table, causing many of the tribe members' wells to begin to run dry, leaving them without water for their livestock or crops. A geologist predicts that all wells on the Reservation will go dry in five years if Acme's methane extraction continues.

In response to the Tribal Court complaint, Acme filed an answer denying liability and jurisdiction. At the same time, Acme commenced an action in federal court requesting a declaratory judgment that the Tribal Court has no jurisdiction over Acme and seeking an injunction against prosecution of the Tribal Court action. Applicants' task is to analyze the law relating to Tribal Court jurisdiction and draft the argument section of a brief in support of a motion for summary judgment in the federal action or to dismiss or stay the federal action to allow the Tribal Court to consider its jurisdiction first.

The File contains: (1) a memorandum from the supervising attorney describing the assignment; (2) a transcript of an interview with the client, Robert Black Hawk; (3) a copy of Acme's complaint filed in U.S. District Court; (4) a draft motion for summary judgment or, in the alternative, to dismiss or stay; (5) an affidavit signed by Robert Black Hawk; and (6) an affidavit by a geologist who has studied the cause of the Reservation water table depletion.

The Library contains excerpts from the Black Eagle Tribal Constitution and Tribal Code, and a Fifteenth Circuit opinion relating to tribal court jurisdiction.

The following discussion covers all the points the drafters intended to raise in the problem. Applicants need not cover them all to receive passing or even excellent grades. Grading is entirely within the discretion of the user jurisdictions.

I. Format and Overview

The supervising attorney's memo requests that applicants draft two arguments: that the court should grant summary judgment to the defendant Tribe members because there is no genuine issue of material fact that the Tribal Court has jurisdiction over Acme; and that, as an alternative basis for relief, the district court should stay or dismiss (without prejudice) Acme's action in federal court to allow the Tribal Court to consider the question of its jurisdiction.

The memorandum provides the template for applicants' argument section of the brief in support of the draft motion. Jurisdictions will have to decide how to weigh the subjective component of "persuasiveness." One guide is that an applicant's work product is not considered responsive to the instructions if it is in the form of an objective memo that takes the on-the-one-hand/on-the-other-hand approach. The argument section of the brief should be broken into its major components with well-crafted headings that summarize applicants' arguments. The arguments should weave the law and facts together into a persuasive statement of the argument, citing to the appropriate authorities and including contrary authorities that are to be addressed, explained, or distinguished. Applicants are instructed that a statement of facts is not necessary.

Applicants should argue that under the two *Montana* exceptions to the general rule against tribal court jurisdiction over nonmembers, the Black Eagle Tribal Court has jurisdiction over Acme. Acme entered into a "consensual relationship" with the Tribe through the lease agreement giving Acme the right to mine the methane gas under the Reservation. Acme's methane operations also threaten the Tribe's economic security by depleting its water supply. Thus, the district court should grant defendants' summary judgment motion. Further, applicants should argue that the Tribal Court has not yet had an opportunity to rule on the jurisdictional issue, and under the exhaustion rule of *National Farmers Union,* the district court should stay or dismiss the federal action to allow the Tribal Court to address the jurisdiction issue first.

II. The Facts

Applicants are to incorporate the relevant facts into the argument sections of their briefs, emphasizing those facts favorable to tribe members' position.

- The eight defendants, Black Hawk et al., are all members of the Black Eagle Tribe (the Tribe) and operate farms and ranches within the Black Eagle Reservation.
- Black Hawk et al. are neighbors of Patrick Mulroney, a nonmember of the Tribe who owns fee land within the Reservation.
- Acme, a mining company, is not a member of the Black Eagle Tribe.
- Mulroney granted a permit to Acme to use his land for the infrastructure necessary to explore for coal bed methane under his land. Acme pays Mulroney a royalty in exchange for access to his land.
- The Tribe owns the mineral rights to the methane under Mulroney's land. It leased to Acme the right to extract the methane in exchange for a 20 percent royalty for the Tribe.
- Acme's methane development requires pumping out huge quantities of groundwater. Within six months of the development of the coal bed methane field, the wells of Mulroney's neighbors, Black Hawk et al., began to run dry.
- Black Hawk and his co-defendants cannot survive economically without water to run their farms and ranches, and there is no other water reasonably available.
- Geologist Jesse Bellingham, Ph.D., defendants' expert, states that all Reservation wells will run dry within five years if the coal bed methane development continues.
- The Black Eagle Constitution recognizes the importance of preserving the Reservation's environment, and the Black Eagle Tribal Code authorizes a civil action by a party aggrieved by another's degradation of the environment.
- Black Hawk et al. brought an action in Black Eagle Tribal Court against Acme for damages and injunctive relief. Acme denied both liability and the Tribal Court's jurisdiction. No further proceedings have been held in tribal court.
- Acme filed an action in federal court seeking declaratory relief and an injunction against prosecution of the tribal court action.
- No federal statute or treaty addresses the Black Eagle Tribal Court's civil jurisdiction.

III. Legal Issues

Applicants must address two issues:

- Whether there is any genuine issue of material fact as to whether the Tribal Court has jurisdiction over the action pending before it and whether summary judgment should be entered in favor of Robert Black Hawk et al., and
- Whether the district court action should be dismissed or stayed because Acme failed to exhaust tribal court remedies before seeking relief in federal court.

Applicants might appropriately frame the questions in any number of ways, but should recognize the jurisdiction and exhaustion of tribal remedies issues.

IV. Argument

To formulate a good argument, applicants must digest the legal authority contained in *AO Architects v. Red Fox et al.*, the Fifteenth Circuit decision, and the cases cited therein as well as the File materials. *AO Architects* summarizes the governing United States Supreme Court precedent regarding tribal court jurisdiction. The following argument headings are suggestions only and should not be taken by the graders as the only acceptable ones.

A. Because Acme Entered Into a Consensual Relationship With the Black Eagle Tribe, and Because Its Mining Poses a Threat to the Tribe's Economic Security, There Is No Genuine Issue of Material Fact as to Whether the Tribal Court Has Jurisdiction Over Acme and, Therefore, Black Hawk Et Al. Are Entitled to Summary Judgment.

- Absent express authorization by Congress or a treaty provision authorizing jurisdiction over nonmembers, a tribal court may not exercise civil jurisdiction over a nonmember. *Montana v. United States*, 450 U.S. 544 (1981).
- There are two exceptions to this general rule: (1) the consensual relationship exception; and (2) the security of the tribe exception. If the controversy arises out of a consensual relationship between the nonmember and the tribe or its members, or if the nonmember's conduct directly threatens the political integrity, economic security, or health and welfare of the tribe, the tribal court may exercise jurisdiction over the nonmember. *Id.*

Applicants should argue that, although Acme is not a member of the Tribe and is engaged in activities on the surface of land held in fee simple by another nonmember (Mulroney), the controversy arises out of a consensual relationship (the lease agreement) and also threatens the economic security of the tribe (no water to raise crops or livestock). Applicants should use the facts in the File to argue that both *Montana* exceptions apply, and should distinguish *Strate* and *Funmaker*, cases cited in *AO Architects* in which the court declined to find a consensual relationship or tribal security exception, and thus found that the tribal court had no jurisdiction over nonmembers.

The Acme/Tribe Lease Constitutes a Consensual Relationship and Therefore the Tribal Court Has Jurisdiction Under the First *Montana* Exception.

- The first *Montana* exception confers civil jurisdiction over a nonmember where the nonmember has a consensual relationship with the tribe through commercial dealings. *AO Architects,* citing *Montana*.
- The Tribe/Acme lease satisfies this commercial dealing requirement: it is a direct business relationship between the Tribe and Acme. It gives Acme a sustained (as opposed to fleeting) presence within the Reservation, and it has significant (as opposed to minimal) financial and environmental implications for Tribe members and the Tribe as a whole.

- The Acme/Tribe relationship is thus distinguishable from a "commonplace" reservation highway accident between two nonmembers that the *Strate* court rejected as an insufficient basis for conferring tribal jurisdiction.

- In *Franklin Motor Credit Co. v. Funmaker* (cited in *AO Architects*), the 15th Circuit Court of Appeals noted that tribal court jurisdiction will not be conferred under the consensual relationship exception unless there is a "direct nexus" between the underlying business relationship and the subject of the lawsuit against the nonmember.

    - Thus, in *Funmaker*, the court rejected tribal court jurisdiction over a car dealership's financing company in a products liability suit brought by a tribe member who was injured while driving a vehicle leased by the tribe and financed by the finance company.

- Here, by contrast, there is a "direct nexus" between Acme and the Tribe.

    - The Tribe and Acme entered into a lease agreement giving Acme the right to extract methane from mineral reserves belonging to the Tribe and located within the Reservation in exchange for a 20 percent royalty payment to the Tribe on all methane produced.

    - The subject of the Tribe members' lawsuit is the harm allegedly caused by Acme's methane mining.

- Applicants might anticipate that Acme will attempt to argue that the consensual relationship at issue, Acme's lease of the mineral rights, is a consensual relationship with the Tribe, and not with one Black Hawk et al., the parties suing Acme.

- However, the applicable case law does not suggest that there must be a direct match between the parties involved in the consensual relationship and the parties to the suit in tribal court. The key is that there be a consensual relationship with the tribe or its members and that there be a connection between the facts giving rise to the litigation in tribal court and that relationship. *See Funmaker.*

Acme's Mining Activities Threaten the Tribe's Economic Security by Depleting the Reservation Water Supply, Thereby Satisfying the Second *Montana* Exception.

The second *Montana* exception permits a tribal court to exercise civil jurisdiction over a nonmember of the tribe where the nonmember's conduct "on fee lands within [the tribe's] reservation . . . threatens or has some direct effect on the political integrity, the economic security, or the health and welfare of the tribe." *AO Architects* (quoting *Montana*). It is important that applicants recognize that a conclusory reference to the negative effect of Acme's activities on the Tribe is not sufficient. Rather, applicants are expected to identify the particular interest(s) of the Tribe (e.g., its economic security) that are at risk from Acme's extraction of coal bed methane.

- Black Hawk et al. have identified a real and substantial risk to the Tribe's economic security: if Acme's mining activities continue, it is likely that within five years all the wells on the Reservation will run dry. (*See* Bellingham Aff.)

- The fact that the wells of eight Tribe members with ranches and farms abutting Patrick Mulroney's land (the site of Acme's methane extraction) began running dry within six months of the start of Acme's mining operations shows the immediate impact that the mining has had and the potential magnitude of the risk. (*See* Black Hawk Aff.)

- The Black Eagle Tribal Constitution, article IV, § 1, stresses the importance of the environment to the Tribe: "The land of the Black Eagle Tribal Reservation shall be preserved in a clean and healthful environment for the benefit of the Tribe and future generations."
- The Tribal Code reiterates this concern for the environment and creates a cause of action in Tribal Court for any person harmed by those who "pollute or otherwise degrade the environment of the Black Eagle Reservation." Tribal Code § 23-5.
- Obviously, depleting the water table in order to extract coal bed methane degrades the environment of the Reservation.
- Moreover, without a stable and plentiful water supply, Tribe members will be unable to raise crops or livestock, in the absence of securing an alternate water supply that is economical and practical. Thus, the lack of water will directly threaten the Tribe's economic security.
- The specific risk here (which threatens the entire Tribe and is directly related to Acme's conduct) stands in sharp contrast to the interest in preventing careless driving on a reservation's public highways at issue in *Strate*, where the Supreme Court refused to find jurisdiction, reasoning that such a broad public safety interest, such as preventing auto accidents, would swallow the rule of *Montana*.
- Applicants may also argue that the Tribe's health and safety and welfare are threatened by Acme's depletion of the water table through its methane mining.
    - While Black Hawk's affidavit and interview focus on the threat to the Tribe's economic security (inability to support crops and livestock), applicants could reasonably argue that tribal health and safety may also eventually be at risk, especially given Bellingham's prediction that *all* wells will run dry in five years. In short, the Tribe could end up without adequate water for basic health and sanitation as a result of Acme's mining.
- Astute applicants might note that Acme could argue that even if the Tribe eventually has to find another source of water, for the term of Acme's lease, the Tribe will receive a royalty of 20 percent of all methane production. Presumably, that is a significant amount (in his interview notes, Black Hawk states that ". . . the promises of easy money carried the day").
- Applicants should contend that the royalty income from Acme cannot offset the permanent damage to the Reservation and the Tribe's long-term economic security if there is no water available on the Reservation.
- The fact that Acme's mining operation is based on land owned in fee simple by Patrick Mulroney, a nonmember of the Tribe, does not deprive the Tribal Court of jurisdiction.
- Acme is extracting coal bed methane that belongs to the Tribe and the aquifer being depleted by Acme's activities serves all the wells on the Reservation.
- The probability, as stated in the Bellingham Affidavit, that *all* the wells on the Reservation will run dry within five years, counters the argument that the economic security of the entire Black Eagle Tribe (as opposed to only the eight tribe members involved in the current litigation) is not at stake.
- Applicants could argue that the fact that the Tribal Council granted Acme a mining concession does not affect defendants' rights, as the Tribal Constitution and Tribal Code addresses threats to the Reservation's environment and provides an independent basis for Tribe members' standing to bring suit.

- In sum, contrary to what Acme alleges in its complaint, it is clear that the Tribal Court has jurisdiction because both exceptions to *Montana*'s main rule apply. Therefore, the court should grant summary judgment to Black Hawk et al.

B. The Tribal Exhaustion Doctrine of *National Farmers Union* Requires the District Court to Dismiss or Stay Acme's Federal Action on the Grounds That the Tribal Court Has Not Been Afforded an Opportunity to Consider Its Own Jurisdiction.

Applicants' argument discussing the exhaustion rule should mention the following points:

- *National Farmers Union Ins. Cos.* v. *Crow Tribe*, 471 U.S. 845 (1985), announced a tribal exhaustion requirement: a tribal court should ordinarily first be given an opportunity to consider its jurisdiction before a party may seek relief in federal court. *See AO Architects*.
- The exhaustion rule is a prudential rule and is to be applied as a matter of comity (deference) unless it is clear that the tribal court lacks jurisdiction over the action involving the nonmember.
- Here, the Black Eagle Tribal Court has not had an opportunity to consider and rule on whether it has jurisdiction over Acme.
    - Acme has answered the complaint in Tribal Court, but no further proceedings have been held there.
- Applicants should argue that the Black Eagle Tribal Court has jurisdiction over the action before it because both *Montana* exceptions apply, and therefore Black Hawk et al. are entitled to summary judgment on that issue. In addition, applicants should state that if the court determines that it is unclear whether the Tribal Court has jurisdiction, the court should, consistent with the principle of comity discussed in *AO Architects* and *National Farmers Union*, dismiss or at least stay the action to give the Tribal Court an opportunity to consider the question.
-
- Acme Resources, Inc. v. Black Hawk et al Sample Answer

Black Eagle Tribal Court has jurisdiction over the present action because it involves a consensual, commercial relationship and directly affects the health, welfare, economic security, and political integrity of the tribe. Although the sovereign powers of an Indian tribal court generally do not govern members of a tribe, Montana, this rule is subject to two important exceptions, both of which permit the Black Eagle Tribal Court to exercise jurisdiction in this case. The Plaintiff, Acme Resources Inc. ("Acme") has entered into a consensual relationship with the tribe concerning the extraction of mineral rights on reservation land. This agreement has had a dire effect on the Tribe's economic security and will continue to impair health, welfare and political welfare of the tribe.

Acme's Lease of Mineral Rights Constitutes a Consensual, Commercial Relationship with Members of Black Hawk Tribe and Therefore Subjects Acme to the Tribal Court's Jurisdiction.

Indian courts have the power to exercise civil jurisdiction over non-members, on reservation land, even when the land is owned by a non-member, where there is a "consensual relationship with the tribe or its members through commercial dealings…"

Montana. There must be a direct nexus between the relationship and the cause of action. See Funmaker.

The court held in Strate that an account between non-members on non-member tribal land was not subject to a tribal courts' jurisdiction. It also held that a lease between a member and non-member did not provide the tribal court with jurisdiction over a products liability action involving the subject matter of the lease. Funmaker. In Red Fox, the Fifteenth Circuit reversed summary judgment and held that there may have been a sufficient consensual relationship to confer jurisdiction where non-member architects contracted with a non-member organization to design a church on tribal land owned by non-members simply because the architects could have foreseen the building would be used by members. . .the design would be "felt on the reservation." Red Fox.

In the case at bar, although the surface rights to the land at issue are owned by a non-member, the Tribe owns the mineral rights to the land. The Tribe entered into a lease with Acme to extract minerals using a process that is known to affect the availability of water (Black Hawk aff, Bellingham aff). The Tribe has a greater ownership claim to the land than the tribes did in Strate, Funmaker, or Red Fox, where the entire land was owned by non-members. In addition, there is a commercial lease between Acme and the Tribe, which did not exist between any of the tribal court litigants and the respective tribes in Strate, Funmmaker, or Red Fox. Furthermore, Fifteenth Circuit had held that a consensual relationship may exist where the effect on the tribe is foreseeable. Red Fox In this case, the depletion of water is a requirement for extracting coal bed methane. (Bellingham off.) The effect on the tribe of the water running out, therefore, is even more foreseeable than the possibility of a design defect in an architect's plans causing personal injury. Finally, the tribal court defendant in Red Fox never came on the land nor supervised the actual building of the church. In this case Acme came on the land and physically extracted minerals. This Court should therefore find that the consensual, commercial relationship between Acme and Black Hawk Tribe is sufficient to subject Acme to jurisdiction regarding the mineral extraction.

The extraction has a direct effect on the political integrity, economic security, health and welfare of the tribe because if affects their ability to farm, the preservation of the land for future generations, their access to water, and their ability to comply with their Tribal Constitution.

A tribe may exercise jurisdiction over the conduct of non-members on reservation land owned by non-members where the conduct has a direct effect on the economic security, political integrity, health or welfare of the tribe. Montana. There must be more than broad public safety concerns like traffic accidents. Strate. The exercise of jurisdiction must further the purpose of protecting tribal self-governance and control of internal regulations. Montana. In this case, the conduct affects the ability of members to make a living by raising crops and producing livestock. An expert estimated that all wells will go dry in 5 years, which would affect health and welfare because land without water is not sufficient for habitation. It affects political integrity because the tribe's constitution requires preservation of the land for future generations. Land is the "soul" of the tribe, and it will be basically useless after Acme is done with it. This is much more of a direct effect than that in Strate where public safety on the government owned highway was at issue.

This court should stay jurisdiction because the tribal court has not ruled in its jurisdiction.

In National Farmers, the Court said that motions of stay require exhaustion of remedies in tribal court before a federal court will act. The rule is disregarded only when the tribal court clearly lacks jurisdiction. As explained above, the tribal court probably does not have jurisdiction. But regardless of this Court's opinion on that issue, it should dismiss this action without prejudice or at least stay the proceedings until the Black Hawk Tribal Court has had an opportunity to rule on this issue.

FILE

NATIONAL CONFERENCE OF BAR EXAMINERS

Palkovich, Van Every Dooley
Attorneys at Law
3034 Sutton Avenue
Banford, Franklin 33518

To: Applicant
From: Lyle Palkovich
Re: Mistover Acres LLC
Date: July 24, 2007

We have been retained by Petra Flynn, one of three members of Mistover Acres LLC ("Mistover"), a Franklin limited liability company, to review a claim made against Mistover by Genesee Trout, Inc., for damage to its trout farm caused by the aerial crop dusting of a pesticide, MU-83, on Mistover's fields. Mistover is a well-respected grower and seller of apples, salad greens, and herbs.

We are representing Petra Flynn in her individual capacity. Mistover has its own legal counsel. Ms. Flynn has come to us because she is concerned about her potential personal liability for the harm claimed by the trout farm. She believes that Mistover's organization completely shields her from personal liability for Mistover's business-related activities, but she is understandably troubled by the demand letter from Genesee Trout's counsel. Another concern I have is whether the aerial crop dusting of MU-83 constituted an ultrahazardous activity, thereby raising the possibility of strict liability. The next meeting with Ms. Flynn on this matter is scheduled for July 31, 2007.

Please prepare an objective memorandum analyzing the following questions under Franklin law:

1) Can Ms. Flynn be held personally liable for the damage done by the aerial crop dusting?
2) Did the aerial crop dusting of MU-83 constitute an ultrahazardous activity?

You need not prepare a separate statement of facts, but in each part of the memorandum you should incorporate the relevant facts, analyze the applicable legal authorities, and explain how the facts and law affect your analysis. A carefully crafted subject heading should precede each discussion section. For the purpose of your analysis, assume that the aerial crop dusting caused the damage to the trout farm.

Client Interview Notes: Petra Flynn

July 17, 2007

Petra Flynn is one of three members of Mistover Acres LLC. The other two members are Petra's brother, Gilbert Flynn, and their cousin, Chip Kendall. They formed Mistover after Petra and Gil inherited two adjoining parcels of land in Sutton Township. Mistover grows apples, herbs, and unusual varieties of lettuce that have become very popular in gourmet restaurants. Under the terms of the Mistover Acres LLC Operating Agreement, Petra and Gil lease their land, about 60 acres, to the business. Petra and Gil do some work for Mistover, but as Chip has the expertise in agriculture, most of the decisions regarding planting are left to him. Petra supervises the marketing and sale of Mistover's produce.

Petra has come to the firm for advice regarding her potential personal liability for claims made by Genesee Trout, Inc., in a demand letter its attorneys sent to Mistover's office. She is concerned about Mistover being liable for such a large claim, as it has yet to turn a profit and Chip invested all the money he had in Mistover when they organized it five years ago. According to Petra, Chip "is essentially judgment proof," and Gil's financial situation has always been precarious. She fears that, because she has substantial assets of her own, any lawsuit by Genesee Trout will try to target her as a "deep-pocket" defendant.

Sutton Township is an area of rolling hills that has long been agricultural. In the 1990s, farmers experienced economic difficulties, but in recent years, small-scale, specialized producers like Mistover have been reviving the local economy. A number of these producers are devoted to organic agricultural practices. For example, across the road from Mistover is Haakon Farms, where the owner sells goat cheese made with the milk from her own herd. And, as noted in the demand letter, Genesee Trout's trout farm lies just east of Mistover.

According to Petra, the three members began Mistover to put into practice their belief that consumers deserved another option besides the bland fruits and vegetables grown by factory farms that dominate the selections in most supermarkets. Nonetheless, neither she nor Gil was particularly thrilled when Chip suggested growing new lettuce varieties. Mistover's heirloom apple varieties were selling well and the lettuce varieties could not be successfully raised in amounts needed for sale without the use of some chemical fertilizers and pesticides, which they generally try to avoid. Chip, however, persuaded them that these rare lettuces would soon be "must have" salad greens in the best restaurants, and that the price Mistover could charge would soon generate enough income to allow it to expand into other vegetable crops. Chip also argued that, as one of the only operations offering a unique and locally grown lettuce variety, Mistover would earn a reputation for being an innovator in the gourmet produce market.

Mistover first grew lettuce two years ago and the crop did well. Last year, however, Chip discovered leaf slugs on the plants. If nothing had been done about the leaf slugs, they could have destroyed one-third of the crop. Chip proposed using a pesticide, but Petra expressed concerns about the marketing consequences, as they had always emphasized that Mistover's produce was locally grown with minimal chemicals. They researched pesticides together and ultimately selected MU-83, a new pesticide. Petra then ordered it last year through an agricultural supplier; MU-83 is not available to the general public. Chip walked through the fields with some of Mistover's seasonal help and sprayed the lettuce crop with MU-83. It was effective, but the labor costs of the pesticide application were high.

When Chip found the leaf slugs again this season, he determined that the slugs were more numerous than last year and that hand spraying would involve even higher labor costs. Before joining Mistover, when he lived in Columbia, Chip had worked one growing season using his small airplane to dust large corn and wheat fields with pesticides and herbicides. He and Petra decided to use aerial crop dusting, and Petra ordered more MU-83. The Franklin Environmental Code requires posting for aerial crop dusting, and Petra ensured that the proper notice was posted on the Sutton Township website, at the Town Hall, and at three other public places.

Chip sprayed the fields with MU-83 on March 28, 2007. Petra was at Mistover that afternoon and watched Chip take off in his airplane, circle the farm buildings, and then fly over the plants at a height of about 20 feet to apply the MU-83. She did not observe the yellow cloud described in the letter from Genesee Trout's attorneys, but does recall that there was a light breeze blowing from the west, which possibly could have carried MU-83 in the direction of the trout ponds. Two days later she and Chip walked through the fields and verified that the MU-83 had killed any visible leaf slugs.

The lettuce, Mistover's best crop yet, was picked and sold at a prime price. Until the letter from Genesee Trout's attorneys arrived, none of the LLC members had heard any complaints about the MU-83 aerial crop dusting or their farming activities in general. Petra will come in next week to discuss the situation.2

FRENCH ISENBERG, LLP
ATTORNEYS AT LAW
222 SHEFFIELD AVE
CENTRALIA, FRANKLIN 33530

JULY 17, 2007

MS. PETRA FLYNN
MISTOVER ACRES LLC
P.O. BOX 572
DERBY, FRANKLIN 38440

RE: GENESEE TROUT, INC.

DEAR MS. FLYNN:

WE REPRESENT GENESEE TROUT, INC., THE OWNER OF THE TROUT FARM THAT ABUTS MISTOVER ACRES ON ITS EASTERN EDGE. ON MARCH 28, 2007, OUR CLIENT'S EMPLOYEES OBSERVED A CROP-DUSTING AIRPLANE FLYING OVER THE FIELDS OF MISTOVER ACRES, SPRAYING A YELLOW-COLORED SUBSTANCE. THEY THEN OBSERVED A YELLOW CLOUD DRIFTING OVER GENESEE TROUT'S FISH PONDS. IN THE MONTHS SINCE THAT DATE, A HIGHER-THAN-EXPECTED PERCENTAGE OF OUR CLIENT'S TROUT STOCK HAS DIED, AND THE NUMBER OF SUCCESSFUL EGG HATCHINGS HAS SUBSTANTIALLY DECLINED. THE WATER IN THE FISH PONDS HAS BEEN TESTED AND HAS BEEN FOUND TO CONTAIN SIGNIFICANT LEVELS OF THE PESTICIDE MU-83. THE COST TO CLEAN THE PONDS AND RESTOCK THE TROUT WILL EXCEED $1 MILLION. GENESEE TROUT IS ALSO CONCERNED THAT MU-83 WILL LEECH INTO THE LOCAL WATER SUPPLY.

THE PRESENCE OF MU-83 IN THE GENESEE TROUT FISH PONDS, THE RESULTING DECLINE IN THE TROUT STOCK AND EGG HATCHINGS, AND THE POTENTIAL DAMAGE TO THE WATER SUPPLY WERE CAUSED BY MISTOVER ACRES LLC'S AERIAL CROP DUSTING ON MARCH 28, 2007.

GENESEE TROUT, INC., IS WILLING TO SETTLE ITS CLAIMS AGAINST MISTOVER ACRES LLC. HOWEVER, IF A SETTLEMENT CANNOT BE REACHED, OUR CLIENT HAS INSTRUCTED US TO PURSUE LEGAL ACTION AGAINST MISTOVER ACRES LLC AND ITS MEMBERS. IF YOU ARE WILLING TO DISCUSS SETTLEMENT, PLEASE RESPOND TO THIS LETTER WITHIN TWO WEEKS OF ITS RECEIPT.

SINCERELY,

WALTER FRENCH
WALTER FRENCH

OPERATING AGREEMENT OF MISTOVER ACRES LLC

This OPERATING AGREEMENT is entered into by Petra Flynn, Gilbert Flynn, and Chip Kendall for the purpose of organizing a limited liability company pursuant to the Franklin Limited Liability Company Act, § 601 *et seq*.

1. **Name and Purpose**: The limited liability company shall be known as MISTOVER ACRES LLC (hereinafter "the LLC"). Its purpose is to grow and market apples and other produce for sale at farmers' markets and to restaurants and other commercial establishments.

2. **Members**: The members of the LLC are Petra Flynn, Gilbert Flynn, and Chip Kendall.

3. **Capital Contributions:** The capital contributions of the respective members shall be as follows:
   a. Chip Kendall: $50,000 (fifty thousand dollars).
   b. Petra Flynn: $10,000 (ten thousand dollars).
   c. Gilbert Flynn: $10,000 (ten thousand dollars).

4. **Lease of Agricultural Land**: On or before the date of filing of the Articles of Organization, leases will be entered into between the LLC and Petra Flynn, and the LLC and Gilbert Flynn, for the two adjoining 30-acre parcels on Schmidt Road, Derby, Franklin, identified as Tracts 37 and 38 of Sutton Township Certified Survey 2713. The LLC shall have the exclusive right to lease these parcels for as long as the LLC continues in existence or until such time as the members agree to terminate the leases.

5. **Management**: With respect to acquisition of capital assets by the LLC, or the addition of new members or employees of the LLC, the undersigned members shall in all cases act as a group, with a majority vote or consent of the members required to take action. Day-to-day decisions regarding planting and harvesting are delegated to Chip Kendall until the members agree otherwise. The marketing and sale of the LLC's produce shall be supervised by Petra Flynn.

6. **Sharing in Distributions and Profits**: For the first five (5) years of the LLC's existence, the profits, if any, will be reinvested into the LLC's operations. If any profit is realized in subsequent years, 50 percent (50%) will be reinvested into the LLC, and the remainder will be distributed in equal shares to the members.

7. **Accounting:** Members shall receive annual financial reports containing the LLC's balance sheet and a statement showing the net capital appreciation or depreciation.

8. **Applicable Law**: All questions concerning the construction, validity and interpretation of this agreement and the performance of the obligations imposed by this agreement shall be governed by the laws of the State of Franklin.

Dated: **February 15, 2002**

Petra Flynn

____

Petra Flynn

Gilbert Flynn

____

Gilbert Flynn

Chip Kendall

____

Chip Kendall

USER'S GUIDE FOR MU-83 APPLICATION

Thank you for selecting an AgriShield, Inc., product to protect your crops! MU-83 is an effective pesticide for use on all crops, including those intended for human consumption. Studies by the University of Franklin Agricultural College have demonstrated that it is 98% successful in completely eradicating pests such as rootworm, boll weevils, and leaf slugs, when applied according to directions. It is suitable for application by hand, tractor-pulled spraying rig, or aerial dusting by airplane. Aerial dusting should occur at a distance no higher than 30 feet from the intended target area.

* * * *

As with all pesticides, persons applying MU-83 should use caution and be aware that pesticide "drift" (the movement of pesticide droplets or particles in the air from the targeted field to non-target areas) is always a risk of pesticide application. Drift and runoff may be toxic to aquatic organisms in neighboring areas. Drift will occur with every application. The amount of drift is subject to various controllable and uncontrollable factors, such as time of application, concentration, wind gusts, weather changes, and the physical characteristics of pesticide droplets or aerosols. Apply this product only in accordance with application instructions found on the label.

WARNING: Improper use or application of MU-83 may cause serious injury or death.

SUTTON TOWNSHIP

PUBLIC NOTICE

In accordance with the Franklin Environmental Code, § 22(1), Mistover Acres LLC hereby gives public notice that it will conduct aerial crop dusting of the following pesticide on the date indicated:

Pesticide: MU-83

The pesticide application will occur on March 28, 2007 on the following described property in Sutton Township:

The two adjoining 30-acre parcels identified as Tracts 37 and 38 of Sutton Township Certified Survey 2713, according to the records of the Clerk and Recorder of Washington County, Franklin, and also known as Mistover Acres LLC, 200 W. Schmidt Rd.

For further information, contact:

Petra Flynn
200 W. Schmidt Road
Derby, Franklin 33510
(920) 555-1085

Dated this 25th day of March, 2007

Mistover Acres LLC

by Petra Flynn
Petra Flynn, its authorized representative

LIBRARY

§ 601 General Purposes.

(1) A limited liability company may be organized under this Act for any lawful purpose....

(2) Unless otherwise provided in an operating agreement, a limited liability company organized and existing under this Act has the same powers as an individual to do all things necessary and convenient to carry out its business, including but not limited to all of the following:

(a) Sue and be sued, complain and defend in its own name.

(b) Purchase, take, receive, lease, or otherwise acquire and own, hold, improve, use, and otherwise deal in or with real or personal property or any legal or equitable interest in real or personal property, wherever situated.

(c) Sell, convey, mortgage, lease, and otherwise dispose of all or any part of its property....

(d) Make contracts and guarantees; incur liabilities....

* * * *

(g) Elect or appoint managers, agents, and employees of the limited liability company, define their duties, and fix their compensation.

* * * *

§ 605 Liability of members.

(1) The debts, obligations, and liabilities of a limited liability company, whether arising in contract, tort, or otherwise, shall be solely the debts, obligations, and liabilities of the limited liability company.

(2) Except as otherwise provided in this Act or by written agreement of a member, a member of a limited liability company is not personally liable solely by reason of being a member of the limited liability company for any debt, obligation, or liability of the limited liability company, whether that liability or obligation arises in contract, tort, or otherwise, or for the acts or omissions of any other member, agent, or employee of the limited liability company.

(3) Nothing in this section shall be construed to affect the liability of a member of a limited liability company to third parties for the member's participation in tortious conduct.

(4) A member of a limited liability company is not a proper party to a proceeding by or against a limited liability company solely by reason of being a member of the limited liability company, except where the object of the proceeding is to enforce a member's right against or liability to the limited liability company or as otherwise provided in an operating agreement.

Hodas v. Ice LLC

Franklin Court of Appeal (2004)

This is an action to recover damages for injuries sustained in a motor vehicle accident. The complaint alleged that on March 18, 2000, between 12:00 a.m. and 1:45 a.m., Tony Veit and Todd Hodas were patrons of the Firefly Bar in Groton, Franklin. The Firefly Bar is owned by Ice LLC. Defendants Duncan O'Malley, Joe Kaufman, and Victor Casellano are the only members of Ice LLC.

While at the Firefly Bar, Veit consumed large quantities of alcohol. Despite his being obviously intoxicated, the defendants and/or their employees continued to serve him. Veit and Hodas, both grossly intoxicated, left the Firefly in Veit's car. While speeding, Veit lost control of the vehicle and hit a tree. Veit died at the scene and Hodas was seriously injured.

Hodas claims that the defendants were negligent and reckless in their conduct by selling any alcohol to an obviously intoxicated person. O'Malley, Kaufman, and Casellano argue that they were entitled to summary judgment because liability cannot attach solely by virtue of the fact that they were members of Ice LLC, the entity that owned the bar. The trial court denied the summary judgment motion. We granted O'Malley, Kaufman, and Casellano leave to bring this interlocutory appeal.

DISCUSSION

It is undisputed that Ice LLC is a Franklin limited liability company organized under the Franklin Limited Liability Company Act (FLLCA), § 601 *et seq*. The original property lease agreement identifies Ice LLC as Lessee, acting through its members O'Malley and Kaufman. A liquor license application for the bar states that Casellano invested $80,000 in Ice LLC to be used for the purpose of renovating the building in Groton that houses the Firefly Bar. The Ice LLC operating agreement names the three as the sole members of the LLC.

A limited liability company, or "LLC," is a business entity that combines the attributes of a partnership for federal income tax purposes with the limited liability protections that a corporation provides to shareholders. Like a partnership, an LLC allows the owners, called members, to participate in the management of the business. LLCs are typically governed by operating agreements. The provisions pertaining to the liability of LLC members are found in § 605 of the FLLCA.

The FLLCA generally provides that a member of an LLC is not personally liable for acts or debts of the company solely by reason of being a member. Nevertheless, a member may be personally liable if the person participates in tortious conduct.

O'Malley and Kaufman contend that tort liability of an LLC member is limited to conduct committed *outside* the member role. We reject this approach as contravening the corporate and agency principles upon which the liability of LLC members is based. Nor does the language of the FLLCA support such a restriction. We recognize, however, that the "participation in tortious conduct" standard does not impose tort liability on a member for performing what is merely a general administrative duty. *See Lee v. Bayrd* (Franklin Ct. App. 1985) (no tort liability where corporate officer not shown to have authorized, directed, or participated in tortious act). There must be some participation; liability of individuals is derived from individual activities. This standard thus comports with the principle that members are not liable based only on their status.

O'Malley, Kaufman, and Casellano argue that this view of limited liability defeats the language of § 605(2) that bars tort liability predicated solely by reason of an individual's status as a member of the LLC. We disagree. The phrase "solely by reason of" refers to liability based upon membership or management *status*. It does not immunize a member's *conduct*. It is not inconsistent to protect a member from vicarious liability (e.g., for the tortious acts of another LLC member or employee), while imposing liability when the member participates in a tort. In short, liability of LLC members is limited, but not to the extent claimed by O'Malley, Kaufman, and Casellano.

O'Malley and Kaufman

The complaint alleges that O'Malley and Kaufman failed to properly supervise and train their personnel and failed to monitor their patrons to ensure safety.

O'Malley and Kaufman both admitted at their depositions that they were at the bar on March 17, 2000, into the morning hours of the 18th, and that the place was very busy. Kaufman stated that he usually deals with the customers and personnel. O'Malley testified that on that night, he was "all over the place, making sure everyone was doing what they were supposed to, greeting customers and doing other 'PR' work." Neither defendant could affirm or deny whether he had personally served alcohol to Veit.

O'Malley and Kaufman would not be liable solely because of their status as members of Ice LLC. But the FLLCA does not affect the liability of an LLC member who participates in tortious conduct, whether or not that conduct is on behalf of the LLC. *See* § 605(3). Given the participation of O'Malley and Kaufman in the operations of the business, there are material issues of fact which precluded the granting of summary judgment. *See Goff v. PureMilk LLC* (Franklin Ct. App. 1997) (summary judgment inappropriate where agreement required LLC's member/manager to provide human resources and consulting services to LLC and extent of member's/manager's participation in tortious conduct was unknown). A trial is necessary to develop the facts relating to allegations of O'Malley and Kaufman's participation in the alleged torts. For this reason, the court affirms the denial of summary judgment as to O'Malley and Kaufman.

Casellano

There was no evidence before the trial court that Casellano was at the Firefly Bar on March 17, 2000, or that he participated in the business operations at any point in time relevant to the allegations in the complaint. To support his claim for Casellano's liability, Hodas referred to the liquor license application that was signed and filed by Casellano, a trade name certificate recorded in the Groton Land Records listing Casellano as one of the persons involved in the business known as the Firefly Bar, and the operating agreement designating Casellano as a member of the LLC.

These documents clearly demonstrate that Casellano was a member of Ice LLC in March 2000. Nothing else has been presented as a basis for Casellano's liability. Hodas could not overcome the fact that his claim for liability is based solely upon Casellano's status as a member of the LLC. Section 605(2) of the FLLCA precludes liability based on membership status alone. Further, a member is not liable for the acts or omissions of any other member of the limited liability company. For this reason, the court reverses the denial of summary judgment as to Casellano.

Affirmed in part, reversed in part, and remanded for further proceedings.

Thurman v. Ellis

Franklin Court of Appeal (2003)

Defendant Gwen Ellis appeals from a judgment entered on a jury verdict awarding damages to plaintiff Adele Thurman in the amount of $50,000. The issue before us is whether the trial court erred in instructing the jury that breeders of pit bull dogs are strictly liable for any harm caused by their animals on the basis that raising pit bulls is an ultrahazardous activity.

Ellis has bred pit bulls for several years. Thurman was injured when, on a visit to Ellis's home, the mother of the current litter attacked her while she was holding a puppy. Thurman suffered deep wounds to her arm and hand before Ellis could restrain the dog. Although Thurman alleged three other counts in her complaint, only the claim for strict liability based on an ultrahazardous activity is before us on appeal.

Those who engage in ultrahazardous activities are, as a general rule, subject to strict liability for the harm caused to the innocent as a result of the activity. When determining whether an activity is ultrahazardous, we apply § 520 of the Restatement (Second) of Torts, which requires analysis of six factors: (1) existence of a high degree of risk of some harm to the person, land, or chattels of others; (2) likelihood that the resulting harm will be great; (3) inability to eliminate the risk by the exercise of reasonable care; (4) extent to which the activity is not a matter of common usage; (5) inappropriateness of the activity to the place where it is carried on; and (6) extent to which the activity's value to the community is outweighed by its dangerous attributes. *Sisson v. City of Bremerton* (Franklin Sup. Ct. 1975). This is a totality of the circumstances test. No one factor is determinative.

In Franklin, assessment of the § 520 factors has resulted in the imposition of strict liability for firework displays; rock blasting where injury occurred to property on an adjacent lot; emissions from chemical separation as part of weapons-grade plutonium production; and a common carrier's transportation of large quantities of gasoline. Under the same analysis of the factors in § 520, Franklin courts have held that the following activities are *not* ultrahazardous: household use of water, electricity, or gas; operation of oil and gas wells in rural areas; and ground damage caused by the crash landing of aircraft.

Sisson provides a detailed example of the court's reasoning when applying the § 520 factors. There, it was alleged that the city's demolition project, which caused the collapse of the retaining walls that protected the plaintiffs' homes, constituted an ultrahazardous activity rendering the city strictly liable for the damage. The court emphasized that the inability to eliminate the risk by the exercise of reasonable care would generally carry more weight than the other factors, but that this factor alone was not dispositive of whether an activity is ultrahazardous. Moreover, while the availability and relative costs, economic and otherwise, of alternative methods for conducting the activity are basic to the inquiry, the court stressed that an activity that was ultrahazardous in one context is not necessarily ultrahazardous for all occasions. Ultimately, the court held that the record was inadequate to determine whether the demolition project was ultrahazardous.

Fredricks v. Centralia Fire Dept. (Franklin Ct. App. 1999) explained that the value of an activity to the community will at times negate factors that would otherwise favor imposing strict liability. In *Fredricks*, it was claimed that the fire department had conducted an ultrahazardous activity in putting out a fire and that water used to put out the fire had spread toxic waste to adjoining properties, requiring costly cleanup. The court reasoned that, while firefighting presented a high degree of risk, the value to the community far outweighed the inherent dangers of the activity. In addition, referring to the fifth factor, the court noted that there was no reasonable basis for the plaintiff's claim, as it "defied logic to argue that it is inappropriate to carry out firefighting at the site of a fire." *Id.*

Here, Ellis disputes the evidence of a high degree of risk of harm. She testified that, until the attack on Thurman, none of her dogs had behaved violently. Her expert, a nationally known breeder, opined that pit bulls are good-tempered, loyal animals, unless specifically trained to be aggressive. Thurman, however, presented the opinions of a veterinarian and an authority on pit bulls to show that years of breeding had created an aggressive breed that was easily provoked, especially if an animal thought its young were in danger.

While the precise degree of risk posed by pit bulls is uncertain, it is undisputed that because of the pit bull's powerful jaw structure, it is extremely difficult to open the dog's mouth once it bites someone or something. This practically ensures that anyone bitten by a pit bull will sustain a severe injury. In addition, the fact that Ellis was breeding pit bulls in her home in a residential neighborhood, in close proximity to young children, as opposed to a less populated area or at least a location with sufficient space for an outdoor dog kennel, leads us to conclude that the activity was being conducted in an inappropriate place. Ellis correctly points out that no city ordinance banned breeding dogs such as pit bulls within city limits. However, the fact that an activity is legal is not a defense to a claim that the activity is ultrahazardous. The first, second, and fifth factors support holding Ellis strictly liable for the harm caused by her dogs.

Turning to the fourth factor, we recognize that dog breeding in general is a common activity. While not as numerous as many breeds, pit bulls are not so rare that raising them should be considered uncommon. Nevertheless, we conclude that, with this breed, exercise of reasonable care is unlikely to eliminate the risk of severe injury, as pit bulls that have never bitten might, without warning, attack an individual perceived to be a threat and inflict grave injury. There was testimony from both parties' experts that preventive measures were possible, such as keeping muzzles on the adult dogs. But dogs cannot be muzzled all the time, and we are not persuaded that the availability of such measures overcomes the other factors favoring the conclusion that raising pit bulls in the circumstances identified here is an ultrahazardous activity. Finally, unlike the situation in *Fredricks*, the public benefit of the activity does not justify insulating the defendant from strict liability.

It is undisputed that the attack by Ellis's pit bull resulted in Thurman's injuries and therefore causation is not in doubt. Accordingly, we conclude that there is sufficient evidence to establish that by raising pit bulls in a residential neighborhood, Ellis engaged in an ultrahazardous activity. The trial court did not err in giving the ultrahazardous instruction.

Affirmed.

INSTRUCTIONS

1. You will have 90 minutes to complete this session of the examination. This performance test is designed to evaluate your ability to handle a select number of legal authorities in the context of a factual problem involving a client.

2. The problem is set in the fictitious state of Franklin, in the fictitious Fifteenth Circuit of the United States. Columbia and Olympia are also fictitious states in the Fifteenth Circuit. In Franklin, the trial court of general jurisdiction is the District Court, the intermediate appellate court is the Court of Appeal, and the highest court is the Supreme Court.

3. You will have two kinds of materials with which to work: a File and a Library. The first document in the File is a memorandum containing the instructions for the task you are to complete. The other documents in the File contain factual information about your case and may include some facts that are not relevant.

4. The Library contains the legal authorities needed to complete the task and may also include some authorities that are not relevant. Any cases may be real, modified, or written solely for the purpose of this examination. If the cases appear familiar to you, do not assume that they are precisely the same as you have read before. Read them thoroughly, as if they all were new to you. You should assume that the cases were decided in the jurisdictions and on the dates shown. In citing cases from the Library, you may use abbreviations and omit page references.

5. Your response must be written in the answer book provided. In answering this performance test, you should concentrate on the materials in the File and Library. If you are taking the examination on a laptop computer, your jurisdiction will provide you with specific instructions. What you have learned in law school and elsewhere provides the general background for analyzing the problem; the File and Library provide the specific materials with which you must work.

6. Although there are no restrictions on how you apportion your time, you should be sure to allocate ample time (about 45 minutes) to reading and digesting the materials and to organizing your answer before you begin writing it. You may make notes anywhere in the test materials; blank pages are provided at the end of the booklet. You may not tear pages from the question booklet.

7. This performance test will be graded on your responsiveness to the instructions regarding the task you are to complete, which are given to you in the first memorandum in the File, and on the content, thoroughness, and organization of your response.

Point Sheet

In re Mistover Acres LLC
DRAFTERS' POINT SHEET

In this performance test item, applicants' law firm represents Petra Flynn, one of the three members of Mistover Acres LLC ("Mistover"), a Franklin limited liability company. A limited liability company is a business entity that provides the liability protections of a corporation but has the attributes of a partnership for federal income tax purposes. Mistover grows and sells apples, salad greens, and other produce. Recently, Mistover received a demand letter from counsel for Genesee Trout, Inc., the corporate owner of a neighboring trout farm. The demand letter claims that a substantial amount of Genesee Trout's fish stock has died as a result of aerial pesticide spraying by Mistover. According to Genesee Trout's demand letter, it will cost upwards of $1 million to clean and restock the trout ponds, and Genesee Trout will bring suit against Mistover if a settlement cannot be agreed upon.

Mistover has its own legal counsel. Petra, however, is seeking legal advice in her individual capacity because she is concerned that the LLC business structure may not protect her from being held personally liable for the alleged harm to the trout farm. Unlike the other two members of Mistover (one of whom she describes as "judgment proof"), Petra has significant assets of her own and thus she fears that she could be an attractive "deep-pocket" defendant from Genesee Trout's perspective. Applicants' task is to write an objective memorandum evaluating Petra's potential liability for Genesee Trout's claim. In addition, applicants are asked to address whether Mistover's pesticide spraying constituted an ultrahazardous activity.

The File contains the memorandum from the supervising partner, notes from the client interview, a demand letter from counsel for Genesee Trout, the LLC operating agreement, an excerpt from the pesticide user's guide, and a copy of the public notice of pesticide application on Mistover's fields. The Library contains excerpts from the Franklin Limited Liability Company Act and two cases, one discussing the circumstances under which a member of an LLC is personally liable for tortious conduct involving the LLC and one describing the Franklin courts' approach to the ultrahazardous doctrine.

The following discussion covers all of the points the drafters intended to raise in the problem. Applicants need not cover them all to receive passing or even excellent grades. Grading decisions are entirely within the discretion of the user jurisdictions.

I. Format and Overview

Applicants' work product should be objective in tone and resemble a legal memorandum such as an associate would write to a supervising partner. It should discuss the range of possibilities (i.e., on-the-one-hand, on-the-other-hand) and reach a reasoned conclusion on each of the issues presented. No separate statement of facts is expected, but it is anticipated that applicants will incorporate the relevant facts from the client interview, the operating agreement, etc., in their analysis. Applicants are instructed to use separate headings for each issue discussed. However, it is left to the jurisdictions to determine whether to credit, and by how much, the format of the answer.

Applicants are directed to focus on two issues:

(1) Can Petra be held personally liable for the damage done by the aerial crop dusting?

(2) Did the aerial crop dusting of MU-83 constitute an ultrahazardous activity?

APPLICANTS SHOULD CONCLUDE THAT WITH RESPECT TO PETRA FLYNN'S PERSONAL LIABILITY FOR MISTOVER'S ACTS, REASONABLE ARGUMENTS CAN BE MADE BOTH FOR AND AGAINST FINDING HER PERSONALLY LIABLE. ON BALANCE, HOWEVER, IT IS MORE LIKELY THAT HER ACTIVITIES RISE TO THE LEVEL OF PARTICIPATION IN TORTIOUS CONDUCT, AND THEREFORE SHE CANNOT RELY ON MISTOVER'S ORGANIZATION AS A LIMITED LIABILITY COMPANY TO INSULATE HER FROM PERSONAL LIABILITY FOR THE DAMAGE CLAIMED BY GENESEE TROUT. MISTOVER'S AERIAL SPRAYING OF THE MU-83 PESTICIDE, WHILE A CLOSE CALL ON SOME OF THE RELEVANT FACTORS, CONSTITUTES AN ULTRAHAZARDOUS ACTIVITY FOR WHICH MISTOVER CAN BE HELD STRICTLY LIABLE.

II. DISCUSSION

A. Petra's Personal Liability for Damages Claimed by Genesee Trout

Applicants' first task is to analyze whether under Franklin law Mistover's organization as a limited liability company will insulate Petra from personal liability for the damage to the trout farm caused by the pesticide spraying. Applicants are expected to frame their discussion using the relevant provisions of the Franklin Limited Liability Company Act (FLLCA) and the standard for finding an LLC member liable in tort as explained in *Hodas v. Ice LLC* (Franklin Ct. App. 2004).

A limited liability company is often referred to as a "hybrid" form of business entity that offers the limited liability protection of a corporation with the tax advantages of a partnership. Like the LLC statutes enacted by most states, the FLLCA provides that "[t]he debts, obligations, and liabilities of a limited liability company, whether arising in contract, tort, or otherwise, shall be solely the debts, obligations, and liabilities of the limited liability company." FLLCA § 605(1). Further, unless otherwise specified in the statute, or by the written agreement of an LLC member, "a member of a limited liability company is not personally liable solely by reason of being a member of the limited liability company for any debt, obligation, or liability of the limited liability company, whether that liability or obligation arises in contract, tort, or otherwise, or for the acts or omissions of any other member, agent, or employee of the limited liability company." FLLCA § 605(2).

In *Hodas*, the Franklin Court of Appeal discussed the extent of protection against tort liability afforded to LLC members by the phrase in § 605(2) that "a member of a limited liability company is not personally liable solely by reason of being a member of the limited liability company . . . ." The court explained that imposition of personal liability on an LLC member is not limited to tortious conduct that is outside of the member role. On the other hand, tort liability will not be imposed on an LLC member for performing what are essentially administrative duties. Actual participation in the tortious conduct is required.

A thorough discussion of Petra's position as a member of Mistover Acres LLC would include these points:

- It is clear from the operating agreement and FLLCA § 605(1) that Petra has not agreed in writing to be personally liable for actions attributable to Mistover.
- However, Petra cannot claim that because she is a member of the LLC, she can never be personally liable for tortious acts. Under *Hodas*, the provision of the FLLCA stating that "a member of a limited liability company is not personally liable *solely by reason of being a member*" means that a member can be liable for tortious conduct, even when such conduct was performed as a member of and benefited the LLC.
- Thus, applicants must discuss the extent to which Petra participated in the pesticide spraying that damaged Genesee Trout's fish stock. While *Hodas* does not provide a comprehensive definition of the participation standard, it does state that no tort liability will be imposed for "performing what is merely a general administrative duty." The relevant facts are as follows:

- Petra had ordered MU-83 the year before, and ordered more for the aerial application that Genesee Trout complained of.
- Together, she and Chip decided that the lettuce should be sprayed aerially, as opposed to manual pesticide application, to address the worsening leaf slug problem.
- She performed marketing and sales duties for the LLC.
- She posted the required notices that Mistover would be spraying pesticide on a particular date.
- She was at Mistover on the date of the spraying, and watched Chip fly his plane over the fields spraying the lettuce crop.
- Two days after the spraying, she and Chip walked through the fields to verify that the leaf slugs had been eradicated.

- Many of Petra's activities could be deemed essentially administrative in nature. Clearly her marketing and sales activities are not directly related to the tortious conduct. Even ordering the MU-83 and posting the pesticide spraying notices could be considered simply administrative. Similarly, walking through the fields after the spraying to verify that the MU-83 had worked does not meet the participation standard. At that point, the tortious activity had been completed.
- However, Petra appears to have participated equally with Chip in the decision to use an aerial pesticide application and the decision to use MU-83 as opposed to another pesticide. These facts, when combined with her being the LLC member who ordered the MU-83, strongly favor the conclusion that her actions exceeded those of a mere member of Mistover and that she was an actual participant in the alleged tortious conduct.
- Applicants who focus on Chip's liability as a basis for Petra's personal liability have missed the point. The FLLCA shields LLC members from liability for tortious conduct by other LLC members. Chip's potential liability is beyond the scope of this item.

Accordingly, it appears likely that, while there are a number of facts to support the argument that her actions were merely administrative in nature, Petra faces a substantial risk that her involvement in the decision to use MU-83 rises to the level of actual participation in tortious conduct. Therefore, the LLC business structure will not shield her from personal liability for the harm suffered by Genesee Trout.

B. Ultrahazardous Activity

Applicants' second task is to determine whether the aerial spraying of the pesticide MU-83 constituted an ultrahazardous activity under Franklin law. If it is determined to be ultrahazardous, strict liability will attach. In other words, if Mistover's aerial pesticide spraying was ultrahazardous, Mistover (and Petra, as a result of her participation in the tortious conduct) will be held liable without Genesee Trout needing to prove negligence. For purposes of their analysis, applicants are instructed to assume that the pesticide spraying caused the alleged harm to Genesee Trout's fish stock.

Applicants should look to *Thurman v. Ellis* (Franklin Ct. App. 2003), which explains that when determining whether an activity is ultrahazardous, Franklin courts follow § 520 of the Restatement (Second) of Torts. Application of § 520 requires analysis of six factors:

(1) Existence of a high degree of risk of some harm to the person, land, or chattels of others;
(2) Likelihood that the resulting harm will be great;
(3) Inability to eliminate the risk by the exercise of reasonable care;
(4) Extent to which the activity is not a matter of common usage;
(5) Inappropriateness of the activity to the place where it is carried on; and

(6) Extent to which the activity's value to the community is outweighed by its dangerous attributes.

As demonstrated by the Restatement factors, the ultrahazardous activity doctrine emphasizes the dangerousness and inappropriateness of the activity. The policy underlying the doctrine reflects a goal to attribute costs to those who benefit from introducing an extraordinary risk of harm into the community by imposing strict liability on them.

In *Thurman*, the court emphasized that the test is one of the totality of the circumstances and no one factor is determinative, although some factors may carry substantially more weight than others. Further, the ultrahazardous label does not attach to a particular substance, such as the pesticide at issue here, in the abstract—it is the activity in which the substance is used that is examined under the § 520 criteria. Applicants should also recognize that Franklin courts do not limit the ultrahazardous category to those activities that are rarely conducted or unusual; the context in which an activity is performed can render it ultrahazardous. Thus activities that are ultrahazardous in one situation are "not necessarily ultrahazardous for all occasions." *Thurman*.

A discussion of whether the pesticide spraying will be considered an ultrahazardous activity should address the following points:

- **High degree of risk of harm**. The cases cited in *Thurman* and § 520 of the Restatement make it clear that harm from ultrahazardous activities is not limited to injuries to people, but also extends to property damage. The statements in the MU-83 User's Guide that "[pesticide] drift will occur with every application" and that pesticide "drift and runoff may be toxic to aquatic organisms" indicate that there is a substantial risk that pesticide will drift to a nontarget area and cause some harm.
- **Likelihood of great harm**. A plaintiff must show that the activity engaged in by the defendant was *likely* to produce *great* harm, not simply that the plaintiff suffered harm as an alleged result of the defendant's activities. In other words, the mere fact that a plaintiff suffered injury as a result of the defendant's actions does not establish that the activity at issue presented a likelihood of great harm. Here, the likelihood of harm from aerial spraying of MU-83 is unclear; it is not certain that harm to Genesee Trout was necessarily the likely result of applying MU-83 on a nearby field. The excerpt from the pesticide user's guide, however, includes an explicit warning that "Improper use or application of MU-83 may cause serious injury or death." This warning, and the warning about aquatic populations, combined with Genesee Trout's claim that the MU-83 killed its fish (evinced by the high levels of MU-83 found in the trout ponds) is probably sufficient to demonstrate a likelihood of great harm.
    - **Note:** Applicants may conflate factors (1) and (2). This should not be a basis for taking off points if applicants recognize the distinct concepts of the risk of harm and the seriousness or severity of any resulting harm.
- **Inability of reasonable care to eliminate risk**. Although no single factor is determinative, this factor is at the heart of an ultrahazardous assessment. Thus, in *Thurman*, the court states that this factor "would generally carry more weight than the other factors, but that this factor alone was not dispositive of whether an activity is ultrahazardous." The court's discussion includes a list of cases where the inherent dangerousness of the activities rendered them ultrahazardous: shooting fireworks, rock blasting, preparation of weapons-grade plutonium, and transportation of large amounts of gasoline. In all of these examples, even the exercise of reasonable care would not eliminate the risk of injury.

    Here, the MU-83 User's Guide refers to "improper use" as presenting a risk of serious injury or death, thereby suggesting that, properly used, MU-83 does not pose a danger to humans, livestock, aquatic life, or crops. At the same time, the pesticide manual states that there is always a risk of "pesticide drift" in every application, depending upon various controllable and uncontrollable factors (temperature, wind gusts, etc.). The user's guide also states that MU-83 poses a danger to aquatic life. The implication is that even reasonable care cannot eliminate all risks, particularly those to aquatic life, inherent in MU-83 use. Applicants might reasonably conclude that the risks from aerial spraying of MU-83 are substantially greater than the risks associated with applying the pesticide by hand, and therefore it is an ultrahazardous activity under Franklin law.

- **Uncommon activity**. The facts that the township posts notices of pesticide spraying and that Chip has previous experience as a crop duster suggest that aerial pesticide application is not an uncommon activity, at least in an agricultural area. Further, crop dusting by airplane is listed in the user's guide as an acceptable method of applying MU-83. Franklin courts have declined to impose liability under an ultrahazardous theory for activities that are a common part of daily life. However, per *Thurman*, applicants should recognize that the legality of an activity (e.g., giving proper notice or compliance with other requirements) does not preclude an activity from being labeled ultrahazardous. Applicants should ultimately conclude that this factor weighs against finding the pesticide spraying to be ultrahazardous.
- **Inappropriateness of the activity where it is conducted**. In *Thurman*, the court held that the defendant's raising of pit bulls constituted an ultrahazardous activity, giving significant weight to the fact that she was breeding the animals in an inappropriate place—a residential neighborhood with many young children. In contrast, in *Fredricks v. Centralia Fire Department* (cited in *Thurman*), the court noted that the only logical place to engage in the dangerous activity of firefighting was at the site of a fire. The pesticide spraying at Mistover falls somewhere between these two extremes. As a farm that grows vegetables for sale and is located in an agricultural area, it seems entirely appropriate that Mistover uses pesticides to protect its crops. And, as noted above, aerial application of pesticides is lawful in the township, as long as the proper permits are obtained and posted. However, the fact that Mistover is close to several organic producers suggests that aerial pesticide spraying may not be appropriate because of the risk of drifting chemicals. This determination is a close call, and applicants can probably go either way on this factor. Better answers may even draw distinctions between ground application of the pesticide during the first year and aerial application of the pesticide during the second year.
- **Activity's value to the community**. Application of pesticides is a beneficial, and often necessary, activity to ensure production of food. Thus there is significant value to the community in the responsible use of pesticides. This weighs against the conclusion that the pesticide spraying is ultrahazardous and that strict liability should be imposed for any harm caused by the activity. On the other hand, in the interview, Petra mentions that the area surrounding Mistover is home to many small producers of organic crops; even Mistover Acres LLC was organized with the intention of raising crops with minimal chemicals. Thus, following *Thurman*'s observation that Franklin courts have refused to employ a narrow application of the ultrahazardous doctrine and that the context of the activity, and not just the activity itself, is a relevant consideration, applicants could conclude that the value to the community of aerial pesticide spraying is not so great as to overcome other factors favoring the conclusion that it is an ultrahazardous activity.

Considering the § 520 factors overall, this is a much closer case than the raising of pit bulls in *Thurman* because of the significant public benefit of protecting the food supply. (Indeed, the jurisdictions are split on whether spraying of herbicides/pesticides is ultrahazardous.) However, the inherent dangerousness of the activity (as described in the excerpt from the pesticide manual), the fact that even with reasonable care there is a risk of pesticide drift and potential harm to aquatic life, and the fact that the spraying was conducted in close proximity to farms devoted to organic agriculture suggest that it would be deemed ultrahazardous and strict liability for the harm caused would attach. Applicants who conclude that the pesticide spraying is not ultrahazardous can receive substantial credit (or even full credit) provided that their analysis is reasonably supported by the relevant facts and law.

Memorandum

To: Lyle Palkovich

From: Applicant

1. Can Ms. Flynn, as a member of a Franklin LLC, be held personally liable for the damage done by the crop dusting her company authorized?

The Franklin Limited Liability Company Act [FLLCA] is the controlling authority pertaining to LLC member liability. The general rule is LLC members are not personally liable for acts of the company based on membership status alone. 605(2). However, members can be liable if the person participates in tortious conduct. The court looks to authorization: direction or participation in defining conduct, thus if the courts find "participation" in a tortious activity, the courts will impose liability on that member.

As noted above, Petra will not be found liable based solely on her membership in the company. Her membership in the company is clear however and therefore she may be liable under recent precedent based on her activities [Hodas (2004)]. As noted above, personal liability will be found if the member participates in some tortious conduct. Assuming this threshold is satisfied [see point 2 below for analysis], "participation" as defined above must be assessed.

Analysis of Ms. Flynn's "participation" in the crop dusting activities.

Ms. Flynn, who is generally solely responsible for marketing responsibilities for her company, concedes she played a role in determining both the use and subsequent crop dusting using the chemical in question. Her role was couched in the context of marketing concerns - she did not want the negative implications of using pesticides to affect the marketability of the company's food. Therefore, she helped Chip, the member who specialized in the agricultural operations, select the particular pesticide, she ordered and once it was decided conventional hand application of the chemical was insufficient to treat the pest issues, she and Chip agreed to the crop dusting and she subsequently ordered more.

Ms. Flynn's activities likely satisfy the definition of "participation"

While it is clear from the facts Ms. Flynn did not specifically fly the plane and apply the chemical herself, her role in the decision making process likely satisfies the authorization or direction necessary to find "participation." While courts have found that involvement in mere ministerial [Bayrd] and public relations task [Hodas] is insufficient in themselves to confer personal liability, Ms. Flynn's actions went beyond those standards and raise enough of a presumption of participation that she will certainly not win a motion for summary judgment on the issue and may very likely lose on this issue at trial. This of course hinges on whether there was a tortious activity.

2.Did the crop dusting of MU-83 constitute an Ultrahazardous activity thus raising the possibility of involvement in a strict liability tort for purposes of analysis 1 above?

When causation is not in doubt, as is the case here, the courts determine whether an activity qualifies as ultra hazardous [UH] by assessing the six factors enumerated in 520 of the restatement torts. These factors are: 1) existence of a high degree of risk of some harm to…land or chattels; 2) likelihood the harm will be great; 3) inability to eliminate the risk by exercise of due care; 4) whether the activity is of common usage; 5) inappropriateness of the activity where it is carried on; and 6) extent to which the activity's value to the community is outweighed by its dangerous attributes. [Thurman].

The activity in question is crop dusting in an area long held to be agricultural. Therefore in considering if the activity is of common usage, we probably need more facts on the prevalence of crop dusting, but it is likely that the activity was both common for the area, and was appropriate for the area - thus speaking to elements 4 and 5 above. With regard to element 6, agricultural growers' ability to successfully produce is important to the community and the use of pesticides is an important factor in growing food. This perspective is undermined however by recent precedent that found that firefighting was not ultrahazardous because the benefits to the community "far outweighed the inherent dangers." [Thurman]. While it is very unlikely that a court will find crop dusting analogous to fire fighting for the purposes of this analysis, this is probably the outer bound of the standard and therefore other inherently dangerous activities are properly defined as valuable to the community - it is just unclear whether crop dusting would satisfy this standard - likely not.

Furthermore, it may not matter, because of the significant number of factors that appear satisfied - thus likely causing this activity to fall into the definition of "ultrahazardous." The courts have held while no single factor is dispositive of defining an activity as UH, the courts have generally found the ability to eliminate risk with due care tends to carry more weight than others. The chemical in question "MU-83," is sold with a user guide that provides that "drift" [unwanted movement of the pesticide to no target areas] is always going to occur and that it may be toxic to aquatic organisms in neighboring areas. While Chip did use due care in not flying over the recommended 30 feet, in fact he flew at 20, according to the user guide, while drift can be mitigated with care [time of day; concentration, etc.] it cannot be eliminated. In addition to satisfying the 3rd element, this high degree of risk also satisfies elements 1 and 2, given that toxicity does strongly imply both high degree of risk and likelihood of great harm. Furthermore, because of the warning regarding toxicity to aquatic organisms, it is probable a court may find the activity was inappropriate for the area [near a pond] - which undermines the position above [the agricultural nature of the area made it likely that this was appropriate].

Given this analysis, it is likely that this activity satisfies the definition of ultrahazardous - and that Ms. Flynn will likely face personal liability.

NATIONAL CONFERENCE OF BAR EXAMINERS

FILE

Hall Gray LLP
Attorneys at Law
730 Amsterdam Ave.
Banford, Franklin 33701

MEMORANDUM

To:	Applicant
From:	Deanna Hall
Re:	Liability waiver for Velocity Park
Date:	February 26, 2008

Our client, Zeke Oliver, is about to open his new business venture, "Velocity Park," an outdoor skateboarding park (also referred to as a "skate park"). To reduce his liability to those who may be injured while skateboarding, Zeke has brought in a waiver form that he proposes to use. To help me advise him, please review his proposed waiver and prepare a memorandum:

- analyzing whether the proposed waiver will protect Velocity Park from liability for injuries occurring at the skate park;
- suggesting specific revisions to the proposed waiver, including replacement language as well as any changes in the waiver's design and layout (however, you should not redraft the entire waiver); and
- discussing whether any waiver will be enforceable if signed only by a minor.

Client Interview—Zeke Oliver

February 22, 2008

Atty: Zeke, come on in. How are things coming along with your new business?

Zeke: I am totally pumped! The construction is right on schedule, and on April 30, 2008, Velocity Park, Banford's first and only skateboarding park, will be open to the public!

Atty: Great. So what can I help you with today?

Zeke: Well, my brother told me that I should require everyone who uses the skateboard park to sign a liability waiver so if someone gets hurt, they can't sue me. I found an entry form from a triathlon in the state of Columbia that I entered last year. It had some stuff about waiving liability, so I just made some changes and added the Velocity Park logo. I was all set to send it to the printer, but then I thought that I should have you look it over first.

Atty: A liability waiver is an excellent idea. And you're right—waivers aren't necessarily interchangeable from one situation to another. Before we discuss your proposed waiver form, let's talk a bit about who will be using the skateboarding park and what activities they will be able to do there.

Zeke: Okay. According to my market research, I expect that most of Velocity Park's visitors will be teenagers and young adults. There will be a minimum age of 10 for using the park. It will have all the basic stuff skateboarders love: a large concrete bowl, a beginners' area, and jumps, sliding rails, and two half-pipes, so advanced skaters can do ollies, kickflips, grinds, and other stunts. I plan to hold skills clinics and offer private lessons. Also, I've hooked up with a couple of skateboard manufacturers to sponsor some competitions, although I don't have anything definite yet. By the way, I've brought a newspaper article that mentions the park.

Atty: Thanks. Will you charge admission for the park? What about equipment rentals?

Zeke: Admission will be $10 for a three-hour block of skateboarding. I want it to be affordable for teenagers. Right now, I have no plans to rent equipment, but the park will have a shop to sell boards, helmets, T-shirts, and accessories. Of course, there will be a concessions area for soft drinks and snacks.

Atty: I assume that skateboarders get a fair number of bumps and bruises. Do you have any particular concerns about injuries at your park?

Zeke: Injuries are just part of skateboarding. Usually they're nothing more than scrapes, bruises, and the occasional sprained wrist from taking a fall. There will be signs posted stating that skateboarders have to wear helmets while using the park.

Atty: Where will skateboarders fill out your waiver form? I notice that it's two pages—that's a fair amount of reading for a teenager waiting to get into the park.

Zeke: Hey, I thought I was doing well to have only a two-page waiver. If I included everything I wanted to, it would be five pages. Anyway, the waivers will be handed out where skateboarders pay the admission fee, and whoever is staffing the cash register will collect them. I suppose some kids may not read it closely, especially if they're anxious to get in and skateboard, but short of reading the waiver to them, I don't know how to get around that. Also the waiver can be printed off of the park's website.

Atty: Will your staff be trained to deal with medical emergencies?

Zeke: I'm in the process of putting together a first-aid station, but kids won't get much more than a bandage there. For anything more serious, staff will be trained to call the skateboarder's emergency contact or an ambulance. I'm not too worried about serious injuries. In my experience, skateboarders have a good sense of what tricks they can do safely. Besides, it's so much better to have kids skateboarding in a park designed for that purpose than on the streets.

Atty: Where do most skateboarders go now in Banford?

Zeke: It's really sad. As soon as the kids find a good place, like a parking lot or cul-de-sac with a nice incline, they get chased out by the neighbors. The city council doesn't like skateboarders either. It's voted to ban skateboarding downtown. That's why I'm opening the park. Unless kids can get to another town in the area with a skateboard park, there's no place to skateboard, apart from streets and driveways in the outlying neighborhoods. Eventually, if Velocity Park succeeds, I'd like to partner with the city of Banford to operate the park and make it free, but until then, I've got my work cut out for me just to make Velocity Park recoup its costs.

Atty: With your business experience, I'm sure it will turn a profit in no time. I'll review this liability waiver and see if it meets your needs. Then we'll meet next week to discuss it.

Zeke: Thanks. I appreciate it. I really need to have this taken care of before the park opens.

Welcome to Velocity Park! Before you hop on your skateboard and start work on your grinds, kickflips, and ollies, be sure to read and complete this form.

Admission Fees
$10 per skateboarder for a three-hour session in the park. $20 gets you an all-day pass. Unlimited monthly passes available for $75.

Hours of Operation
Monday–Friday, noon–8 p.m.
Saturday–Sunday, 10 a.m.–8 p.m.
Hours of operation subject to change without notice. Unanticipated closures will be posted at www.velocityparkskate.com.

Park Rules

Ø Must be 10 years of age or older to enter the skate park.
Ø Only skateboards and in-line skates may be used in the skate park.
Ø To enter and remain inside the skate park, you must wear a helmet.
Ø Inspect your equipment to make sure it is in good working order.
Ø Be considerate of fellow skateboarders, especially those who are younger and/or less skilled.
Ø No food, drink, or smoking allowed inside the skate park except in designated areas. No alcohol or drugs allowed.
Ø Skate park visitors must abide by staff instruction at all times.
Ø Velocity Park is not responsible for lost or stolen items.
Ø Failure to abide by these rules may result in expulsion from Velocity Park.

1. I understand and appreciate that participation in a sport carries a risk to me of serious injury and/or death. I voluntarily and knowingly recognize, accept, and assume this risk and hereby forever release, acquit, covenant not to sue, and discharge Velocity Park, its employees, event sponsors, and any third parties from any and all legal liability, including but not limited to all causes of action, claims, damages in law, or remedies in equity of whatever kind I have or which hereafter accrue to me, whether such injuries and/or claims arise from equipment failure, conditions in the park, or any actions of Velocity Park, its employees, third parties, or other skateboarders. Velocity Park is not responsible for any incidental or consequential damages, including, but not limited to, any claims for personal injury, property damage, or emotional distress. This release is binding with respect to my heirs, executors, administrators, and assigns, as well as myself.

2. I have been informed of Velocity Park Rules and agree to abide by them.

3. In connection with any injury I may sustain, or illness or other medical condition I may experience during my participation in skateboarding or attendance at Velocity Park, I authorize any emergency first aid, medication, medical treatment, or surgery deemed necessary by attending medical personnel if I am not able to act on my own behalf.

4. In consideration of permission to use the skate park facility, I agree that Velocity Park, its agents, and its employees may use my appearance, name, and likeness in connection with my use of the facility in any Velocity Park publication, including news releases. I further agree that I am not entitled to any compensation for such use of my appearance, name, or likeness.

Name (please print):________________________ Sex:____ Age:_____

(Signed):________________________________ Date:______________

Emergency Contact Information
Name: ______________________________ Phone No.:______________
Address: ____________________________

How did you hear about Velocity Park? ____
Would you like e-mail updates about Velocity Park events? Yes No
If yes, e-mail address: ____________________

The Banford Courier February 2, 2008

SKATEBOARDING: OLD AND NEW INJURIES ON THE RISE

Each year in Franklin, skateboarding results in about 500 visits to hospital emergency rooms, with some 50 skateboarders (usually children and adolescents) requiring hos-pitalization, usually because of head inju-ries. Nationally, in 2007, some 15,000 emergency room treatments were skate-board-related. Wrist injuries are the most common, either sprains or fractures. Although rare, deaths from falls and collisions with motor vehicles can occur.

Protective gear, such as helmets, slip-resistant closed-toe shoes, and wrist guards can greatly limit the number and severity of injuries. However, according to J.P. Clyde, a professional skateboarder, injuries could be further reduced if skateboarders paid more attention to the surfaces they ride on. "Studies by the U.S. Consumer Product Safety Commission found that 35 percent of all skateboarding-related injuries could have been avoided if skateboarders really paid attention to the skating environment," he said. "One-third of injuries happen because there's a flaw in the riding surface, whether it's a street, a parking lot, or a skate park. Innocuous objects like pebbles, twigs, bottle tops, or other debris can cause a skateboarder to take a spill. Cracks, potholes, and ruts also pose hazards to the unwary skateboarder."

Dr. Sanford Takei, a sports medicine specialist, agrees. "Beginning skate-boarders—those who have been riding for less than a week—account for one-third of skateboarding injuries overall," he said. "Obviously, beginners fall more often and may not know how to fall correctly. When experienced riders are injured, it is usually from falls caused by rocks and other irregularities in the riding surface."

But what really has parents in Banford up in arms is a new trend in skateboarding-related injuries: injuries that occur when teenagers mix alcohol or marijuana and skateboards. There has been a rise in reports of teenagers gathering in the Library Mall, drinking alcohol and then skateboarding on home-made ramps and trying risky stunts. Maggie Alden, a student at Banford High School, said that she quit skateboarding in the Mall after seeing a rider fall and break his nose after colliding with another skateboarder. "Those guys are clueless about where they're going," Alden said. "Someone is always trying to start a fight or take someone else's skateboard," she added.

For his part, Zeke Oliver, owner of Velocity Park, which will be Banford's first skate park when it opens in April, appeared relaxed about the risks of skateboarding injuries and aggressive skateboarders. "Look, skateboarding is only going to grow in popularity," he said. "It's a great way for kids to get outside, blow off some steam, and get some exercise."

LIBRARY

§ 41 Contracts involving minors; limitations on authority of minor.

This section is intended to protect minors and to help parents and legal guardians exercise reasonable care, supervision, protection, and control over minor children.

(a) A minor cannot make a contract relating to real property or any interest therein.

* * * *

(b)(1) The contract of a minor may be disaffirmed by the minor himself, either before his majority or within a reasonable time afterwards, unless the contract at issue is one for necessaries, such as food or medical care.

(b)(2) Where a minor enters into a contract, whether one for necessaries or not, said contract may be enforced against that individual if, upon reaching the age of majority, the individual expressly or implicitly ratifies the contract.

(b)(3) Subsections (b)(1) and (b)(2) shall not apply to contracts made on behalf of a minor by the minor's parent or guardian.

Lund v. Swim World, Inc.

Franklin Supreme Court (2005)

Tim Lund sued Swim World, Inc., for the wrongful death of his mother, Annie Lund, who suffered a fatal head injury at its facility. The trial court granted summary judgment to Swim World, ruling that the waiver signed by Lund released Swim World from liability. The court of appeal affirmed. For the reasons set forth below, we reverse.

Swim World is a swimming facility with a lap pool open to members and visitors. On May 3, 2001, Lund visited Swim World as part of a physical therapy program. Because Lund was not a Swim World member, she had to fill out a guest registration card and pay a fee before swimming.

The guest registration, a five-inch-square preprinted card, also contained a "Waiver Release Statement," which appeared below the "Guest Registration" section, requesting the visitor's name, address, phone number, reason for visit, and interest in membership. The entire card was printed in capital letters of the same size, font, and color. The waiver language read as follows:

WAIVER RELEASE STATEMENT.
I AGREE TO ASSUME ALL LIABILITY FOR MYSELF, WITHOUT REGARD TO FAULT, WHILE AT SWIM WORLD. I FURTHER AGREE TO HOLD HARMLESS SWIM WORLD, AND ITS EMPLOYEES, FOR ANY CONDITIONS OR INJURY THAT MAY RESULT TO ME WHILE AT SWIM WORLD. I HAVE READ THE FOREGOING AND UNDERSTAND ITS CONTENTS.

The card had just one signature and date line. Lund completed the "Guest Registration" portion and signed at the bottom of the "Waiver Release Statement" without asking any questions.

After swimming, Lund used the sauna in the women's locker room. The bench she was lying on collapsed beneath her, causing her to strike her head against the heater and lose consciousness. Lund was rushed to the hospital but died the next day as the result of complications from her head injury.

The complaint alleged that Swim World was negligent in the maintenance of its facilities and that its negligence caused Lund's death.

Summary judgment is granted when there is no genuine issue of material fact and the movant is entitled to judgment as a matter of law. *Samuels v. David* (Franklin Sup. Ct. 1991). The case at bar turns on the interpretation of Swim World's waiver form and whether it relieves Swim World of liability for harm caused by its negligence.

Waivers of liability, also known as exculpatory contracts,5 are permitted under Franklin law except when prohibited by statute or public policy. As no statute bars the contract at issue, we proceed to a public policy analysis of the exculpatory clause.

Public policy can restrict freedom of contract for the good of the community. Thus, claims that an exculpatory contract violates public policy create a tension between the right to contract freely without government interference and the concern that allowing a tortfeasor to contract away responsibility for negligent acts may encourage conduct below a socially acceptable standard of care.

We examine the particular facts and circumstances of the case when determining whether an exculpatory contract is void and unenforceable as contrary to public policy. Exculpatory contracts are generally construed against the party seeking to shield itself from liability. In *Schmidt v. Tyrol Mountain* (Franklin Sup. Ct. 1996), we set forth two requirements for an enforceable exculpatory clause: "First, the language of the waiver cannot be overbroad but must clearly, unambiguously, and unmistakably inform the sign-

---

5 The words "release," "waiver," and "exculpatory agreement" have been used interchangeably by the courts to refer to written documents in which one party agrees to release another from potential tort liability for future conduct covered in the agreement.

er of what is being waived. Second, the waiver form itself, viewed in its entirety, must alert the signer to the nature and significance of what is being signed." *Id.* We also noted that a relevant consideration in the enforceability of such a clause is whether there is a substantial disparity in bargaining power between the parties.

Thus, a release having language that is so broad as to be interpreted to shift liability for a tortfeasor's conduct under all possible circumstances, including reckless and intentional conduct, and for all possible injuries, will not be upheld. Likewise, release forms that serve two purposes and those that are not conspicuously labeled as waivers have been held to be insufficient to alert the signer that he is waiving liability for other parties' negligence as well as his own.

In *Schmidt,* an action on behalf of a woman who fatally collided with the base of a chair- lift tower while skiing, the plaintiff alleged that the defendant ski resort negligently failed to pad the lift tower. The resort moved for summary judgment, relying on the exculpatory clause in the ski pass signed by the skier. The waiver read, in part: "There are certain inherent risks in skiing and I agree to hold Tyrol Mountain harmless for any injury to me on the premises."

The court in *Schmidt* held that the release was void as against public policy. First, the release was not clear; it failed to include language expressly indicating the plaintiff's intent to release Tyrol Mountain from its own negligence. Without any mention in the release of the word "negligence," and the ambiguity of the phrase "inherent risks in skiing," the court held that the skier had not been adequately informed of the rights she was waiving.

As to the second factor, the form, in its entirety, did not fully communicate its nature and significance because it served the dual purposes of an application for a ski pass and a release of liability. Furthermore, the waiver was not conspicuous, in that it was one of five paragraphs on the form and did not require a separate signature. In addition, we noted that there was a substantial disparity in bargaining power between the parties.

Following *Schmidt*, we hold that Swim World's exculpatory clause violates public policy. First, the waiver is overly broad and all-inclusive. The waiver begins: "I AGREE TO ASSUME ALL LIABILITY FOR MY-SELF, WITHOUT REGARD TO FAULT. . . ." Here, it is unclear what type of acts the word "fault" encompasses; it could potentially bar any claim arising under any scenario.6 We reject Swim World's claim that negligence is synonymous with fault and conclude that the word "fault" is broad enough to cover a reckless or an intentional act. A waiver of liability for an intentional act would clearly violate public policy. *See* Restatement (Second) of Contracts § 195(1) (term exempting party from tort liability for harm caused intentionally or recklessly is unenforceable on grounds of public policy).

Exculpatory agreements that, like this one, are broad and general will bar only those claims that the parties contemplated when they executed the contract. Here, we must determine whether the collapse of a sauna bench was a risk the parties contemplated when the exculpatory contract was executed. If not, the contract is not enforceable.

Here, given the broadness of the exculpatory language, it is difficult to ascertain exactly what was within Lund's or Swim World's contemplation. Nevertheless, it appears unlikely that Lund, when she signed the guest registration and waiver form, would have contemplated receiving a severe head injury from the collapse of a sauna bench.
Further, Swim World's guest registration and waiver form failed to provide adequate notice of the waiver's nature and significance. Like the contract in *Schmidt*, the form served two purposes: it was both a "Guest Registration" application and a "Waiver Release Statement." The exculpatory

6 While including the word "negligence" in exculpatory clauses is not required, we have stated that "it would be helpful for such contracts to set forth in clear terms that the party signing it is releasing others for their negligent acts." *Schmidt*.

language appeared to be part of, or a requirement for, a larger registration form. The waiver could have been a separate document, giving Lund more notice of what she was signing. Also, a separate signature line could have been provided, but was not. Clearly identifying and distinguishing those two contractual arrangements could have provided important protection against a signatory's inadvertent agreement to the release.

Another problem with the form is that the paragraph containing the "Waiver Release Statement" was not conspicuous. The entire form was printed on one card, with the same letter size, font, and color. It is irrelevant that the release language is in capital letters; *all* of the words on the form were in capital letters. Further, the only place to sign the form was at the very end. This supports the conclusion that the waiver was not distinguishable enough such that a reviewing court can say with certainty that the signer was fully aware of its nature and significance.

Finally, we consider the bargaining positions of the parties. This factor looks to the facts surrounding the execution of the waiver. We hasten to add that the presence of this factor, by itself, will not automatically render an exculpatory clause void under public policy.

Here, the record suggests that there was an unequal bargaining position between the parties. Lund had no opportunity to negotiate regarding the standard exculpatory language in the form. In his deposition, Swim World's desk attendant testified that Lund was simply told to complete and sign the form; the waiver portion was not pointed out, nor were its terms explained to her. No one discussed the risks of injury purportedly covered by the form. The desk attendant further testified that Lund did not ask any questions about the form but that there was pressure to sign it because other patrons were behind Lund waiting to sign in. These facts undeniably generate, at a minimum, a genuine dispute of material fact regarding the parties' disparity in bargaining power.

For these reasons we conclude that the exculpatory clause in Swim World's form violates public policy, and, therefore, is unenforceable.

Reversed.

Holum v. Bruges Soccer Club, Inc.

Columbia Supreme Court (1999

Pamela Holum registered her seven-year-old son, Bryan, for soccer with Bruges Soccer Club, Inc. (the Club), a nonprofit organization that provides local children with the opportunity to learn and play soccer. Its members are parents and other volunteers. As part of the registration process, Mrs. Holum signed a release form whereby she agreed to release "the Club from liability for physical injuries arising as a result of [Bryan's] participation in the soccer club."

Bryan was injured when, after a soccer practice, he jumped on the goal and swung on it. The goal tipped backward and fell on Bryan's chest, breaking three ribs. Bryan's parents, Phil and Pamela Holum, sued the Club, alleging negligence on their own behalf and on behalf of Bryan. The trial court granted summary judgment to the Club, holding that the release signed by Bryan's mother barred the Holums' action against the Club.

The court of appeal affirmed in part and reversed in part. It held that the release barred Mr. and Mrs. Holum's claims. However, it went on to hold that the release did not bar Bryan's claim. Thus, while the parents' claims were barred, Bryan still had a cause of action against the Club, which a guardian could bring on his behalf, or which he could assert upon reaching the age of majority.

We agree with the court of appeal that the release applies to the injuries at issue. As to whether the release executed by Mrs. Holum on behalf of her minor son released the Club from liability for Bryan's claim and his parents' claims as a matter of law, we conclude that the release is valid as to all claims. Accordingly, we reverse that portion of the court of appeal decision holding that the release would not prevent Bryan from asserting a claim for his injuries.

We first consider whether the release is valid. In Columbia, with respect to adults, the general rule is that releases from liability for injuries caused by negligent acts arising during recreational activities are enforceable, whether the negligence is on the part of the participant in the recreational activity or the provider of the activity, in this case, the Club. This approach recognizes the importance of individual autonomy and freedom of contract.

For that reason, the release agreement is valid as to the parents' negligence claim. Mrs. Holum acknowledged that she read the agreement and did not ask any questions. Mr. Holum did not sign the release, but he accepted and enjoyed the benefits of the contract. In fact, when the injury occurred, he was at the practice field, thereby indicating his intention to enjoy the benefits of his wife's agreement and be bound by it. It is well settled that parents may release their own claims arising out of injury to their minor children. Accordingly, we find that Bryan's parents are barred from recovery as to their claims.

Here, however, the release was executed by a parent on behalf of the minor child. The Holums contend that the release is invalid on public policy grounds, citing the general principle that contracts entered into by a minor, unless for "necessaries," are voidable by the minor before the age of majority is reached. The Club, however, argues that the public interest justifies the enforcement of this agreement with respect to both the parents' and the child's claims.

Organized recreational activities provide children the opportunity to develop athletic ability as well as to learn valuable life skills such as teamwork and cooperation. The assistance of volunteers allows nonprofit organizations to offer these activities at minimal cost. In fact, the Club pays only 19 of its 400 staff members. Without volunteers, such nonprofit organizations could not exist and many children would lose the benefit of organized sports. Yet, the threat of liability deters many individuals from volunteering. Even if the organization has insurance, individual volunteers could find themselves liable for an injury.

Faced with the threat of lawsuits, and the potential for substantial damage awards, nonprofit organizations and their volunteers could very well decide that the risks are not worth the effort. Hence, invalidation of exculpatory agreements would reduce the number of activities made possible by the services of volunteers and their sponsoring organizations.

Therefore, although when his mother signed the release Bryan gave up his right to sue for the negligent acts of others, the public as a whole received the benefit of these exculpatory agreements. Because of this agreement, the Club can offer affordable recreation without the risks and overwhelming costs of litigation. Bryan's parents agreed to shoulder the risk. Accordingly, we believe that it is in the public interest that parents have authority to enter into these types of binding agreements on behalf of their minor children. We also believe that the enforcement of these agreements may promote more active involvement by participants and their families, which, in turn, promotes the overall quality and safety of these activities.

A related concern is the importance of parental authority. Parents have a fundamental liberty interest in the care, custody, and management of their offspring. Parental authority extends to the ability to make decisions regarding the child's school, religion, medical care, and discipline. Invalidating the release as to the minor's claim is inconsistent with parents' authority to make important life choices for their children.

Mrs. Holum signed the release because she wanted Bryan to play soccer. In making this family decision, she assumed the risk of physical injury on behalf of Bryan and the financial risk on behalf of the family as a whole. Apparently, she determined that the benefits to her child outweighed the risk of physical injury. The situation is comparable to Columbia Stat. § 2317, which gives parents the authority to consent to medical procedures on a child's behalf. In both cases, the parent weighs the risks of physical injury to the child and its attendant costs against the benefits of a particular activity.

Therefore, we hold that parents have the authority to bind their minor children to exculpatory agreements in favor of volunteers and sponsors of nonprofit sport activities where the cause of action sounds in negligence. These agreements may not be disaffirmed by the child on whose behalf they were executed. We need not decide here whether there are other circumstances, beyond the realm of nonprofit organizations, which will support a parent's waiver of a child's claims.

Accordingly, we hold that the release is valid as to the claims of both the parents and the minor child.

Affirmed in part and reversed in part.

Point Sheet
DRAFTERS' POINT SHEET

This performance test requires applicants, as associates at a law firm, to analyze the provisions of a liability waiver for a recreational activity. The client, Zeke Oliver, owns Velocity Park, set to be the first skateboarding park in Banford, Franklin, when it opens in April. Zeke has asked the law firm for advice regarding an appropriate liability waiver that users of the skate park will be required to sign in order to use the park.

In analyzing whether the waiver that Zeke provided is enforceable under Franklin law, applicants are expected to address both the waiver's language and its format. Applicants also must grapple with the issue of whether liability waivers signed only by minors will be enforced to bar actions for negligence arising from the minors' skateboarding injuries.

The File contains the task memorandum from the supervising partner, a client interview transcript, a liability waiver Zeke assembled by taking language from a triathlon entry form/liability waiver, and a newspaper article about the risks of skateboarding. The Library includes a Franklin statute regarding civil actions, a Franklin case, and a case from Columbia.

The following discussion covers all of the points the drafters intended to raise in the problem. Applicants need not cover them all to receive passing or even excellent grades. Grading is entirely within the discretion of the user jurisdictions.

I. Format and Overview

Applicants' work product should resemble a legal memorandum such as an associate would write to a supervising partner. Applicants should analyze the waiver Zeke has proposed, identifying problems with its content and design that may preclude it from being found enforceable by a court. Applicants are told not to rewrite the entire waiver. However, if certain language is overbroad or ambiguous, applicants should suggest replacement language that better conforms to the standards set forth in the cases and explain why the changes are necessary for an enforceable waiver. Further, applicants should recognize that the reach of a waiver is tied to the characteristics of the activity (and potential injuries) at issue. Thus they should incorporate the relevant facts from the client interview and the news article in their analysis of the issues. The task memorandum does not require applicants to organize their answers in any particular order, but the order presented below is a logical manner in which to address the issues.

Applicants should conclude that (1) Zeke's proposed waiver contains significant content and format defects, and (2) while the precise issue has not been addressed by Franklin courts, it is unlikely that a court will enforce an exculpatory contract executed by a minor in this situation.

II. Discussion

In Franklin, a party may use an exculpatory contract to limit its liability exposure, but a court may refuse to enforce such a contract on the grounds that its terms violate public policy. A court considers two factors when determining whether an exculpatory contract is enforceable: whether the waiver of liability language is overly broad and ambiguous and whether the exculpatory clause is conspicuous such that it notifies the signer of the nature and significance of what is being waived. Courts will also consider a third, nondispositive factor: whether there exists a substantial disparity in bargaining power between the parties. *Lund v. Swim World, Inc.* (Franklin Sup. Ct. 2005).

A. Whether the Velocity Park Waiver Is Overly Broad and Ambiguous

Franklin courts construe the language of an exculpatory contract against the party seeking to enforce the contract. *Lund.* To survive a public policy challenge, the exculpatory contract must include a description that "clearly, unambiguously, and unmistakably inform[s] the signer of what is being waived." *Id.* (quoting *Schmidt v. Tyrol Mountain* (Franklin Sup. Ct. 1996)). In *Lund*, the deceased swimmer had signed a waiver in which she agreed "to assume all liability for myself, without regard to fault." The Franklin Supreme Court concluded that, by using only the word "fault," the exculpatory clause was overly broad because it could be construed as waiving any and all claims, even those for the defendant's intentional or reckless acts and omissions.

The key to determining whether the exculpatory language is overly broad is whether the risks that the parties contemplated at the time the waiver was executed can be ascertained. In *Lund*, the court held that the waiver's broad language prevented it from concluding that, at the time Lund signed the waiver, she anticipated the risk of a severe head injury when a sauna bench collapsed under her. Not only did the Swim World waiver refer generally to "fault," it failed to spell out any particular risks for which Lund was waiving the right to sue Swim World.

Here, the Velocity Park waiver fails to satisfy *Lund*'s requirement that exculpatory contracts "clearly, unambiguously, and unmistakably inform the signer of [the rights he or she is waiving]." The relevant paragraphs of the proposed waiver read as follows:

> 1. I understand and appreciate that participation in a sport carries a risk to me of serious injury and/or death. I voluntarily and knowingly recognize, accept, and assume this risk and hereby forever release, acquit, covenant not to sue, and discharge Velocity Park, its employees, event sponsors, and any third parties from any and all legal liability, including but not limited to all causes of action, claims, damages in law, or remedies in equity of whatever kind I have or which hereafter accrue to me, whether such injuries and/or claims arise from equipment failure, conditions in the park, or any actions of Velocity Park, its employees, third parties, or other skateboarders. Velocity Park is not responsible for any incidental or consequential damages, including, but not limited to, any claims for personal injury, property damage, or emotional distress. This release is binding with respect to my heirs, executors, administrators, and assigns, as well as myself.
>
> 2. I have been informed of Velocity Park Rules and agree to abide by them.

1. The language of the waiver is overbroad.

- Exculpatory clauses are strictly construed against the party seeking to shield itself from liability. *Lund.*
- The waiver at issue ostensibly releases Velocity Park "from any and all legal liability, including but not limited to all causes of action, claims, damages in law, or remedies in equity of whatever kind . . . ."
- The phrase "any and all legal liability" would presumably cover injuries resulting from intentional and reckless acts, as well as from negligence. As stated in *Lund*, a release that is "so broad as to be interpreted to shift liability for a tortfeasor's conduct under all possible circumstances, including reckless and intentional conduct, and for all possible injuries, will not be upheld."
    - Waivers are not effective to bar liability for intentional acts. *See Lund* (citing Restatement of Contracts (Second) § 195(1)).
    - The word "negligence" need not appear in a waiver for it to be enforceable, but the better practice is to clearly state that by signing the waiver, the party is releasing others from negligence claims. *Lund*, fn.2.
- Thus, Zeke's waiver is too broad to inform a skateboarder of the precise rights waived.

- Further, the waiver attempts to be a release of claims against not just Velocity Park and its employees, but also against "any third parties."
    - This attempt to extend the waiver to unknown third parties is most likely unenforceable under *Lund*.
- The exculpatory clause also contains repetitive and confusing language (e.g., "[I] hereby forever release, acquit, covenant not to sue, and discharge Velocity Park . . ."), making it more likely that the average skateboarder at the park—according to Zeke, most Velocity Park visitors will be teenagers and young adults—will not carefully read or understand the agreement before signing it.

2. **The waiver fails to alert the signer to the risks involved in skateboarding.**

- Overbroad and general exculpatory agreements will be construed to bar only those claims that the parties contemplated when they executed the contract. *Lund*. A waiver that only vaguely refers to the activity at issue will not be deemed sufficient to inform the signer of the risks of the activity and the rights being waived. In *Schmidt v. Tyrol Mountain*, cited in *Lund*, a waiver's reference to the "inherent risks in skiing" was insufficient to inform the skier of the risks she was assuming.
- The Velocity Park waiver states that the signer "understand[s] and appreciate[s] that participation in a sport carries a risk to me of serious injury and/or death."
    - This language is even more vague than the language in *Schmidt* ("the inherent risks in skiing"); it gives no information to the signer about particular risks associated with skateboarding.
- Thus the waiver should be revised to include language expressly informing the signer of specific skateboarding injury risks and possible causes.
    - The *Banford Courier* article states that the most common skateboarding injuries are wrist sprains and fractures, but that serious head injuries may also occur.
- Applicants could redraft the Velocity Park waiver as follows: "I understand and appreciate that skateboarding carries a risk to me of injury from falls or collisions with objects or other skateboarders, including but not limited to bruises, abrasions, sprains and fractures (especially to the wrist), and head injuries, and that these injuries could be severe or even result in substantial disability or death."
    - A revised waiver could also mention something to the effect that using the half-pipes, jumps, etc., increases the risk of harm to the skateboarder.
    - A thorough waiver might also state that falls are likely due to debris on or irregularities in the riding surface (thus insulating Velocity Park for claims based on a skater falling because he or she ran over a piece of trash).
- The waiver also should clearly and expressly convey the risks of skateboarding in a park with other skateboarders.
- Applicants might note that many park users will be teenagers, so the language of the waiver should use terms understandable to someone of a relatively young age, even if the form will have to be signed by parents (*see* discussion *infra* II.D.).

- Moreover, given the rise in injuries associated with aggressive behavior in skateboarders (e.g., risky stunts, fights), the waiver should include language denying liability for injuries caused by Velocity Park's negligent failure to supervise skateboarders.
- Applicants could also note that there are other injuries that even a well-drafted waiver may not cover because they were not within the parties' contemplation when the waiver was executed. (For example, a skateboarder gets food poisoning from a hot dog sold by the Velocity Park concession stand.)

B. Whether the Velocity Park Waiver Is Conspicuous

Second, a liability waiver must "alert the signer to the nature and significance of what is being signed." *Lund*. The exculpatory clause must be conspicuous to the signer; its format must visually communicate that the waiver language is important.7 In *Lund*, the court noted that documents that serve two purposes generally are not sufficiently conspicuous, especially when there is only a single signature line, because the importance of the exculpatory clause may not be clearly distinguishable from the rest of the document. Further, the exculpatory clause in *Lund* was not conspicuous because it was in the same size, font, and color as the rest of the form.

- *Lund* provides specific examples of how a dual-purpose document may be improved.
    - The waiver could be a separate document.
    - There could be a separate signature line for the exculpatory clause.
- Zeke's form serves many purposes and the exculpatory clause is not conspicuous.
    - The form contains information on park hours, prices, and rules. It also has paragraphs whereby the skateboarder agrees to waive liability, consents to the use of his or her likeness, authorizes medical treatment, provides emergency contact information, and agrees to receive park e-mails.
    - There are headings for the sections regarding fees, hours, and park rules, but there is no heading for the exculpatory clause or the medical care and use of likeness paragraphs (although these paragraphs are numbered).
    - The exculpatory clause is in a *smaller* font than is the first part of the form.
    - There is only one signature line; arguably, the exculpatory clause, consent to medical treatment, and use of likeness parts warrant separate signatures.
    - The clause does not have any language to the effect of "I have read this form and understand that by signing it I am waiving important rights." (Even the waiver in *Lund* contains the sentence "I have read the foregoing and understand its contents.") Adding such language would emphasize to the skateboarder the nature and significance of the waiver.

C. Whether There Is a Disparity in Bargaining Power Between the Parties

The third public policy factor addressed in *Lund* is the question of whether there is a substantial disparity in bargaining power between the parties. In making this determination, the court will consider "the facts surrounding the execution of the waiver," including whether the signer has an opportunity to negotiate its terms. *Lund*.

---

7 Applicants are not expected to redraft the entire waiver or attempt to re-create it in a better format in their answer books (e.g., by redrafting the waiver language using a larger font). However, as directed by the task memo, they should suggest those changes that should be incorporated into the waiver's design and layout.

- In *Lund*, there was no opportunity to negotiate the waiver's terms; Lund either signed or didn't swim.
- The Swim World employee did not alert Lund that the entrance form included a liability waiver, let alone explain its terms to her.
- The court also noted that there was not enough time to read Swim World's form and make a reasoned decision about the consequences of signing it, because there were other Swim World patrons waiting in line to check in.
- The court concluded that, at a minimum, there was a genuine dispute of material fact regarding the parties' disparity in bargaining power.
- Regarding the expected circumstances of skateboarders' execution of Zeke's proposed waiver, a substantial disparity of bargaining power could be found.
    - As in *Lund*, skateboarders will have to sign the exculpatory contract to use the park; there is no "opt-out" provision.
    - Velocity Park would-be patrons, similar to the deceased in *Lund*, may be under pressure to sign the waiver as quickly as possible so as not to delay the entry of other skateboarders waiting in line.
- Applicants should suggest that park employees alert skateboarders and their parents (*see* below) to the form's liability waiver portion, warning them to carefully read it.
- They should also suggest that all patrons (and their parents) be told that if they have any questions about the waiver, they should ask park employees, who should be familiar with the waiver's terms.
- Also, Zeke should be sure to fully staff the park at peak times (e.g., opening and after school) when there might be many impatient kids and parents waiting in line.
- Applicants thus should suggest measures Zeke can take to minimize a substantial disparity in bargaining power between the parties. However, even if there is some disparity (i.e., patrons are not allowed to opt out of signing), it is unlikely that the presence of this one negative factor would lead a court to find an otherwise enforceable waiver void as against public policy. *See Lund*. Indeed, the *Lund* court appears to give more weight to the first two factors: whether the language is overbroad and ambiguous, and whether the form notifies the signer to the significance of what is being waived.

D. Whether a Waiver Is Enforceable If Signed Only by a Minor

- *Lund* does not address whether a release signed by a minor, or by a parent on a minor's behalf, would be contrary to public policy. Thus, it appears that the enforceability of waivers against minors is an issue of first impression in Franklin.
- The relevant case law on this issue is a Columbia case, *Holum v. Bruges Soccer Club, Inc.* (Col. Sup. Ct. 1999). *Holum* discusses the effectiveness of a waiver signed by a parent on behalf of her minor child as a condition of the child's participation in a soccer club. The court held that enforcing the waiver against the parents and the child was in the public's interest, largely because the defendant was a nonprofit soccer club that relied on volunteers to offer soccer to many children at low cost. The court reasoned that protecting the

club and its volunteers from liability was critical to the existence of such recreational activities because volunteers might be reluctant to help if doing so meant subjecting themselves to liability. The court said that enforcing the club's liability waiver allocated the risk of injury from the club to parents, thereby benefiting the community as a whole by making soccer more accessible to all children.

- The court in *Holum* also emphasized that parents have authority to make decisions regarding the welfare of their children, comparing the club's waiver to the parents' statutory right to consent to medical procedures involving their children. The court assumed that a parent signing a release of future claims would be in a position to consider the alternatives and make a reasoned decision that the cost of waiving the right to sue was outweighed by the benefit to the child of being able to participate in the activity.
    - In *Holum,* the mother signed a release on behalf of her seven-year-old child. Most of the patrons at Velocity Park will be teenagers. Applicants will have to address how *Holum* applies where teenagers are involved and to an activity which, unlike the soccer club, is not sponsored by a volunteer-driven organization.

Application of *Holum* to the proposed Velocity Park waiver form

- Zeke's proposed waiver has a single line for the skateboarder's signature, and places for indicating sex and age. Zeke says in his interview that 10 is the minimum age to use the park and that he expects most skateboarders to be teens or young adults. In short, a substantial number of park patrons will be minors.
- Also, because beginning skateboarders account for one-third of skateboarding injuries, liability for claims by underage skateboarders is a real concern.
- The fact that Velocity Park is a for-profit enterprise weighs against enforcing a release that purports to waive a minor's right to sue for negligence under *Holum*.
    - While Zeke states that, at some point, he would like to partner with the City of Banford and make the skate park free, Velocity Park will clearly open as a for-profit business.
    - Thus, the rationale that enforceable liability waivers ensure volunteer participation and the provision of community-based recreation (so central in the *Holum* holding) is not a consideration here.
    - That does not mean that Velocity Park won't benefit Banford: it gives skateboarders a supervised space in which to skate and one that was expressly designed for that purpose. Thus, it will be an improvement over teens skateboarding in neighborhood cul-de-sacs and the Library Mall.
    - Applicants must recognize that *Holum,* a Columbia case, is persuasive only.
    - However, the *Holum* court based its holding equally on the fact that parents have authority to make life choices for their children and that they assume the risk of injury to their children in exchange for the privilege and benefit of participation in low-cost recreational sports.
- Applicants must grapple with the Franklin statute regarding enforceability of contracts entered into by minors. It seems clear that under § 41, a liability waiver signed by an underage skateboarder, without being co-signed by a parent or guardian, will not be enforceable.
    - For example, under § 41(b)(1), a minor can disaffirm a contract, unless the contract was for "necessaries" (e.g., food). Because skateboarding is not a necessary, an under-18 skateboarder could sign but then disaffirm a Velocity Park waiver. On the other hand, the waiver could be enforced against the skateboarder if he or she ratified the agreement after turning 18 by, for example, continuing to

use the park. (The assumption here is that once a waiver is signed, Velocity Park keeps it on file and a skateboarder doesn't need to sign a new one every time he or she uses the park.)

- Applicants should note that under *Holum*, parents in Columbia can waive claims on their own behalf and on behalf of their children for negligence that results in injuries to their children. Given that exculpatory contracts in Franklin will be enforceable if they meet the standards for scope and clarity in *Lund*, applicants should suggest that the Velocity Park waiver be signed by the parents of any skateboarder who is under 18. This will help insulate Velocity Park from negligence claims by injured skateboarders' parents.

Note: Applicants could receive extra credit for observing that, strategically, even if it is uncertain whether a waiver will be enforced, some provisions may be desirable to discourage people from suing the park after an injury.

In Re Velocity Park Sample Answer

(1) Will the proposed waiver protect Velocity Park?

The proposed waiver likely will not protect Velocity Park as Mr. Oliver intends. For a waiver to be effective, three requirements must be met: (1) the language of the waiver must be clear and not over broad, (2) the waiver taken as a whole "must alert the signor to the nature and significance of what is being signed." Lund. Courts will also consider the relative bargaining positions of the parties and construe ambiguities against the party seeking to obtain a waiver. Lund. For waivers by minors, the waiver should additionally be "made on behalf of a minor by the minor's parent or guardian;" otherwise, the minor may disaffirm the contract. 41(b)(1)-(3).

The proposed waiver suffers from several flaws. First, the language of the waiver, including phrases such as "participation in a sport", "condition in a park," "any actions of velocity part," etc are ambiguous. In Lund, the court noted that the phrase "inherent risks in skiing" was too ambiguous to clearly inform the person of rights being waived.

The language is also over broad. Because waivers are construed against the party obtaining it, waivers for intentional acts violate public policy in their entirety. Lund. Quoting R2d 195. Here, the proposed waiver releases "all legal liability" for "any actions of Velocity Park," (which would include intentional acts), both for the skateboarder and the skateboarder's heirs and assigns (cf. Holum, where for a parent to release their claims the parent signed a waiver). And, the waiver seeks to void liability not only for Velocity Park, but also for all third parties. These provisions taken alone would probably void the entire waiver.

Also, the language of the waiver should more clearly indicate that it is a waiver. The proposed waiver does not include a header or title drawing the reader's attention to the fact that it is actually a waiver, in contrast with proper waivers. Lund. The waiver also lacks signature lines on each page, or perhaps even beside each paragraph that significantly waives liability. Accordingly, a party signing the waiver may not appreciate the content of the waiver. Moreover, the waiver uses smaller font than the rest of the document, without capitals or bold to draw attention to particular portions of significance. See Lund.

The waiver also may fail because it is incorporated into a single document along with general information about Velocity Park. It therefore does not clearly call attention to seriousness of the signature. See Holum.

Although the Holum court upheld a waiver that did not use any capitals, Holum was decided in a neighboring jurisdiction and is therefore not binding in Franklin. Holum is also further distinguished as applying to non-profit situations, whereas Mr. Oliver will be charging admission for profit. Rather than run the risk that a Franklin court would rely on these distinguishing characteristics, the proposed waiver should be amended.

Regarding the bargaining power of the parties, Velocity Park appears to have most of the power: Velocity is the only park in the area, a large portion of their business will be from minors, the minor may have to sign the form while standing in line with others waiting (see Lund), and the terms may not be explained to the minor (indeed, Mr. Oliver indicates many would not read it). The proposed waiver should be amended to address the concerns.

The proposed waiver also would only be signed by a minor, and therefore could be disaffirmed in accordance with 41(b)(1)-(2).

(2) Suggested revisions

I have prepared the following list of suggested revisions to bring the waiver into compliance with the public policy considerations set forth in Holum. Notably, the Holum decision involved enforceability by a minor for a harm to her parent, rather than a child's injuries.

- The waiver should be on a separate document and clearly titled "WAIVER, RELEASE, AND EXCLUPATORY AGREEMENT."
- The waiver should be signed by a parent and not just a minor. The parent and child should be asked if he or she have any questions before signing. A separate entrance line be used for people coming to the park a first time to avoid the feeling of being rushed. The parent and child's waiver can be kept on file. Waivers may only cover certain areas (e..g. beginner).
- Signatures should be required for each page.
- The waiver should address liability from all anticipated sources, such as choking hazards related to selling food within the park. The waiver could include language that "I agree to eat food and drinks within a designated area of the skate

park and not enter the ramp area with any such food and drinks. I UNDERSTAND NO MEDICAL STAFF WILL BE PRESENT on site."

- The waiver should specifically reference Velocity's negligence, such as: "I agree to ASSUME ALL LIABILITY FOR MYSELF, WITH REGARD TO NEGLIGENT ACTIONS PERFORMED OR NOT, BY VELOCITY PARK. I understand, DEBRIS, INCLUDING TWIGS, ROCKS AND THE LIKE may be present in the park and WAIVE LIABILITY." References to "any and all" liability should be replaced with "negligence," as waivers for intentional or reckless behavior will not be upheld.
- The waiver should require wearing wrist guards and closed toe shoes.
- Include language "I agree NOT TO ENTER an area occupied by ANOTHER SKATEBOARDER until the area is clear," to avoid collisions.

(3) Enforceability against a minor

Waivers signed only by a minor will not be enforceable against the minor because he or she will have the right to disaffirm the contract. 41(b)(1).

Once the minor reaches the age of majority, however, a waiver signed only by a minor may be enforceable where the minor expressly or implicitly ratifies the contract. 41(b)(2). Therefore, although the contract may not be enforceable while a minor, if the minor reaches the age of majority and signs a new waiver (express), or continues to use the skate park (arguably implied ratification), the waiver may be enforceable thereafter.

NATIONAL CONFERENCE OF BAR EXAMINERS

FILE

Black, Fernandez Hanson LLP

Attorneys at Law
Suite 215
396 West Main Street
Greenville, Franklin 33755

MEMORANDUM

To: Applicant
From: Henry Black
Re: Peel subpoena
Date: February 26, 2008

Our client, Lisa Peel, has just been subpoenaed by the local district attorney to testify before a grand jury. The subpoena directs her to bring notes concerning any and all persons interviewed regarding an item she posted on her Web log (blog). These notes will reveal the identities of her sources for the information she posted on her blog. Peel promised to protect the confidentiality of her sources. She seeks our advice on whether she has grounds to resist the subpoena.

I am somewhat familiar with the Franklin Reporter Shield Act (FRSA). However, I do not know if the FRSA applies to Peel and her blog. Please draft an objective memorandum for me analyzing whether we can use the FRSA to move to quash Peel's subpoena.

You need not include a separate statement of facts, but be sure to use the facts in your analysis. Be sure to address both sides of the issue; that is, discuss any facts or law that may prevent Peel from claiming the protection of the FRSA.

Do not concern yourself with any First Amendment issues; another associate is researching those arguments.

Transcript of Interview with Lisa Peel

February 22, 2008

Attorney: Lisa, nice to see you. What can I do for you?

Peel: You can make this subpoena go away.

Attorney: Tell me more. Why don't you start at the beginning?

Peel: A couple of years ago, I retired from teaching, and my husband and I moved to Greenville here in Montgomery County. To find out more about my new community, I started attending the meetings of several public bodies—the library and school boards, the park district board, and the town council. The more I went, the more I got to know people, and the more I became part of the scene. People got to know and trust me. Soon, I realized that there was a lot going on that the public should know about.

Attorney: Did you think about getting the local newspaper involved?

Peel: Most of the towns in this county are too small to support a daily paper. So there is only one daily paper covering all of Montgomery County. The publisher believes the paper should boost the local communities, and he discourages the reporters from doing any stories and investigations that might portray the communities in a bad light.

Attorney: So what did you do?

Peel: About a year ago, I started an Internet blog. As you know, often the owner of the blog starts a discussion and others can post comments.

On my blog, I posted the agendas of the Greenville town council, library and school boards, and sometimes the planning commission. After the meetings, I posted the minutes, my summary of the minutes, and my own commentary about how these decisions would affect the town. Within weeks, over 400 people visited the blog, and about a quarter of them commented on what I wrote or added questions that others would respond to. I actually had citizens engaged in learning what their government was doing.

At first I updated the blog only occasionally. Then it generated so much interest that I decided to update it more often.

Attorney: How often do you update it?

Peel: I generally post new items on Friday, but sometimes I may not get around to it until later in the weekend. I have movie reviews and gardening tips on the blog and also share news of my family. I post pictures of my pets and places where I've traveled. I'll also post announcements about the library's bake sale and events like that.

Attorney: Do your readers pay for access to your blog?

Peel: No, it's free. At first, I kept the blog wide open; anyone could access it and post anything—anonymously if they wanted to. But then I decided that letting anyone post anything might not be wise. So now, anyone can access it at no cost. But if you want to post a comment or a question, you have to register. Registering is also free. In the past two months, I've had over 3,500 registrants in this town of 38,000 people, and people have visited the site more than 15,000 times. I've also picked up a couple of local businesses, which pay me to post their ads on my blog.

Attorney: So, tell me about the subpoena.

Peel: One day, I got a call from an individual familiar with the school district administration. This person told me that the Greenville School District was losing the use of $10,000 worth of audiovisual and computer equipment purchased with district funds because the stuff was going to the home of the assistant superintendent. Well, $10,000 isn't a lot of corruption, I concede, but it is public money and it was intended to buy equipment for schoolchildren.

So I investigated and got confirmation from a couple of sources. I wrote a piece about what I found out and posted it on my blog. I brought you a hard copy of the posting. Now the Montgomery County District Attorney wants to know the sources of my information.

Attorney: Why not reveal your sources?

Peel: To get to the truth, especially the truth about public corruption, I have to talk to people on the inside. But insiders will never talk to me if they think their names will become public because they're worried about losing their jobs. So I get inside information from confidential sources, let people know about it by getting the word out, and suddenly the government starts investigating or the public starts asking questions.

Attorney: Do you get paid for this work?

Peel: Not much. The little income that comes from the sponsors' ads, I use for my expenses: computer upgrades, copy costs, telephone costs, gas for traveling, that sort of thing.

Attorney: Do you know why the district attorney subpoenaed you?

Peel: I have a couple of guesses. Now that I've exposed this scandal, he has to investigate. I suspect he is embarrassed to learn about this from my blog. Also, the district attorney is just being lazy. Think about it—how many people are in a position to know about this going on at the school? He just needs to start asking the right people and the information will come out. But, regardless of the reason, I have to protect my sources. I may be retired and this blog may be my hobby, but right now it is the only avenue for real news in this county.

Attorney: I'm somewhat familiar with the Franklin Reporter Shield Act—we may have an argument that you are protected by it, but I doubt that "blogs" or "bloggers" are specifically mentioned in the Act. I am also concerned that you've never worked as a reporter before.

Peel: But I work just like a real reporter. I attend public meetings, read agendas, minutes, budgets, etc. I make calls to the officials and other staff members and interview them. I then post the official agendas and minutes, along with my summaries and comments. The amount of time varies, but I usually spend 12-15 hours a week on my blog.

Attorney: I see your point. Well, we'll do some research and get back to you soon.

Peel: Thanks. I look forward to hearing from you.

$10,000 in School Equipment Diverted from Schools to Home of Assistant Superintendent

January 4, 2008: Greenville, Franklin
by Lisa Peel

The Greenville School District approved the purchase of $70,000 worth of new audiovisual and computer equipment for the schoolchildren of the Greenville School District this year, but not all of the equipment is in the schools. As the equipment arrived at the district offices, selected items were redirected to the home of Assistant Superintendent Frank Peterson, according to several sources closely associated with the school district. Sources estimate that Peterson has school district equipment worth over $10,000 at his home at the present time.

According to sources, who would speak only on the condition of anonymity, Peterson took selected items home "to test them out." But instead of returning these materials to the school, he kept them at his home.

At this time Peterson reportedly has at home two fully equipped desktop personal computers with two color printers, two laptop computers, one high-performance scanner, and a digital camera. He also has a classroom multimedia system in his home. That's $10,000 worth of *public* school equipment that he's using to create his own multimedia studio!

When asked for a response on Peterson's alleged activities, Greenville School Board President Annette Gross said, "We have policies in place to ensure that the public's dollars are spent according to budget."

Citizens should immediately ask President Gross for a full accounting of the purchases and for an investigation of Assistant Superintendent Peterson.

IN THE DISTRICT COURT FOR MONTGOMERY COUNTY
STATE OF FRANKLIN

SUBPOENA DUCES TECUM

In re Grand Jury Investigation

Grand Jury Case Number 08-7703

TO:

Elliot Wallace

Lisa Peel
9853 S. Elm Street
Greenville, Franklin 33755

YOU ARE COMMANDED TO APPEAR before the Grand Jury duly empaneled in the above-captioned case at the Montgomery County Courthouse, Room 346, March 10, 2008, at 10:00 a.m. YOU ARE COMMANDED TO PRODUCE all reports, files, notes, and other documentation regarding Greenville School District equipment in the possession of Assistant Superintendent Frank Peterson, including all files, notes, reports, and any other documentation taken of or from any and all persons interviewed for or sources described or quoted in the GREENVILLE CITIZEN BLOG operated by Lisa Peel and dated January 4, 2008.

Subpoena requested by the Montgomery County District Attorney's Office.

DATE ISSUED: February 20, 2008

Elliot Wallace
District Attorney

NOTICE:

FAILURE TO COMPLY WITH THIS SUBPOENA MAY RESULT IN FINES OR IMPRISONMENT OR BOTH.

AMERICA TODAY July 5, 2007

BLOGS COMPETING WITH NEWSPAPERS AND NETWORKS

Blogs—slang for Web logs—started out as online personal diaries or journals but have rapidly become part of the everyday Web vernacular and are replacing news websites for many readers.

Blog owners or "bloggers" establish Web pages on which they post news items, commentary, information, and links to other sources for readers. Readers are often invited to respond. For example, the blogger might post a movie review, and ask readers to post their opinions. Or the blogger might comment on the latest appropriations bill before Congress and encourage readers to share their views with their representatives.

According to recent surveys, at least 8 million adults in the United States have created blogs, and 30 percent of Americans read one or more blogs regularly. Blogs cover every topic imaginable—technology, sports, medicine, art, entertainment, business, news, and politics. Of course, many blogs still serve as forums for sharing personal experiences, from weddings to the contents of a blogger's junk drawer.

Journalists and politicians have learned the power of blogs and recognize that they are now a force to be reckoned with. For example, during the 2006 Congressional campaigns, bloggers challenged many of the candidates' statements. Several major bloggers have received press credentials for political events. Most major news outlets have several staff bloggers.

Blogging software is easy to use and inexpensive. Blogging is said to give a voice to those not given attention in the traditional media. It is just this ease of blogging that makes some professional journalists uncomfortable. "The blogger is the reporter, editor, and publisher. Where is the check on the blogger to ensure the truth?" asked Al Rains, Franklin Newspaper Association director. "Blogging isn't reporting, it's just writing. Any hack can offer half-baked commentary on the news of the day and post it online. How is that different from the millions of people who post items on their MySpace or Facebook pages?"

Other journalists see blogging as just another development in journalism—from newspapers to radio to TV to cable news, talk radio, and YouTube. "More means of sharing the news and inviting commentary is better than fewer means. I trust the public to learn from many sources and decide for themselves," says Tanya Browne, a journalism professor at Franklin University. "With so much media consolidation, there are many voices, especially local ones, that will be heard only through these 'alternative' forms of journalism."

LIBRARY

Franklin Reporter Shield Act

§ 900 Preamble

The primary purpose of this Act is to safeguard the media's ability to gather news. It is intended to promote the free flow of information to the public by prohibiting courts from compelling reporters to disclose unpublished news sources or information received from such sources.

§ 901 Definitions

As used in this Act:

(a) "reporter" means any person regularly engaged in collecting, writing, or editing news for publication through a news medium.

(b) "news medium" means any newspaper, magazine, or other similar medium issued at regular intervals and having a general circulation; a radio station; a television station; a community antenna television service; or any person or corporation engaged in the making of newsreels or other motion picture news for public showing.

(c) "source" means the person from whom or the means through which the information was obtained.

§ 902 Nondisclosure of source of information

No court may compel a reporter to disclose the source of any information or any unpublished material except as provided in this Act.

* * * *

Dictionary Definitions

The American Heritage Dictionary of the English Language (4th ed. 2000)

Blog: *noun* [shortened form of Web log], a website that contains an online personal journal with reflections, comments, and often hyperlinks provided by the writer.

Circulation: *noun*, movement in a circle or circuit, especially the movement of blood through blood vessels; .... free movement or passage; the passing of something, such as money or news, from place to place or person to person; the condition of being passed about and widely known, distribution; dissemination of printed material, especially copies of newspapers or magazines among readers; the number of copies of a publication sold or distributed.

Publication: *noun*, the act or process of publishing printed material; the communication of information to the public.

Publish: *verb*, to prepare and issue material for public disclosure or sale; to bring to public attention; to announce.

Reporter: *noun,* a writer, investigator, or presenter of news stories; a person who is authorized to write and issue official accounts of judicial or legislative proceedings.

In re Bellows

Franklin Court of Appeal (2005)

During Terrence Johnson's trial for murder, Johnson served a subpoena *duces tecum* upon respondent Peggy Bellows, a newspaper photographer employed by the *Springfield Review*. The subpoena required Bellows to produce certain photographs that she took during a police search of Johnson's residence prior to his arrest. When Bellows refused to produce the photos, the trial court found her in civil contempt and sentenced her to jail. This appeal followed.

The sole issue on appeal is whether Bellows is a reporter whose unpublished photographs are protected by the Franklin Reporter Shield Act (FRSA). In Franklin, reporters have a statutory, qualified privilege protecting their sources and unpublished material from compelled disclosure. FRSA § 902. It is the burden of the party claiming the privilege to establish his or her right to its protection. *Wehrmann v. Wickesberg* (Fr. Sup. Ct. 2002).

We note at the outset that testimonial privileges, in general, are not favored because they "contravene a fundamental principle of our jurisprudence that the public has a right to every man's evidence." *United States v. Bryan*, 339 U.S. 323 (1950). The preamble to the FRSA, on the other hand, states that the FRSA seeks to promote the free flow of information to and from the media by protecting the media's confidential sources. Hence, competing interests must be addressed in determining the FRSA's scope.

We have found few cases that discuss who, beyond members of the traditional media, has status to claim the journalist's privilege. In 2002, the Franklin Supreme Court rejected using the FRSA to protect the identities of those paying for newspaper ads disguised as journalism. *St. Mary's Hospital v. Zeus Publishing* (Fr. Sup. Ct. 2002). The full page ads recounted a hospital's alleged illegal labor practices and urged a boycott. Similarly, the Columbia Supreme Court rejected the argument that defamatory messages posted on a sports Internet bulletin board (GolfNet) could be construed as "news" or as being "published at regular intervals," and therefore held that the poster of the messages was not protected by the Columbia Reporter Shield Act. *Hausch v. Vaughan* (Col. Sup. Ct. 1995).

In contrast to these cases, the Franklin Supreme Court did grant FRSA protection to a freelance writer for a magazine, *Kaiser v. Currie* (Fr. Sup. Ct. 2004), and to the author of a medical journal article, *Halliwell v. Anderson* (Fr. Sup. Ct. 2002), holding that neither could be compelled to divulge their sources of information.

What we glean from these cases is that the test does not grant "reporter" status to any person simply because that person has a manuscript, a computer, a Web page, or a film. Rather, it requires an intent at the inception of the newsgathering process to disseminate investigative news to the public. Thus in *Hovey v. Fellenz* (Fr. Ct. App. 1989), the court held that the FRSA did not shield two reporters from having to testify about a crime that they happened to witness on their way home from work—when they witnessed the crime, they had no intent to disseminate news to the public. As we see it, the privilege is available only to persons whose purposes are those traditionally inherent to the press: gathering news for publication.

The FRSA defines a reporter as "any person regularly engaged in *collecting,* writing, or editing news for publication through a news medium." § 901(a) (emphasis added). Johnson claims Bellows is not covered by the FRSA for the simple reason that the Act doesn't mention "photographers." He claims that had the legislature intended to protect photographers, it would have included photographers in the statute.

Franklin law concerning statutory construction is clear. The principal rule of statutory construction is to ascertain and give effect to the legislature's intent. To determine the legislature's intent, courts first look to the statute's language. A court must give the legislative language its plain and ordinary meaning and construe the statute as a whole, giving effect to every word therein. When interpreting a statute, words and phrases must not be viewed in isolation but must be considered in light of other relevant provisions of the statute.

Where the language of the statute is clear and unambiguous, the only legitimate function of the courts is to enforce the law as enacted by the legislature. Courts should not depart from the plain language of the statute by reading into it exceptions, limitations, or conditions which conflict with the intent of the legislature. No rule of statutory construction authorizes the courts to declare that the legislature did not mean what the plain language of the statute says.

The record is clear from testimony of the *Springfield Review* editor that Bellows is employed as a photographer for the newspaper and that her permanent assignment is to "photograph newsworthy events." There is no dispute that the *Springfield Review*, a daily newspaper with a daily circulation of more than 100,000 readers, is a news medium. The record is also clear that, in her capacity as a photographer, Bellows does not write or edit.

The question then is whether she collects news by photographing newsworthy events. Where the legislature has supplied a definition, we are constrained to use only that definition. However, the legislature does not define the term "collecting" in the FRSA. In interpreting "the plain and ordinary meaning" of a word, where the legislature has not defined the term, courts may use a dictionary to assist in determining the plain and ordinary meaning. Turning to MERRIAM WEBSTER'S COLLEGIATE DICTIONARY 720 (10th ed. 1998), we find that collecting means "to bring together, gather, assemble." Taking photographs of events is one way to gather or assemble news. Bellows, by photographing newsworthy events, is regularly engaged in the gathering or assembling of news, and her activities fall within the statutory meaning of "collecting" news for publication.

Furthermore, extending the protections of the FRSA to photographers is consistent with the purpose of the Act. When it enacted the FRSA in 1948, the legislature stated the purpose of the Act as encouraging the free and unfettered flow of information to the public. The more recent amendments to the FRSA extend the protections to undisclosed materials as well as sources. *See* FRSA § 900. This provision protects the discretion of journalists to determine when and how to publish their materials.

Accordingly, Bellows meets the statutory definition of a reporter as she is a person regularly engaged in collecting news for publication through a news medium. Bellows is protected by the FRSA.

Reversed.

Lane v. Tichenor

Franklin Supreme Court (2003)

The sole question on appeal is whether the term "recreational purpose," as used in the Franklin Landowner's Recreational Immunity Act ("the Act"), § 730, includes hayrides. Lane brought this action against Tichenor for damages sustained during a hayride on Tichenor's land. On Tichenor's motion, the trial court dismissed the case and the appellate court affirmed.

The Act provides that landowners owe no duty of care to keep their premises safe for entry or use by any person for recreational purposes. The stated purpose of the Act is to "encourage owners of land to make land and water areas available to the public for recreational purposes by limiting their liability toward persons entering thereon for such purposes." § 730(1). Thus, the Act provides immunity only if the land is entered upon or used for a "recreational purpose."

The Act defines the term "recreational purpose" as follows: "'[r]ecreational purpose' includes any of the following, or any combination thereof: hunting, fishing, swimming, boating, snowmobiling, motorcycling, camping, hiking, cave exploring, nature study, water skiing, water sports, bicycling, horseback riding, and viewing or enjoying historical, archaeological, scenic or scientific sites, or other similar activities." § 730(2)(c).

Lane argues that because hayrides are not listed among the items defined in the Act, the legislature meant to exclude them from the definition of "recreational purpose," and therefore the Act does not apply here. Tichenor responds that the term "other similar activities" indicates the legislature's intent to broadly define the term "recreational purpose."

In interpreting a statute, the court is constrained to ascertain and give effect to the intent of the legislature. The statutory language is the best indication of the drafters' intent. Where that language is unambiguous, courts must enforce the law as enacted. Each word in the statute, as well as the punctuation used, is to be examined. Where the statute enumerates various covered activities, such enumeration implies the exclusion of all others.

However, in this case the statutory language is not clear, and the enumeration is neither exclusive nor exhaustive. While the legislature provided a list of activities intended as a definition of "recreational purpose," the question is what the legislature meant by "other similar activities." The question, more precisely, is whether hayrides fit within the phrase "other similar activities."

Where the language of a statute is unclear, the court may avail itself of external aids to interpret the statute. One such aid is the rules of construction of statutes, also called the canons of statutory interpretation. These rules or canons guide the court in ascertaining the intent of the legislature.

One canon, *ejusdem generis*, states that when general words follow particular and specific words in a statute, the general words must be construed to include only things of the same general kind as those indicated by the particular and specific words.

When we examine the items specifically enumerated in the Act, we find that the quality or characteristic common to all of them is the enjoyment of nature. While some may find enjoyment in fishing or hunting, others will find enjoyment in viewing historical or scientific sights, and still others in horseback riding or motorcycling. All of these activities take place outdoors and involve nature: the study of nature, the enjoyment of nature, or even travel through a natural setting.

Applying that quality to the present situation, a hayride is just another form of the enjoyment of nature. It is hard to see how hayrides are significantly different from horseback riding, motorcycling, or bicycling—all of which involve transporting oneself or others across the outdoors for enjoyment. One can imagine a group climbing onto a farm wagon, traveling along in the open, watching the stars, and communing with nature.

Lane further argues that while we should not apply this canon of construction at all, if we do, we must conclude that the quality common to all the enumerated or specific activities is that they occur by day. In this case, the hayride was conducted at night. However, we note that camping occurs overnight and that some fishing does as well. A starlit night far away from the lights and noise of a city, the crisp night air of an October evening, the snap and crackle of fall leaves accompanied by the sounds of night birds, the moonlight faintly illuminating old trees and fallen leaves, can all be enjoyed on a hayride at night under cover of darkness.

Because we hold that hayrides fall within the term "other similar activities" of the Act, we conclude that the trial court properly dismissed the case.

Affirmed.

Point Sheet
DRAFTERS' POINT SHEET

In this performance test item, applicants are employed by a law firm. Applicants' task is to prepare an objective memorandum evaluating whether a motion to quash will be successful with respect to a subpoena served on the firm's client, Lisa Peel. Peel operates an Internet Web log or "blog," which functions much as a newspaper, reporting news items and commentary; she is not a professional reporter. She recently posted to her blog a report that Greenville School District Assistant Superintendent Frank Peterson was using school district equipment in his home. The report was based on information from anonymous sources. Soon after the story was posted, Peel was served a subpoena duces tecum by the district attorney and ordered to appear before a grand jury and to bring notes and other documents concerning the sources of her information. Peel seeks the law firm's advice on whether there are grounds to resist the subpoena.

Applicants must analyze whether Peel is entitled to claim the protection of the Franklin Reporter Shield Act (FRSA), which provides that a reporter cannot be compelled to reveal his or her sources of information except as provided by the Act. The instructional memo instructs applicants not to address any First Amendment issues. To complete the assigned task, applicants must parse and interpret the statute and, in particular, the definitions of "reporter" and "news medium."

The File consists of the instructional memo from the supervising partner, a transcript of the interview with Peel, a copy of the item posted on the blog, the subpoena, and a news article about blogs. The Library consists of excerpts from the FRSA, several dictionary definitions, and two cases bearing on the subject.

The following discussion covers all of the points the drafters intended to raise in the problem. Applicants need not cover all of them to receive passing or even excellent grades. Grading is entirely within the discretion of the user jurisdictions.

I. Overview

The task is to draft an objective memorandum assessing whether there are grounds to quash the subpoena. The work product should resemble a legal memorandum such as one an associate would prepare for a supervising partner. The key issue is whether Peel qualifies as a "reporter" as defined in the Act; if so, she cannot be compelled to reveal the sources of her report, except as provided in the Act.

This is primarily an exercise in statutory interpretation. Applicants should thus examine the definitions provided in the Act, determine the elements of the definitions that must be met if Peel is to be protected by the Act, and reach a conclusion regarding whether Peel's blogging activities meet each element. With respect to the key definitions in the Act, it is expected that applicants will arrive at the following conclusions:

- **A "reporter" is any person regularly engaged in collecting, writing, or editing news for publication through a news medium.**
  - **Peel regularly engages or involves herself in collecting, writing, or editing the news, specifically, by attending meetings, analyzing public information, interviewing public officials, and writing summaries of and commentaries on their activities.**

- **The news written by Peel is published through a news medium.**
  - **A "news medium" is any newspaper, magazine, or other similar medium issued at regular intervals and having a general circulation.**
  - **Peel's blog is a publication issued at regular intervals and with a general circulation. Therefore, it qualifies as a news medium within the meaning of the Act.**

II. Relevant Facts

Applicants are instructed that they need not draft a separate statement of facts, but that they are expected to incorporate the relevant facts into their analysis. Some applicants may wish to set forth the facts at length. Others may wish to state only enough facts to set the scene and import other facts as necessary into their discussion of the issues.

A thorough discussion of whether Peel's blogging activities bring her within the Act's coverage would include the following facts:

- Peel began an Internet blog in which she publishes information about public bodies, including the agendas and minutes of public meetings, summaries of the meetings, and her own comments about the importance of these meetings.
- Peel attends meetings, obtains public documents, prepares summaries of the meetings and documents, and writes commentaries about the business of several public bodies. Peel's activities generally take about 12 to 15 hours per week.
- Peel's blog, the Greenville Citizen Blog, has at least 3,500 persons who are registered as readers. In order to post comments to the blog, readers must register with the blog; registration is free. There are likely many additional readers who are not registered.
- Peel usually posts items to the blog every Friday.
- There is no town newspaper and the only newspaper available is a countywide one that does not publish anything critical of the local communities.
- On January 4, 2008, Peel posted a news item to the blog reporting that Greenville School District Assistant Superintendent Frank Peterson was keeping school district audiovisual and computer equipment, worth approximately $10,000, in his home for his personal use.
- The blog posting about Peterson is based on information provided by confidential sources.
- The district attorney has subpoenaed Peel to appear before a grand jury and to bring notes concerning the source of her information about Frank Peterson.

III. Analysis

Applicants are told to analyze applicable legal authority and explain how the facts and law support their conclusions. The instructional memo emphasizes that both sides of the issue should be addressed; that is, applicants should discuss not only those facts that support a motion to quash but also those facts that weigh against the motion's success. Applicants should take care to address each of the elements of the definition of a reporter found in the Act. One format is for each element of the definition to be the subject of a separate heading followed by analysis related to that heading. Alternatively, applicants may organize their work product in other ways. The headings appearing below are exemplars only and are not intended as the only acceptable headings.

Whether Peel engages in the activities of a reporter for the purposes of the FRSA

- At the outset, applicants should note that the person claiming the privilege under the FRSA has the burden to establish his or her right to its protection. *In re Bellows* (Franklin Ct. App. 2005). Thus, in order to successfully resist the subpoena, the burden is on Peel to demonstrate that her blogging activities come within the ambit of the FRSA.
- The FRSA defines a reporter as "any person regularly engaged in collecting, writing, or editing news for publication through a news medium." FRSA § 901(a). Some of the terms in the statutory definition are further defined by statutes and others are not defined. Each of them must be interpreted.
  - In interpreting the FRSA, the court must ascertain and give effect to the intent of the legislature. Ordinarily the best indicator of the legislature's intent is the plain and ordinary meaning of the words used in the statute. Where the language is unambiguous, the court must rely on that language, giving effect to all the words in the statutory provision at issue. Where the legislature has defined terms, the court must use the definitions provided in the Act. *Bellows.*
  - NOTE: Applicants who rely on the dictionary definition of the term "reporter" have misconstrued the nature of statutory interpretation as explained in *Bellows*. The court is clear that where the legislature has defined a term, the court must rely on that definition.
    - Peel collects, writes, and edits news.
      - To collect news means to "gather or assemble" it. *Bellows.*
        - Peel gathers and assembles the news by obtaining public documents from public bodies, attending their meetings, and interviewing public officials.
      - Peel writes and edits the news by preparing summaries of minutes and other public documents and commentaries on the activities of several public bodies and posting them to her blog.
    - The term "news" is not defined in the Act. The plain and ordinary meaning of the term "news" involves activities of public bodies and the use of public monies.
      - Many of Peel's blog postings involve the activities of public bodies.
      - However, Peel's blog is not entirely devoted to news items. She posts recipes, gardening tips, and items about her family, as well as her vacation and pet photos, presumably none of which would be considered newsworthy.
    - The FRSA describes a reporter as someone who "regularly engages" in news-gathering activities. FRSA § 901(a). The term "regular" is not defined. However, common usage of the term would include weekly activities of attending meetings and posting items to the blog.
    - In addition, in *Bellows*, the court emphasized that the protections of the FRSA will be extended only to those individuals and organizations having "an intent at the inception of the news-gathering process to disseminate investigative news to the public."
      - Clearly Peel has the intent when she is attending civic meetings and interviewing officials to disseminate the news to the public via her blog. *Cf. Hovey v. Fellenz* (cited in *Bellows*) where

two reporters were not entitled to claim the protection of the FRSA when they witnessed the commission of a crime on their way home from work.

- Nevertheless, Peel has no training as a reporter and she is not employed by the traditional media. By contrast, the person deemed a "reporter" for FRSA purposes in *Bellows* was a professional news photographer.
- Likewise, *Kaiser v. Currie* and *Halliwell v. Anderson*, two cases cited in *Bellows* as examples of situations in which the Franklin courts have granted FRSA protection, involved persons writing for traditional media: a magazine and a medical journal.

Whether Peel's blog qualifies as a "news medium" under the FRSA

- A reporter collects, writes, or edits news for publication through a news medium. FRSA § 901(a). Thus applicants must determine whether Peel's blog is a "news medium" for purposes of the FRSA.
  - The term "news medium" is defined in the FRSA as "any newspaper, magazine, or other similar medium issued at regular intervals and having a general circulation . . . ." FRSA § 901(b).
  - Neither the term "Web log" nor "blog" is listed in the statute. Thus applicants must discuss whether an Internet blog like Peel's meets the definition of a "news medium."
    - The examples of news media provided in the statute are not an exhaustive or exclusive listing, because the definition includes the term "other similar medium." *See Lane v. Tichenor* (Franklin Sup. Ct. 2003).
    - Arguably, the use of the term "other similar medium" indicates the intent of the legislature to interpret "news medium" in a broad manner.
    - One canon of statutory construction, *ejusdem generis*, is helpful in interpreting the term "other similar medium." The canon states that when general words follow particular and specific words in a statute, the general words must be construed to include only things of the same general kind as those indicated by the particular and specific words. *Lane.*
      - In this case, one key quality common to the particular and specific words listed (i.e., newspapers and magazines) is that they are publications that occur on a regular basis.
      - However, it is also possible that the court may focus on the fact that newspapers and magazines are primarily print media.
      - Arguably, an indication that the legislature intended that the term "news medium" be interpreted in a broad manner is the long list of various forms of media listed in the statute; these media are not limited to print media, but encompass a broad range of means of communication. FRSA § 901(b).
      - And applicants could note that it is now common for newspapers and magazines to have online versions.
    - There is a strong argument that, like the listed forms of news media in § 901(b), Peel's blog is published at regular intervals and has a general circulation.

        - The word "publish" means "to prepare and issue material for public disclosure or sale; to bring to public attention; to announce." *American Heritage Dictionary.*
        - Peel posts items to the blog in order to bring them to the attention of the public. This is analogous to the printing and distribution of a newspaper or magazine.
            - Indeed, she states that, because of her blog, "I actually had citizens engaged in learning what their government was doing." Peel interview.
        - As a general rule, Peel posts new items to the blog on a regular basis— she tries to post new items every Friday. But sometimes it may be later in the weekend before new posts are on her website.
            - Thus, Peel's blog lacks the reliability of most traditional media (e.g., the morning newspaper or 11 p.m. news broadcast).
        - Nonetheless, Peel's blog can be distinguished from the Internet bulletin board in *Hausch v. Vaughan* (Col. Sup. Ct. 1995). In that case, the Columbia Supreme Court, interpreting the Columbia Reporter Shield Act, held that messages posted to an Internet bulletin board, which were posted intermittently, failed to meet that Act's requirement that to be a news medium, the claimed "news" had to be "published at regular intervals."
            - Peel's blog is updated every week.
            - And, unlike an Internet bulletin board, Peel's blog is not designed to be primarily a forum for readers to post messages for others to read. (In fact, she modified her blog so that only registered users could post comments.) Her blog is intended to inform members of her community about local government activities.
        - The term "circulation" is not defined in the Act, but the dictionary defines "circulation" as "the condition of being passed about and widely known, distribution; . . . the number of copies of a publication sold or distributed." *American Heritage Dictionary.*
        - In order to post to the blog, a reader must register with the blog. This is an act like subscribing, although there is no cost. The current registration for the blog totals over 3,500, or almost 10 percent of the Greenville population.
        - The large number of visitors (15,000) to Peel's blog indicates that, in addition to the more than 3,500 registered readers, there are many other regular or intermittent readers.
            - This relatively large readership is consistent with the statistics showing that millions of Americans either operate, read, or otherwise participate in blogs. *See America Today* article.
    - Additionally, the fact that the legislature used a broad range of means of communication or types of media when defining "news medium" suggests that an Internet blog is a news medium.
        - Words in statutes are not to be viewed in isolation but in light of other relevant provisions of the statute. *Bellows.*
    - Other news media included in the Act are radio, television, community antenna television, and news-

reels. FRSA § 901(b).

- Including a blog in the definition of "news medium" is consistent with the inclusion of more "modern" forms of communication in the Act.
  - Even though "blogs" and "bloggers" did not exist when the Franklin legislature enacted the FRSA in 1948, they are now, as indicated in the *America Today* article, a journalistic force to be reckoned with.

<u>Whether including Peel's blogging activities within the coverage of the FRSA serves the legislative intent underlying the Act</u>

- The intent of the legislature in enacting the statute was discussed in *Bellows*.
  - The Franklin legislature, in 1948, stated that the purpose of the Act was to encourage the free flow of information. *See* FRSA § 900 ("The primary purpose of this Act is to safeguard the media's ability to gather news. It is intended to promote the free flow of information to the public . . . .").
  - The purpose of promoting the free flow of information to the public applies here where Peel's blog is dedicated to that purpose, where the item posted on the blog reported on misconduct by a public official, where there is no town newspaper, and where the only newspaper in the county does not engage in investigative journalism.

IV. Conclusion

- Even though Peel is not a professional reporter employed by traditional media, because she is regularly engaged in collecting, writing, and editing the news for publication on her blog, which is a news medium, being published at regular intervals and having a general circulation, she should be deemed a reporter under the FRSA.
- Because she is a reporter under the FRSA, she cannot be compelled to reveal the identity of the source of the information for the article that appeared in the blog.

Therefore, it is probable that a motion to quash the subpoena based on the FRSA privilege will be successful.

In Re Lisa Peel Sample Answer

MEMORANDUM

TO: Henry Black
FROM: Applicant

RE: Peel Subpoena

DATE: February 26, 2008

After reviewing the relevant authority, it is my opinion that the Franklin Reporter Shield Act (FRSA) will apply to Ms. Peel and her blog. My conclusion is based on current case law as well as the rules of statutory construction. I base my findings on the In Re Bellows and Lane v. Tichenor. The key issues to focus on when determining whether the statute is applicable are the intended meanings of the term "reporter" and "news medium" in the FRSA.

<u>Definition of Reporter</u>

In Bellows the court discussed the test utilized when determining whether one would be deemed a reporter. The court indicated that the focus should be on the "intent at the inception of the newsgathering process to disseminate investigative news to the public." Ms. Peel clearly has satisfied this burden. While her blog does contain extraneous portions (i.e. gardening tips and personal photos), there is an intention on her part to accurately investigate, uncover, and publish newsworthy information on her blog. Although this was not the initial purpose of the blog, it does appear to be one of the primary goals now. Therefore, I believe she should be classified as a reporter.

We must also look at the face of the statute itself when trying to ascertain the proper definition of a reporter. The FRSA defines a reporter as "any person regularly engaged in collecting, writing, or editing news for publication through a news medium." The main rule of statutory construction requires us to look at the face of the statute first to garner the intended meaning of terms. If the meaning is ambiguous on the face of the statute, then it is acceptable to give words their plain, ordinary meaning (p. 12). In Bellows 'collecting' was given its dictionary definition to help the court decide whether a photographer came under the heading of a reporter. In our present case, this interpretation is extremely useful. Collecting, according to the Bellows court, meant to bring together, gather, and assemble. That is precisely what Ms. Peel does. She herself has said she attends public meetings, reads documents, and performs investigations in a similar manner as a traditional reporter, She gathers the information with the previously discussed intent to disseminate it.

When we apply the everyday meaning to a term of a statute, we must ensure that the legislature's intent remains intact. And in our case, it does. The intent is clear on the face of the statute. The FRSA is designed to promote the free flow of information to the public and by allowing Ms. Peel to protect her sources, there is a greater chance others will come forward with information pertaining to matters of public concern.

<u>Definition of News Medium</u>

Ms. Peel's blog constitutes a news medium for purposes of the FRSA. Again, we are allowed to utilize additional sources because the language of the statute is ambiguous. In Lane, the court utilized a canon of statutory interpretation known as ejusdem generis to help clarify the reaches of a statute. The canon states that when general words follow particular specific words in a statute, the general words must be construed to include only things of the same general kind as those indicated by the particular and specific words (p. 15). This canon can be applied to the FRSA's section defining a news medium. The FRSA begins by stating specific mediums such as newspapers and magazines, then proceeds to use the general description of other similar medium issued at regular intervals. It is my opinion that Ms. Peel's blog has the same vital characteristics as a newspaper or magazine. Both mediums involve investigation of matters of public interest. The facts discovered are then compiled, edited, and published at regular intervals for the general public. These are the defining characteristics of all 3 and as such, serves as evidence that the blog should be considered a news medium.

Possible Adverse Arguments

There are a few points that should be noted, which may be raised by opposing counsel. First, in the case of St. Mary's Hospital v Zeus Publishing, the court held that a full page ad revealing illegal activity was not news. Similarly, the Columbia Supreme Court has rejected the argument that defamatory messages posted on a Sports Internet Bulletin constitute news. These two cases are important to note because when one thinks of a blog, one often thinks of a series of internet postings versus something akin to the New York Times. Therefore, opposing counsel may try to argue that Ms. Peel's blog is more like the online bulletin or full page ad than a traditional news source. These two examples can be distinguished from the case at hand. The full page ad was not the result of consistent investigatory work that continually produces newsworthy information and articles for the general public. It was not a medium but rather a one time announcement. The Sports bulletin case dealt with defamatory statements being posted with no particular time intervals specified. There is no evidence that the contents of the online bulletin was the result of work akin to that of an investigative reporter, whose main intent is to disseminate truthful information to the public for their benefit.

One important factor to note is that neither the full page ad nor the Sports bulletin seemed to have set intervals for publication. Opposing counsel may try to argue that this is also the case for Ms. Peel's blog since it is not updated at the same time each week. However, the time frame for the blog's entries (every 7-9 days) is fairly consistent and would probably be able to withstand such an argument.

For the above mentioned reasons, it is my opinion that Ms. Peel should be able to claim the protection of FRSA.

NATIONAL CONFERENCE OF BAR EXAMINERS

Petrilla and Associates
Attorneys at Law
222 Van Every Place
Centralia, Franklin 33703

Office Memorandum

To: Applicant
From: Charles Petrilla, Managing Partner and Pro Bono Coordinator
Date: July 29, 2008
Re: Jessica Bohmer/Interstate Custody Case

Our law firm, as part of its pro bono program, has agreed to represent Jessica Bohmer in a child custody matter that her husband, Alex Bohmer, has filed in Franklin City, Franklin. Jessica currently lives with their six-year-old daughter, Carrie, in Columbia Heights, Columbia.

No divorce proceeding has yet been filed by either party. On June 30, 2008, Jessica's husband filed a child custody petition in Franklin District Court. We hope to convince the Franklin court that the case should be heard in Columbia where Columbia Legal Services is prepared to help Jessica file a custody action and obtain a civil protection order if necessary.

I just spoke to Columbia Legal Services this morning and will be talking to Jessica and Columbia Legal Services tomorrow. I want to be able to give them some answers regarding jurisdiction. To help me advise them, please prepare a memorandum analyzing the following two issues:

1. Whether Franklin or Columbia was the home-state jurisdiction under the Franklin Uniform Child Custody Jurisdiction and Enforcement Act (UCCJEA) at the time of the filing of the current custody case in Franklin.
2. Assuming for purposes of argument that the Franklin court decides that Franklin is the home-state jurisdiction, whether we are likely to be successful if we file a Motion to Decline Jurisdiction under the Inconvenient Forum provision of the Franklin UCCJEA.

Be sure to provide detailed discussion and analysis, incorporating the relevant facts and addressing the applicable legal authorities. I want to know the weaknesses as well as the strengths of a potential motion on Jessica's behalf. You need not prepare a separate statement of facts.

Transcript of Telephone Call

[Kathleen Murphy (KM), Columbia Legal Services attorney, and Charles Petrilla (CP), Franklin law firm partner, July 29, 2008]

KM: Charles, thanks very much for calling. I'm glad you've agreed to take Jessica's case because she needs representation in Franklin as well as in Columbia.

CP: Kathleen, I'm happy we can help. Thanks for faxing us a copy of the intake form and the Civil Protection Order issued in 2006 in Franklin against Jessica's husband, Alex. I've reviewed the intake form, but want to know if there have been any new developments. Have you filed a custody action on Jessica's behalf in Columbia?

KM: No, not yet. Jessica came into our office a little over two weeks ago seeking our help in obtaining sole custody of Carrie, and possibly with obtaining another civil protection order if Alex continues to threaten her. However, on June 30, 2008, Alex filed for custody of Carrie in Franklin District Court. We haven't actually seen a copy of Alex's complaint yet.

CP: I will get a copy from the court today and fax it to you. What are Jessica's concerns regarding having custody handled in Franklin?

KM: She's afraid to go back to Franklin City because of Alex's history of violence against her. She says that he owns a hunting rifle and she fears that he might use it to hurt her or Carrie. The most recent threatening episode was on February 1, 2008, when Alex became enraged when Jessica suggested a short visit to Columbia Heights to see her parents and Carrie, who was staying there with Jessica's parents. He ripped up several family photos. That really scared her—she left for Columbia the next day, on February 2, 2008, and hasn't been back since. Jessica also doesn't have the time or the money to go back and forth to Franklin City—the drive takes about an hour and a half, one way, and would require her to take time off from her new job.

CP: Does she intend to stay in Columbia?

KM: Yes. When she left Franklin on February 2, 2008, she didn't really have a plan. She told Alex that she would be back soon. However, after about three weeks in Columbia, she realized that she didn't want to go back to Franklin. She found a job and enrolled Carrie in the first grade in Columbia Heights. On March 1, 2008, she finally got up the courage and told Alex she wasn't coming back to Franklin but was going to stay with Carrie in Columbia.

CP: How did Alex react to that news?

KM: According to Jessica, he "flipped out." For weeks, he phoned her day and night, calling her all sorts of names. He also sent her a series of threatening e-mails like the one attached to the intake form.

CP: How does Jessica want to have the situation resolved?

KM: She wants sole custody of Carrie and wants to continue to live in Columbia, where her parents live. Having them nearby makes her feel safer, and they also help take care of Carrie. Jessica likes her new part-time job at a doctor's office and wants to enroll at the community college to finish her degree. Carrie's doing really well in school and has made a lot of friends. Carrie has told Jessica that she wants to stay in Columbia.

CP: We'll have to figure out which court should handle this matter. The UCCJEA is the law that controls which court has jurisdiction to hear custody cases. Both Columbia and Franklin adopted identical versions of this law. Let's see what the law is on this issue.

KM: We really hope that you can find a way to get the Franklin custody case resolved so that we can go forward here in Columbia. I will begin to prepare pleadings so that we can be ready to proceed in Columbia. Jessica is meeting with us tomorrow.

CP: Okay. I'll call you again tomorrow after we have done some research on our end.

Columbia Legal Services Intake Form

Date: July 14, 2008 **Intake Attorney:** Kathleen Murphy

I. Applicant Name: Jessica Bohmer

DOB: 5/30/1976 **Place of birth:** Columbia Heights, Columbia

Home address: 6226 Berkeley Blvd., Columbia Heights, Columbia 12111

Home telephone: 860-555-5688

Work address: Office of Stephen Tigani, MD, 10 Tulip Ave., Columbia Heights, Columbia

Work telephone: 860-555-3876

Is it safe to call the phone numbers listed? __X__ **yes** ______ **no**

Are the parties married? __X__ **yes** ______ **no**

If so, date and place of marriage: 3/29/2001, Columbia Heights, Columbia

Child(ren) in common. Include name, sex, and date and place of birth.

Carrie Bohmer, female, born 3/22/2002, Memorial Hospital, Columbia Heights, Columbia

Residence of applicant and child(ren) for the past 5 years. Include addresses, dates, and other people living with applicant.

1. 1/15/2003 to 5/31/2004: 28 Lanier St., Columbia Heights, Columbia; both parents and child;
2. 6/1/2004 to 5/30/2006: 1311 Taylor St., Franklin City, Franklin; both parents and child;
3. 5/31/2006 to 4/1/2007: 12 Ivy Lane, Franklin City, Franklin; mother and child only;
4. 4/2/2007 to 2/01/2008: 1311 Taylor St., Franklin City, Franklin; both parents and child (mother and child moved back with father);
5. 2/02/2008 to present: 6226 Berkeley Blvd., Columbia Heights, Columbia; mother, maternal grandparents, and child (mother moved in with her parents and child on February 2, 2008; child had been visiting her maternal grandparents since December 1, 2007).

What legal services is applicant seeking?

Jessica seeks to obtain sole custody of Carrie and protection from her husband's violence.

II. Opposing Party Name: Alex Bohmer

DOB: 10/18/1976 **Place of birth:** Columbia Heights, Columbia

Home address: 1311 Taylor St., Franklin City, Franklin 33068

Home telephone: 514-555-6999

Work address: Franklin Pharmaceutical Co., 101 Industrial Blvd., Franklin City, Franklin

Work telephone: 514-555-2339

Criminal history: n/a

Weapons: owns hunting rifle

Alcohol/drug use: drinks a few beers every weekend

Participation in drug/alcohol treatment: n/a

Participation in domestic violence intervention program: n/a

Has opposing party ever put his/her hands on applicant against applicant's will? Yes

If yes, fill out Section III, Domestic Violence History

III. Domestic Violence History

Has applicant's spouse/partner forced applicant to do something by threatening applicant?

Yes, since Jessica was pregnant with Carrie, Alex has been physically and emotionally abusive. He has pushed her down, grabbed her, pulled her by the hair, slapped her in the face, and tried to choke her. He has refused to give her money, prevented her from going out with friends, and generally tried to interfere with her relationship with her large extended family.

What was the most recent incident?

On February 1, 2008, Alex got mad when Jessica told him she wanted to go for a short visit to Columbia to see Carrie and her family. He grabbed her by the shoulders and shook her. When she tried to get away, he got one of her family scrapbooks and took out several photos of her with her parents and ripped them up. Jessica was scared but managed to act calm. She left the next day for Columbia and told Alex she would be back in a few weeks.

What was the worst incident ever?

On Jessica's 30th birthday (5/30/2006), Alex pushed her down on the floor, then pulled her up and choked her. Jessica thought she was going to lose consciousness. She feared that he might really kill her. She had bruises on her neck and arms. She left the next day with Carrie and filed for a civil protection order, which was granted on 6/10/2006. She and Alex were separated for approximately 10 months before reuniting. She let the civil protection order lapse.

Has/have applicant's child(ren) been abused by applicant's spouse/partner?

Alex has never attacked Carrie directly, but she has witnessed his violence against Jessica. When Alex, Jessica, and Carrie were living together as a family, Carrie frequently said that she was afraid "Daddy would get mad" at her, which Jessica interpreted as Carrie's fear that Alex would also hit Carrie. Carrie used to have nightmares, but those have subsided since she and Jessica moved out.

Additional history:

Jessica has never told anyone all the details about the abuse, although her family has suspected serious problems for a long time. Her family has witnessed the harassing phone calls Alex made after she moved to Columbia. Jessica wants to stay in Columbia because she has a place to live and a good part-time job, and because her mother is available to watch Carrie whenever needed. Jessica also plans to enroll in a community college here and complete her college degree.

Police reports: n/a

Hospital records: n/a

Prior Protection Orders: Yes, see Attachment A.

Date Issued	Jurisdiction	Disposition
6-10-2006	Franklin District Court	Consent Civil Protection Order, expired 6-9-2007

Other documents: See Attachment B.

IV. Income

Applicant employed: yes **Approximate gross income:** $10,000

Opposing party employed: yes **Approximate gross income:** $55,000

DISTRICT COURT OF FRANKLIN

Jessica Bohmer, Petitioner, }
} **DV No. 0569-2006**
vs. }
}
Alex Bohmer, Respondent. }

CIVIL PROTECTION ORDER

Upon consideration of the petition filed in this case, and after a contested hearing, o after a default hearing, x by consent of the parties, the Court has determined:

x that the Petitioner has established by a preponderance of the evidence that there is good cause to believe that the parties have a family relationship and that the Respondent committed or threatened one or more acts of domestic violence within the meaning of Franklin Code § 12-105 *et seq.*, to wit, that the Respondent threatened to seriously harm the Petitioner and that he put his hands on Petitioner's neck in an attempt to choke her.

IT IS HEREBY ORDERED that for a period of 12 months from the date of this order:

x Respondent shall not assault, threaten, harass, or physically abuse Petitioner in any manner.

x Respondent shall stay at least 100 feet away from Petitioner's x person, x home,
x workplace, x vehicle.

x Respondent shall not contact Petitioner in any manner, except by telephone; all telephone calls must be limited to reasonable hours of the day and must abide by the other provisions of this order.

x Respondent may not possess any firearms and must immediately turn over any such weapons he or she owns to the Franklin City Metropolitan Police Department.

THIS ORDER WILL EXPIRE IN 12 MONTHS UNLESS IT IS RENEWED BY THE COURT. FAILURE TO COMPLY WITH THIS ORDER IS A CRIMINAL OFFENSE AND CARRIES A PENALTY OF SIX MONTHS IN JAIL AND/OR A FINE OF $1,000.

nly) Date 6-10-06

6/10/2006

To: jessicabohmer@mpt.com
From: alexbohmer@mpt.com
Date: March 10, 2008

Jessica,

You should think twice about leaving Franklin and taking Carrie. I mean business—if you don't come back soon, I guarantee you that you'll be sorry. I'm not going to sit still and let you walk all over me!

You know you can't take care of Carrie without me. Remember what happened the last time when you ran off and then came back begging for another chance? Besides, you're taking Carrie away from her life here—her school and her friends.

This is it, Jessica. I am not playing any more of your games. For Carrie's own good, I'm not going to let you cut me out of her life.

You know we could make this work if you would just try a little harder instead of quitting and running off to your parents every time we argue. I'm willing to meet you halfway—I know I've got a bad temper, and I've got an appointment with a therapist next week—but Carrie is my daughter and she needs her daddy as well as her mommy.

Alex

LIBRARY

FRANKLIN UNIFORM CHILD CUSTODY JURISDICTION AND ENFORCEMENT ACT (§ 16-101 *et seq.* (1999))

* * * *

§ 16-102. Definitions. In this Act:

* * * *

(3) "Child custody determination" means a judgment, decree, or other order of a court providing for the legal custody, physical custody, or visitation with respect to a child. The term includes a permanent, temporary, initial, or modification order. . . .

* * * *

(7) "Home State" means the State in which a child lived with a parent for at least six consecutive months immediately before the commencement of a child custody proceeding. . . . A period of temporary absence of any of the mentioned persons is part of the period.

* * * *

§ 16-201. Initial Child Custody Jurisdiction.

(a) Except as otherwise provided . . . a court of this State has jurisdiction to make an initial child custody determination only if:

(1) this State is the home State of the child on the date of the commencement of the proceeding, or was the home State of the child within six months before the commencement of the proceeding and the child is absent from this State but a parent continues to live in this State;

(2) . . . or a court of the home State of the child has declined to exercise jurisdiction on the ground that this State is the more appropriate forum under § 16-207 . . . .

* * * *

§ 16-207. Inconvenient Forum.

(a) A court of this State which has jurisdiction under this [Act] to make a child custody determination may decline to exercise its jurisdiction at any time if it determines that it is an inconvenient forum under the circumstances and that a court of another State is a more appropriate forum. The issue of inconvenient forum may be raised upon motion of a party, the court's own motion, or request of another court.

(b) Before determining whether it is an inconvenient forum, a court of this State shall consider whether it is appropriate for a court of another State to exercise jurisdiction. For this purpose, the court shall allow the parties to submit information and shall consider all relevant factors, including:

(1) whether domestic violence has occurred and is likely to continue in the future and which State could best protect the parties and the child;

(2) the length of time the child has resided outside this State;

(3) the distance between the court in this State and the court in the State that would assume jurisdiction;

(4) the relative financial circumstances of the parties;

(5) the nature and location of the evidence required to resolve the pending litigation, including testimony of the child; and

(6) the familiarity of the court of each State with the facts and issues in the pending litigation.

(c) If a court of this State determines that it is an inconvenient forum and that a court of another State is a more appropriate forum, it shall stay the proceedings upon condition that a child custody proceeding be promptly commenced in another designated State and may impose any other condition the court considers just and proper.

In re Marriage of Mills

Franklin Court of Appeal (2002)

William and Jennifer Mills were married in 1993. They have two children. The parties separated in November 1999, when William moved from the family home to a nearby town in Franklin where he had secured a new job. Jennifer and the children remained in the family home in Franklin City.

In June 2000, the children went to Columbia for an extended visit to Jennifer's sister's farm. On August 10, 2000, Jennifer decided to leave Franklin with her mother and permanently move to Columbia and did so with the children. Thereafter, she rented a house, enrolled the children in school, and found a new job in Columbia. Jennifer has resided in Columbia with the children and her mother since moving there. However, Jennifer did not have an explicit conversation with William about her permanent relocation until sometime during the fall—the exact date is disputed, but both agree it was no earlier than November 1, 2000.

On April 1, 2001, William filed a petition in Franklin District Court seeking custody of the parties' two children.8

Jennifer moved to dismiss the petition, arguing that the Franklin court lacked subject matter jurisdiction to determine custody of the parties' children, on the grounds that Columbia was the children's "home state." The trial court granted the motion, concluding that it lacked subject matter jurisdiction under the Franklin Uniform Child Custody Jurisdiction and Enforcement Act (UCCJEA), § 16-101 *et seq*. William appeals. We affirm.

Under the UCCJEA, a Franklin court has subject matter jurisdiction to make a child custody determination if Franklin is the "home state" of the child. "Home state" is defined as the state in which a child lived with a parent for at least six months immediately before the commencement of a child custody proceeding. *See* UCCJEA § 16-102(7). Any period(s) of temporary absence are considered part of and included in the calculation of the six-month home-state requirement. *Id.*

8 It is not unusual for child custody actions to be undertaken without a request to dissolve the marriage.

On appeal William contends that the district court should have asserted jurisdiction under the UCCJEA to decide custody of the children because the children were only temporarily absent from Franklin and temporary absences are considered time in the home state. Specifically, he argues that when Jennifer left the state on August 10, 2000, she did so with the intent of returning to Franklin, and that she did not inform him that she intended to remain in Columbia with the children until at the earliest November 1, 2000. He thus maintains that the children's absence from Franklin was only a "temporary absence," and that they should be considered to have resided in Franklin until November 1, 2000.

While we agree that intent is a significant consideration in determining whether an absence from a state is a "temporary absence," we do not believe that the significance of intent can or should be restricted to the intent existing at the time of leaving. If it were so restricted, then an absence that began with intent to return would remain a "temporary absence" even long after a decision had been reached to permanently relocate and such relocation to another state had in fact occurred. We believe instead that an absence from a state is no longer "temporary" once the absent person has formed the intent to reside permanently in another state and is in fact doing so with such intent.

In this case the children's presence in Columbia beginning in June 2000 was originally intended to be temporary. However, the parties had separated some seven months earlier and, as of August 10, 2000, Jennifer moved to Columbia intending to permanently relocate there with the parties' children. She has since resided there with them, with that intent. We conclude that the relevant six-month period began to run on August 10, 2000. We therefore agree with the trial court that Columbia, and not Franklin, was the children's "home state" when William filed his April 1, 2001, petition for custody, and that under UCCJEA § 16-201(a), the Franklin court did not have jurisdiction to make a child custody determination. In so concluding, we reject William's contention that the children's absence from Franklin must be considered a "temporary absence" until Jennifer expressly informed him in November that her earlier move to Columbia, of which he was aware, had been made with the intent that she and the children would remain in Columbia permanently.

Affirmed.

In re Marriage of Brickman and Young
Franklin Supreme Court (2003)

Mark Brickman commenced this action seeking to modify custody of his four minor children. His former wife, Ruth Young, moved to dismiss under the Franklin Uniform Child Custody Jurisdiction and Enforcement Act (UCCJEA) on the ground that Franklin is an inconvenient forum. She appeals the district court's denial of her motion, as affirmed by the court of appeal. We granted review, and now reverse and remand.

BACKGROUND

Brickman and Young married on October 1, 1988, in Livingston, Franklin. Thereafter, they separated and reconciled numerous times before finally separating in 1996.

Brickman repeatedly battered Young during the marriage, and Young obtained several court-issued protection orders during their multiple separations. Brickman pled guilty to domestic assault in 1990, 1991, 1994, and 1996. The record details Brickman's violations of the protection orders, as well as several incidents involving Brickman's violent behavior after the parties' final separation and before Young's move to Columbia.

In its March 23, 1998, marriage dissolution decree, the Franklin District Court, among other things, awarded custody of the parties' four children to Young. Shortly thereafter, Young relocated to the State of Columbia with her children. In response, Brickman filed a motion in Franklin District Court seeking to modify the court's decree and to obtain custody. Young then subsequently filed a motion requesting the Franklin District Court to decline jurisdiction as an inconvenient forum to allow the Columbia court to assume jurisdiction over the parties' ongoing child custody and visitation arrangements. Brickman opposed the motion. The Franklin District Court denied the motion; the court of appeal affirmed, and we granted review.

DISCUSSION

In this case of first impression we examine the provisions of the Franklin UCCJEA that allow a court to decline to exercise jurisdiction over child custody proceedings when the court determines that it is an inconvenient forum under the circumstances and that a court of another state is a more appropriate forum in which to make the child custody determination.

The Franklin UCCJEA sets forth six specific factors to be considered, which we discuss in turn below. We note that, while some factors may weigh more heavily than others, *all* must be considered by the court. The law does not allocate a burden of proof to either party, but directs the court to conduct an evaluation based upon the relevant information available to determine whether it is appropriate for another state to exercise jurisdiction.

The first inconvenient forum factor inquires "whether domestic violence has occurred and is likely to continue in the future and which State could best protect the parties and the child." UCCJEA § 16-207(b)(1). The UCCJEA places domestic violence at the top of the list of factors that courts are required to evaluate when determining whether to decline jurisdiction as an inconvenient forum for a child custody proceeding. With regard to this factor, the court should determine whether the parties are located in different states because one party is a victim of domestic violence or child abuse. If domestic violence or child abuse has occurred, the issue is which forum can provide greater safety.9

Given the high propensity for recidivism in domestic violence, we hold that when a court finds that domestic violence has occurred or that a party has fled the state to avoid further violence or abuse, the court is authorized to consider whether the party and the child might be better protected if further custody proceedings were held in another state. This factor alone is not dispositive under the UCCJEA; however, courts should give greater weight to this factor than to any other individual factor when considering jurisdictional issues under the UCCJEA.

Brickman asserts on appeal that his last act of reported domestic violence occurred in 1996 and claims that there

9 The compelling need to protect victims from further domestic violence is supported by the research findings of the United States Department of Justice. Those findings suggest that termination of an abusive relationship actually poses an increased risk of escalation in domestic violence. Although divorced women and separated women comprise only 10 percent of all women in America, they account for three-quarters of all battered women and report being battered 14 times as often as women still living with their partners. Divorced or separated men, as opposed to husbands living with their wives, commit 79 percent of all spousal violence.

has been "no apparent problem" during the past three years.

But Brickman's criminal record of domestic violence reveals a pattern of recurrent wife-battering of escalating intensity, which includes severely beating Young during her pregnancies. The record also establishes that Brickman has perpetrated serious injury upon his ex-wife and has exhibited obsessive and controlling behavior. Brickman testified at the May 2001 hearing that he had not received any type of psychological counseling since his last incarceration in 1996 for domestic violence. Moreover, he made no showing to the district court that his potential for future violence has abated.

This history of serious domestic violence and the threat of future domestic violence by Brickman leads us to conclude that with regard to this factor, Columbia is the state that would best protect Young and the children.

The second statutory factor asks how long the children have resided outside Franklin. UCCJEA § 16-207(b)(2). The district court relied heavily on the fact that the children have spent the majority of their lives in Franklin and on the extensive history of the parties in the Franklin courts. However, the four children, ranging in age from four to eleven at the time of the hearing, have now lived in Columbia for five years. Young testified that the children "have significant connections to family, school, and community" in Columbia and have developed relationships that have enhanced their sense of security and well-being, which is "a contrast from the isolation they experienced while living in Franklin." Because it has been the children's home for the past five years, we conclude that, on this factor, Columbia would be an appropriate forum for child custody proceedings.

The third factor evaluates the distance between the courts, which is approximately 400 miles in this case. UCCJEA § 16-207(b)(3). Young testified that the drive between her home and the court in Franklin takes about eight hours each way. As the primary custodial parent, Young must either bring the children with her to court proceedings or arrange for their care in her absence. Because the distance between the Franklin and Columbia courts creates a transportation inconvenience that must be borne by one of the parties, we conclude that the facts suggest that Brickman, as the non-custodial parent, may be in the better position to undertake the necessary travel.

The fourth factor concerns the relative financial circumstances of the parties, which the district court found to be disparate. UCCJEA § 16-207(b)(4). The court determined that Brickman enjoys an annual income of $41,797 while Young has an annual income of $6,500. We conclude that this factor weighs in favor of transfer to Columbia's jurisdiction.

The fifth factor examines the traditional bases for determining venue and inquires about the nature and location of the evidence required to resolve the pending litigation, including testimony of the children. UCCJEA § 16-207(b)(5). Notwithstanding Young's testimony that all current evidence regarding the children's mental health, medical, financial, and school records is in Columbia, the district court concluded that Franklin is just as convenient a forum as Columbia for review of pertinent child records. Although records may be easily transportable, the district court failed to address the convenience of the witnesses, the majority of whom reside in Columbia, including the four children. Three of the children are enrolled in school and receive therapeutic counseling in Columbia. Young maintains that Columbia is now the location of all witnesses and evidence regarding the children. Brickman did not refute Young's assertions regarding the location of evidence and witnesses. This factor weighs in favor of Columbia's jurisdiction.

The final factor is the familiarity of the court of each state with the facts and issues in the pending litigation. UCCJEA § 16-207(b)(6). There has been extensive litigation concerning this marriage in the Franklin court—the case file is now in its fifth volume. But while the Franklin court may be well versed in the conflict, Young argues persuasively that the Columbia court also has had an opportunity to at least become familiar with the facts and issues involved in the case, when she applied for and received a permanent protection order in 2001 from the Columbia court. Therefore, under this factor, while the Franklin court might be the more appropriate forum, we conclude that the Columbia court would not be an inappropriate forum.

CONCLUSION

Weighing all the factors together, and giving added weight to the first factor concerning the existence of past and danger of continuing violence, we conclude that Columbia is the more appropriate forum to resolve this custody dispute.

Accordingly, we reverse the court of appeal's affirmance of the district court's order and remand to the district court with instructions to stay further proceedings and to direct the parties to file in Columbia, the more appropriate forum.

Reversed and remanded.

Bohmer v. Bohmer Sample Answers

MPT I Sample Answer #1

To: Charles Petrilla

From: Applicant

Date: July 29, 2008

Re: Bohmer Custody Case

1. FRANKLIN UCCJEA §16-102(7) ESTABLISHES THAT FRANKLIN WAS THE HOME-STATE JURISDICTION AT THE TIME OF FILING

A Franklin court has jurisdiction to make an initial child custody determination only if Franklin is the child's home-state on the date of the commencement of the proceeding, or was the home-state of the child within 6 months before the commencement of the proceeding and the child is absent from Franklin but a parent continues to live in Franklin. See UCCJEA §§16-102(7); 16-201(a)(1). Franklin is considered the "home-state" of a child if the child has lived with a parent for at least 6 months immediately before the commencement of a child custody proceeding. When calculating the home-state requirement, any period of temporary absence of the child or parent(s) is considered part of and included in the relevant 6 month period. *Id.* An absence from Franklin is no longer "temporary" once the absent person has formed the intent to reside permanently in another state and is in fact doing so. *In re: Marriage of Mills.*

Applying the above standard, Franklin had home-state jurisdiction when Alex Bohmer filed for custody in Franklin District Court on 6-30-2008. On 12-1-07, Carrie, the Bohmer's child, went to visit her grandparents in the state of Columbia. Although she has remained there ever since, the original intention was for Carrie to just visit. Therefore, 12-1-07 cannot be used as the starting point for Carrie's permanent residence in Columbia. Instead, only when the intent for Carrie to remain permanently in Columbia does the 6 month time period begin. Furthermore, UCCJEA requires that the child live with a parent in the home-state for at least 6 months. Here, although Jessica Bohmer has remained in Columbia since 2-2-08, she did not decide to remain there permanently until approximately three months later. Therefore, the 6-month time period when Jessica and Carrie resided in Columbia began at the end of Feb. 2008. Since Franklin was Carrie's home-state within 6 months before Alex filed on 6-30-08 and Alex continues to live in Franklin, the Franklin court, pursuant to UCCJEA §16-201(a)(1) could properly exercise jurisdiction over an initial child custody determination even though Carrie was absent from the state at the time of filing.

2. JESSICA BOHMER IS LIKELY TO SUCCEED IF SHE FILES A MOTION TO DECLINE JURISDICTION UNDER THE UCCJEA'S INCONVENIENT FORUM PROVISION

Franklin UCCJEA§16-207 sets forth 6 specific factors to be considered by the court when determining whether it is an inconvenient forum and that a court of another state is a more appropriate forum. *In re: Marriage of Brickman and Young.* All of these factors must be considered although the court should give more weight to some when making its determination. If Jessica files a motion to decline jurisdiction under the inconvenient forum provision of the Franklin UCCJEA, the Franklin court, upon weighing these factors, is likely to grant her motion so that the proceedings may be filed in Columbia, a more appropriate forum.

The first factor to be considered, whether domestic violence has occurred and is likely to continue and which State could best protect the parties and the child, is given the most weight. When domestic violence has occurred, the issue is which forum can provide greater safety. In this case, Alex has abused Jessica since 2001, when she was still pregnant with Carrie. This abuse has continued until at least 5-30-06 and Alex, who owns a gun, has continued to make threats toward Jessica as late as this summer. These facts establish a history of abuse which is likely to continue, since Jessica has the support of her family in Columbia and is away from Alex's immediate reach, there is little doubt that Columbia is safer for her and Carrie. The second factor to be considered is the length of time the child has resided outside of the state. Here, Carrie has been outside Franklin for nearly 8 months. The facts that she is very young, barely 6 years old, and has made friends and been enrolled in school in Columbia supports the fact that this is a long enough time where Carrie has lost her connections with Franklin and formed new connections with Columbia. The third factor is the distance between the court in Franklin and the court in the state that would assume jurisdiction (Columbia). The drive between the two courts is about 1.5 hours each way. Although it is a shorter distance than that in *Brickman*, in both cases the noncustodial parent is at a better position to travel since they do not have to accommodate for child care. Also, in this case, the inconvenience to Alex is lessened by the shorter drive. The fourth factor considered is the relative financial circumstances of the parties. Here, Jessica makes approximately $10,000 annually while Alex earns approximately $55,000. This is a disparity very close to that found to weight in favor of transferring jurisdiction to the court of the lower earning spouse in *Brickman.* The fifth factor considered by the court is the traditional bases for determining venue and inquiries about the nature and location of the evidence required to resolve the pending litigation, including the child's testimony. Like in *Brickman,* the court to which the case would be transferred to is a more convenient forum for the child to testify. Additionally, although some of the records involved may be located in Franklin these would be easily transported to Columbia. The last factor the Franklin court would weigh is the familiarity of the court of each state with the facts and issues in the pending litigation. Here, Franklin is more familiar since the restraining order was granted by it while Columbia's involvement was limited to issuing the marriage certificate. However, *Brickman* found that transfer was still warranted even when the Franklin court was substantially more involved. Upon weighing these 6 factors, giving special weight to safety, the case should be transferred to Columbia.

Sample Answer #2

TO: Charles Petrilla

FROM: Applicant

RE: Jessica Bohmer/Interstate Custody Case

This memorandum addresses the jurisdiction issues in the Jessica Bohmer case.

1. Which state was the "home-state" jurisdiction under the UCCJEA at the time of filing?

The state of Franklin was probably Carrie's "home-state" for jurisdictional purposes at the time Alex Bohmer filed his child custody petition. The Franklin UCCJEA grants jurisdiction to "a court of this State" where Franklin is either "the home state of the child on the date of the commencement of the proceeding, or was the home state of the child within six months before the commencement of the proceeding and the child is absent from this state but a parent continues to live in this state." (Franklin UCCJEA 16-201(a)(1)) Home state is defined under the UCCJEA, section 16-102(7), as the "State in which a child lived with a parent for at least six consecutive months immediately before the commencement of child custody proceeding." Franklin was Carrie's home state within six months before the commencement of the proceeding *and* Alex Bohmer continues to live in Franklin, thus Franklin can properly claim jurisdiction as Carrie's home state. Whether the absence was temporary or not is irrelevant but under Mills it was not a temporary absence.

It appears that Carrie had lived in Columbia for just under five months at the time Alex Bohmer filed his petition, thus Columbia was not Carrie's "home state" under the UCCJEA, unless the "more appropriate forum" section (16-201(a)(2)) applies, which is addressed below.

2. Since Franklin will likely have subject matter jurisdiction over the matter, the likelihood of success of a Motion to Decline Jurisdiction is paramount. According to In re Marriage of Brickman and Young, a Franklin court, applying UCCJEA section 16-207, *may* "decline to exercise jurisdiction over child custody proceedings when the court determines that it is an inconvenient forum under the circumstances and that a court of another state is a more appropriate forum in which to make the child custody determination." The permissive nature of the inconvenient forum statute aside, the issue is governed by six specific statutory factors, which are addressed individually with reference to the specific facts of Jessica Bohmer's situation below. For purposes of analyzing the relevance of the factors, the Brickman court notes that some facts weigh more heavily than others, but *all* factors must be considered by the court.

Whether domestic violence has occurred and is likely to continue in the future and which State could best protect the parties and the child is the most important factor to be considered. The fact that Alex Bohmer has a history of committing acts of violence against Jessica Bohmer, which can be shown both by testimony and the civil protection order, weighs heavily in favor of holding the custody hearing in Columbia. Brickman directs the court to consider "whether the parties are located in different states *because* one party is the victim of domestic violence," which in this instance seems to be the case. Whether Jessica decided to stay in Columbia for reasons other than Alex's propensity to violence is probably not as important as the fact that she left the state because of a specific instance of violence coupled with a pattern of previous violence. The courts of Franklin also recognize that domestic violence is a high recidivist crime, and thus explicitly authorize their courts to decline jurisdiction in favor of proceedings in another state to protect the child and the party fleeing the violence. Alex Bohmer might try to offer evidence of his having sought psychological counseling as a "mitigating" factor here, but the weight of the evidence will still likely come down in Jessica's (and Columbia's) favor.

The length of time Carrie has resided outside Franklin is about 22 months in total. The court will certainly consider the fact that Carrie has significant family connections in Columbia, but because Franklin has been Carrie's residence for a solid majority of her life, this factor probably weighs in favor of Franklin retaining jurisdiction.

The distance between the courts, the third factor in this case, is apparently a 1.5 hour drive, which does not appear to impose a substantial burden on either party. The Brickman court appears to endorse a position that the non-custodial parent is generally in a better position to travel, however, so this factor may weigh in favor of Columbia's jurisdiction.

The fourth factor, relative financial circumstances, weighs heavily in Jessica and Columbia's favor. Jessica's ability to adequately protect her interests (and Carrie's interests) may be seriously affected by requiring her to travel back and forth to Franklin with limited financial resources.

The fifth factor concerns the traditional bases for determining venue, including the nature and location of evidence. Much of the testimony in this case will come from Jessica and her family, and Carrie, and any records of Carrie's education, etc. in Franklin are easily transported.

The final factor is the familiarity of the court with the case. The fact that the Franklin court issued the prior protection order weighs in favor of the Franklin court's exercise of jurisdiction. Brickman indicates that the Franklin courts will give consideration to an out of state court's ability to familiarize itself with the litigation, and further that unless the out of state court appears to be an "inappropriate" forum, this factor is not dispositive.

Considering all the statutory factors and the precedential weight given to them in prior Franklin case law, it appears to be highly likely that the Motion to Decline Jurisdiction will succeed. If Franklin does, in fact, grant the eventual motion, it will be necessary for Jessica Bohmer to file for custody hearings in Columbia as soon as possible.

Sample Answer #3

TO: Charles Petrilla

FROM: Applicant

RE: Bohmer/Interstate Custody Case

First, you wanted to know whether Franklin or Columbia was the home-state jurisdiction under the Franklin Uniform Child Custody Jurisdiction and Enforcement Act (UCCJEA) at the time of filing of the current custody case in Franklin. I believe that Franklin will have home state jurisdiction under Franklin's UCCJEA.

Section 16-201(1) says that a state will have jurisdiction if it "is the home state of the child on the date of the commencement of the proceedings, or was the home state of the child within six months before the commencement of the proceeding and the child is absent from this state but a parent continues to live in this state." Section 16-102 defines home state as "the state in which a child lived with a parent for at least six consecutive months immediately before the commencement of a child custody proceeding." It also states that "a period of temporary absence of any of the mentioned persons is part of the period."

Carrie has been in Columbia with her grandparents since December 1, 2007, meaning that she had lived in Columbia for 7 consecutive months before the custody proceeding was filed on June 30, 2008. However, she has not lived with a parent that whole time. Before that she had lived in Franklin with her parents for two and a half years, since June 2004.

When Carrie came to Columbia in December 2007, she came with the intent to stay there temporarily. The Mills case said that intent is significant in whether absence from a state is temporary and that absence is no longer temporary once an intent to reside elsewhere permanently has been formed. In this case, Jessica came to Columbia on February 2, 2008, but she did not form the intent for her and Carrie to stay there permanently until three weeks later, on February 23, 2008. Therefore, Carrie can be considered having resided in Franklin until February 23, 2008.

Carrie's permanent residence transferred on February 23rd instead of in December 2007 when she first came to Columbia, less than six months before the custody proceeding was filed. She is currently absent from the state because she resides in Columbia now. Carrie's father, Alex, continues to live in Franklin. Therefore, under section 16-201(1), Franklin has UCCJEA jurisdiction because Franklin was Carrie's home state within six months before the proceeding, she is absent from Franklin now, and her father continues to live there.

Second: Whether a motion to decline jurisdiction under the Inconvenient Forum provision will be successful.

Discussion:

A motion to decline for inconvenient forum is likely to be successful. In determining whether another state should exercise jurisdiction, a court considers the following factors: (1) Whether domestic violence has occurred and is likely to continue in the future, and which state could best protect the parties and the child, (2) length of time the child has resided outside Franklin, (3) distance between the court in Franklin and the state that would assume jurisdiction, (4) relative financial circumstances of parties, (5) nature and location of evidence required to resolve pending litigation, including testimony of child and (6) familiarity of court of each state with the facts and issues in pending litigation.

While some factors weigh more heavily than others, all factors must be considered by the court. The first factor is extremely important and tends to have a lot of weight on the court's ultimate decision. In the case In re: Marriage of Brickman and Young, the Franklin Supreme Court held that when a court finds that domestic violence has occurred or that a party has fled the state to avoid further violence, this factor should be given greater weight than any other individual factor when determining jurisdictional issues under the UCCJEA. In that case, the father was abusive during wife's pregnancy, exhibited obsessive and controlling behavior, perpetrated serious injuries on her, and made no showing that his potential for future violence had ended. Several of these facts exist in the case at bar. When Jessica was pregnant, Alex was physically and emotionally abusive. He pushed her down stairs, slapped her, and tried to choke her. These are serious injuries that should be sufficient to warrant grave concern. The worst incident on Jessica's birthday was so harmful that Jessica almost lost consciousness. In addition to the abusive behavior, his letter also shows signs of obsessive and controlling behavior. Here, he's threatening to make her sorry for leaving. This may be used to show that it is likely that the violence will continue. The fact that he signed up for therapy and is seeking to resolve matters without resorting to abuse may be used by Alex to show he has changed, but since we don't know if he attended therapy or have the therapist's notes, we could possibly still prevail.

As stated in the first issue, the child has spent a majority of her life in Franklin. Some evidence that may help us on the second factor is the fact that Carrie is enrolled in school, Jessica's parents are in Columbia, and since Carrie has witnessed Alex be abusive to her mother, her sense of well-being and security is better in Columbia. Alex may argue that her friends, school, and community contacts are in Franklin making it the more convenient state. This factor could go either way.

The third factor, distance between courts, may also help Jessica. Columbia is an hour and a half away and as the custodial parent, Jessica would have to bring Carrie or arrange for her care. Although Alex may argue that the distance is not very long, unlike the eight hours in the Young case, it nonetheless creates a transportation inconvenience.

The fourth factor also weighs in favor of transfer to Columbia jurisdiction. In the Young case, the husband made over $41,000 in comparison to the wife's $6,500 income. This was enough for the court to conclude that the wife's choice of Columbia should be granted. In this case, Jessica makes $10,000 in comparison to Alex's $55,000. Considering that she would have a lot more expense if also asked to travel, this should lean toward Columbia exercising jurisdiction.

The fifth factor, location of evidence, is debatable. This factor examines where the parties are located, Carrie's health and child records, witnesses, etc. Since Carrie has lived in Franklin most of her life, her records are still there. Although the parties, Jessica and Carrie, are in Columbia, Alex may bring a successful argument that the pertinent evidence outside of location of parties weighs in favor of Franklin.

Additionally, other factors like the location of the protective order, marriage license, and other litigation concerning marriage (6th factor) favor Franklin courts. However, Franklin may conclude similar to the holding in Young, that Columbia will have an opportunity to become familiar with case by virtue of Jessica applying for legal services in Columbia.

Conclusion: Weighing all these factors and giving additional weight to the first factor, like the Franklin Supreme Court, Franklin Court will likely transfer jurisdiction to Columbia.

81970981R00175

Made in the USA
San Bernardino, CA
12 July 2018